Memory and popular film

MANCHESTER
UNIVERSITY PRESS

Inside Popular Film

General editors Mark Jancovich and Eric Schaefer

Inside Popular Film is a forum for writers who are working to develop new ways of analysing popular film. Each book offers a critical introduction to existing debates while also exploring new approaches. In general, the books give historically informed accounts of popular film, which present this area as altogether more complex than is commonly suggested by established film theories.

Developments over the past decade have led to a broader understanding of film, which moves beyond the traditional oppositions between high and low culture, popular and avant-garde. The analysis of film has also moved beyond a concentration on the textual forms of films, to include an analysis of both the social situations within which films are consumed by audiences, and the relationship between film and other popular forms. The series therefore addresses issues such as the complex intertextual systems that link film, literature, art and music, as well as the production and consumption of film through a variety of hybrid media, including video, cable and satellite.

The authors take interdisciplinary approaches, which bring together a variety of theoretical and critical debates that have developed in film, media and cultural studies. They neither embrace nor condemn popular film, but explore specific forms and genres within the contexts of their production and consumption.

Already published:

Thomas Austin *Hollywood, hype and audiences*
Harry M. Benshoff *Monsters in the closet: homosexuality and the horror film*
Julia Hallam and Margaret Marshment *Realism and popular cinema*
Joanne Hollows and Mark Jancovich (eds) *Approaches to popular film*
Nicole Matthews *Gender in Hollywood: comedy after the new right*
Rachel Moseley *Growing up with Audrey Hepburn*
Jacinda Read *The new avengers: feminism, femininity and the rape-revenge cycle*
Aylish Wood *Technoscience in contemporary film: beyond science fiction*

Memory and popular film

edited by
Paul Grainge

Manchester University Press
Manchester and New York
distributed exclusively in the USA by Palgrave

Published by Manchester University Press
Oxford Road, Manchester M13 9NR, UK
and Room 400, 175 Fifth Avenue, New York, NY 10010, USA
www.manchesteruniversitypress.co.uk

Distributed exclusively in the USA by
Palgrave, 175 Fifth Avenue, New York,
NY 10010, USA

Distributed exclusively in Canada by
UBC Press, University of British Columbia, 2029 West Mall,
Vancouver, BC, Canada V6T 1Z2

British Library Cataloguing-in-Publication Data
A catalogue record for this book is available from the British Library

Library of Congress Cataloging-in-Publication Data applied for

ISBN 0 7190 6374 4 *hardback*
   0 7190 6375 2 *paperback*

First published 2003

11 10 09 08 07 06 05 04 03   10 9 8 7 6 5 4 3 2 1

Typeset in Sabon with Frutiger
by Northern Phototypesetting Co. Ltd, Bolton

Printed in Great Britain
by Bell & Bain Ltd, Glasgow

Contents

Notes on contributors

Robert Burgoyne is Professor of Film and English at Wayne State University. His work centres on questions of history, memory, and film. He is the author of *Film Nation: Hollywood Looks at U.S. History* (Minnesota University Press, 1997), *Bertolucci's 1900: A Narrative and Historical Analysis* (Wayne State University Press, 1991) and is co-author of *New Vocabularies in Film Semiotics* (Routledge, 1992).

Neil Campbell is Head of American Studies at the University of Derby. His recent publications as author, editor and co-author are *The Cultures of the American New West* (Edinburgh University Press, 2000), *The Radiant Hour: Youth and American Culture* (Exeter University Press, 2000) and *American Cultural Studies* (Routledge, 1997). He is currently writing on American Western landscape photography.

Philip Drake is Lecturer in Media at the University of Paisley. He is currently researching questions of stardom, performance and industry in contemporary Hollywood cinema. He has published on performance in post-classical comedian comedy, and has forthcoming publications on stardom and cultural value.

Paul Grainge is Lecturer in Film Studies at the University of Nottingham. His work on cultural nostalgia and media memory has been published in journals including *Cultural Studies, The Journal of American Studies, American Studies, The International Journal of Cultural Studies* and *The Journal of American and Comparative Cultures*. He is the author of *Monochrome Memories: Nostalgia and Style in Retro America* (Praeger, 2002).

Heidi Kenaga is Adjunct Assistant Professor at the University of Memphis, where she teaches film, television and literature courses. Her article, 'Edna Ferber's *Cimarron*, Cultural Authority, and 1920s Western historical narratives' will appear in the anthology *Forgotten Feminisms: Popular Women Writers of the 1920s* in 2003. She is currently at work on a book about the

American film studios' production of 'commemorative' films during the postwar era, entitled *Marketing a Usable Past: Historical Commemoration and the Prestige Western, 1923–1931*.

Alison Landsberg is Assistant Professor of American cultural history and film in the Department of History and Art History at George Mason University. Her work on memory has been published in journals including *Body and Society* and *New German Critique* and has most recently appeared in *The Cybercultures Reader* (Routledge, 2000). She is currently finishing a manuscript entitled *Prosthetic Memory: The Logics and Politics of Memory in Modern American Culture*.

Sharon Monteith is Senior Lecturer in American Studies at the University of Nottingham. She is co-editor of *Gender and the Civil Rights Movement* (Garland, 1999) with Peter Ling and *South to a New Place* (Louisiana State University Press, forthcoming) with Suzanne W. Jones, and is the author of *Advancing Sisterhood? Interracial Friendships in Contemporary Southern Fiction* (University of Georgia Press, 2000). She is currently writing a book on popular cinema and the Civil Rights Movement.

Roberta E. Pearson is a Reader in Media and Cultural Studies at Cardiff University. She is the author, co-author and co-editor of numerous books and articles. She has recently co-edited both the *Critical Dictionary of Film and Television Theory* (Routledge, 2001) and *American Cultural Studies: a Reader* (Oxford University Press, 2000). She is also co-editor of *Worlds Apart: Essays on Cult Television*, which will be published by the University of Minnesota Press in 2003.

Jeffrey Pence is Assistant Professor of English and Cinema Studies at Oberlin College. His essays have appeared in such journals as *Public Culture, Poetics Today, MLQ, Film and Philosophy* and *JNT*. Currently, he is working on a manuscript dealing with cinema, technology and spirituality.

John Storey is Professor of Cultural Studies and Director of the Centre for Research in Media and Cultural Studies at the University of Sunderland. His recent publications include *Cultural Theory and Popular Culture: A Reader* (University of Georgia Press, 1998), *Cultural Consumption and Everyday Life* (Edward Arnold, 1999), *Cultural Theory and Popular Culture: An Introduction* (University of Georgia Press, 2001) and *Inventing Popular Culture* (Blackwell, 2003).

Julian Stringer is Lecturer in Film Studies at the University of Nottingham, and editor of *Movie Blockbusters* (Routledge, 2003). He is currently completing a PhD on film festivals at Indiana University.

Sarah Stubbings is currently completing a PhD entitled 'From Modernity to Memorial: Changing Meanings of the 1930s Cinema in Britain' at the University of Nottingham. She is a contributory writer in Mark Jancovich and Lucy Faire, *The Place of the Audience: Cultural Geographies of Film Consumption* (BFI, forthcoming).

Acknowledgements

I would like to thank Mark Jancovich for his encouragement and unfailing generosity, and to colleagues at the University of Derby and the University of Nottingham for sharing thoughts and memories throughout this project, specifically Neil Campbell, Dave Holloway, Alasdair Kean, Simon Philo, Sharon Monteith, Julian Stringer and Peter Ling. My thanks go to all the contributors, to everyone at Manchester University Press and, most of all, to Claire who with great patience let me tap away upstairs.

Finally, my thanks go to the editors of the online journal *Markszine* for permission to reprint a version of Robert Burgoyne's essay, and to the *San Francisco Chronicle* for the image that appears on page 54.

Introduction: memory and popular film

Paul Grainge

As a technology able to picture and embody the temporality of the past, cinema has become central to the mediation of memory in modern cultural life. While, in representational terms, the past has been figured in variations of the history film, the costume drama and the heritage picture from early cinema to the present, rituals of remembrance have come to surround the culture of film. Whether in the form of commercial reruns, generic recycling, critical retrospectives or popular reminiscence, the memory of film scenes and movies screens, cinema and cinema-going, has become integral to the placement and location of film within the cultural imagination of this century and the last.

This volume uses memory as a specific framework for the study of popular film, intervening in growing debates about the status and function of memory in cultural life and discourse. Susannah Radstone has usefully mapped the boom in memory's valuation in recent decades, a contemporary resurgence that has led to an explosion of academic interest in questions of memory and memory work.[1] This cross-disciplinary field of enquiry, which has become loosely known as 'memory studies', has addressed itself both to historical and methodological concerns: how to understand the rising stock of memory in particular periods of history, and how to evaluate particular sites and texts of memory as they invoke the past in specific ways and for specific ends. At the centre of analysis is a fundamental concern with what the CCCS Popular Memory Group has called the 'past-present relation'.[2] While akin to the province of history, with it disposition towards 'knowing' and interpreting the past, memory suggests a more dialogic relationship between the temporal constituencies of 'now' and 'then'; it draws attention to the activations and eruptions of the past as they are experienced in and constituted by the present.

Despite the clear entanglements of history and memory, there remain important differences between them that prevent any simple conflation of terms. These differences have been mapped politically. Michel Foucault, for example, has discussed the tensions between official histories and their contestation in 'popular' or unofficial memory, analysing the bearing of historical and memorial knowledge on formations of identity and operations of power. In a discussion of 'film and popular memory' in French cinema of the 1970s (specifically, a number of films dealing with the French Resistance), Foucault suggests that memory is 'a very important factor in struggle . . . if one controls people's memory, one controls their dynamism'.[3] Memory, in this context, is seen as a political force, a form of subjugated knowledge that can function as a site of potential opposition and resistance, but that is also vulnerable to containment and 'reprogramming'. In a more recent study, Marita Sturken draws upon Foucault but refines his conceptual position. Rather than categorise memory as inherently oppositional, Sturken develops a concept of 'cultural memory' that is more varied and ambiguous, that lays stress on memory's production through images, sites, objects and representations, but that neither inherently celebrates nor castigates manifestations of memory in the cultural terrain. Adapting her argument to events in American history and culture, she writes that:

> [The] process of cultural memory is bound up in complex political stakes and meanings. It both defines a culture and is the means by which its divisions and conflicting agendas are revealed. To define a memory as cultural is, in effect, to enter into a debate about what that memory means. This process does not efface the individual but rather involves the interaction of individuals in the creation of meaning. Cultural memory is a field of cultural negotiation through which different stories vie for a place in history.[4]

In this definition, memory is socially produced and is bound in the struggles and investments of cultural and national identity formation. It retains a notion of contestation but does not give memory a prescribed politics or cultural orientation. Unlike Foucault, who equates 'popular memory' with the force of resistance, Sturken provides a useful model for the *negotiation of memory* in popular film, especially as it is produced within the context of American culture. If, as Erica Carter and Ken Hirschkop suggest,[5] memory depends less on a conscious decision to record than an inability to forget, the negotiation of memory describes the echo and pressure of the past as it is configured in present-based struggles over the meaning of lived experience.

While the study of memory and film extends itself to a number of national cinemas, with potentially different stakes in the form and nature of cinematic remembrance, this volume takes Hollywood, and the cultural history of the United States, as its principal focus of concern. Notwithstanding the dominance of Hollywood in world cinema, and its capacity to harness debates about the nature of popular film, America has become central to critical discussions about the status and bearing of memory in the cultural sphere. As I have written elsewhere, these discussions have focused on two principal questions or concerns.[6] Firstly, the question of what (or not) is remembered in cultural life and practice has been carried into a number of debates within the United States figured around the content and transmission of memory within educational curricula and public and popular representation. This has derived, not least, from a deepening sense of the plural and discontinuous histories that have challenged ideas about the singularity of American experience, and that have led to battles of value fought over the (re)conception of the cultural centre. The balance of memory and forgetting in American culture – what is remembered, by who and for who – has in recent years become entwined in hegemonic struggles fought and figured around the negotiation of America's national past.

These struggles sharpened significantly in the late 1980s and early 1990s, a moment of reported 'culture war' where consensual narratives of American identity were (seen to be) challenged by an emergent politics of difference. According to Robert Burgoyne, Hollywood played its part in these struggles, in some cases reasserting traditional narratives of nation and, in others, addressing the 'recovered memory' of the American nation-state – taking on traumas such as slavery, genocide, political assassination and the war in Vietnam – to express a reconfigured sense of American identity.[7] The 1990s, in particular, were a time when the metanarratives of American memory began to strain for legitimacy against the multiple pasts of the marginalised. This must be set within a broad climate where national identity itself was, and continues to be, called into question by transnational political and economic restructuring. If memory discourses have accelerated in response to crucial changes in the ideological structure of US society – symptomatic, according to Andreas Huyssen, of a more

general challenge to progressive Western paradigms of history, modernity, and nation[8] – Hollywood has functioned strategically in the articulation and codification of the cultural past. Although varied in its
discursive contribution to the 'field of national imaginings' that Burgoyne describes, Hollywood has shown a concerted fascination with
cinematic renderings of American history and memory, levied in films
such as *Glory* (1989), *Born on the Fourth of July* (1989), *Dances with
Wolves* (1990), *JFK* (1991), *Malcolm X* (1992), *Forrest Gump* (1994),
Nixon (1995), *Lone Star* (1996), *Amistad* (1997), *Titanic* (1997),
Pleasantville (1998) and *Saving Private Ryan* (1998), to name just a
few. Whether or not these films represent an anxious response to the
'end of history', a revisionist programme of alternative remembrance,
or something more benign, memory has garnered a powerful currency
in the discursive operations of contemporary American film.

Of course, Hollywood's bearing on constructions of memory and
identity are not constrained to the domestic sphere alone. Hollywood film has been taken up in discussions about the degree to
which its products advance, adumbrate or even 'Americanise' the
memory of events and peoples that belong, figuratively, to other cultures and contexts. Steven Spielberg's treatment of the Holocaust in
Schindler's List (1993) is a marked example, generating discussion
about the capacity of American/popular film to address the gravity
of a subject that has become an encompassing trope of twentieth-
century trauma. On the one hand, *Schindler's List* was accused of
representing events within conventional narrative frames, for concentrating on survivors rather than victims, and for presenting,
within its documentary mode, the 'voluptuous anguish and ravish-
ing images' that Saul Friedlander has linked with the re-evocation of
Nazism in the West.[9] On the other hand, Spielberg's film was praised
for problematising Nazi clichés, for its mood of visual gravity and
seriousness, and for the way that *Schindler's List* dealt with the
Holocaust in affective terms. The debates that unfurled posed a
series of questions not simply about the capacity of Hollywood to
understand and respect the Holocaust, but also, and perhaps more
fundamentally, about the nature of popular film and its function as
an approbate or 'authentic' memory text.

The question of authenticity is a complex one that has frequently
come to manifest itself in debates about the fidelity of popular
film to historically remembered events. The brouhaha over Oliver
Stone's depiction of events surrounding the assassination of

President Kennedy in *JFK* was an especially publicised example of this, figured around questions of historical accuracy and the perception of Stone's obfuscating conspiratorial obsessions. For its part, *Schindler's List* generated fears that 'authentic cultural memory' was being compromised by the film's particular blending of fictive and factual elements. These debates were embroiled in larger questions about the limits of representing the Holocaust. However, the distinction between real and imagined pasts became a central focus of complaint for critics like Claude Lanzmann who objected to the film's very pretensions of being able to approximate, in representational terms, the Nazi genocide.

The concept of 'authentic memory' is, of course, highly problematic. The desire for memory as stable, reassuring, and constant has always been plagued by the fear of its instability and unreliability, and its disposition towards fantasy and forgetting. The impact of digital mediation further compounds and complicates the question of authenticity, as Robert Burgoyne outlines in his essay for this volume. In certain kinds of critique, however, a notion of memorial authenticity has endured, linked negatively to presumptions about the deracinating effects on memory produced by and within particular forms of technological media. In his sweeping theory of modern memory, Pierre Nora suggests that the 'real' or 'unbidden' experience of memory has been replaced by its trace and secretion in particular sites, or *lieux de memoire*.[10] This is a type of memory 'deformed and transformed' by its essential materialisation within mass culture. The attendant 'collapse of memory' that Nora posits is based on a premise that memory is a matter of retrieving and reliving experience rather than something that is bound in, and structured through, representation and narrative. While not all would agree with Nora's romanticised notion of spontaneous memory, there is enough critical scepticism felt towards the forms and narratives of popular culture (not least, by documentary filmmakers like Lanzmann) to make certain of Nora's observations resonate in theories that suggest an essentially fallacious or inauthentic rendering of memory in mainstream commercial film.

The narrative imperatives of popular cinema in both classical and post-classical forms – largely character-driven, marked by continuous editing, demanding resolute closure – have led historians and cultural critics alike to form of ring of suspicion around Hollywood's treatment of the historically remembered past. More recently, however, theories about the narrative character of history itself, powerfully addressed by Hayden White, have inspired a re-appraisal of the workings of history and memory in film.[11] Addressing the shibboleths of objective modernist history and the tendency on the part of many historians to dismiss film as distorting, subjective and trivial, Robert A. Rosenstone points out that such a view does not give due attention either to the narrative dimensions of history-writing or to the specificity of film as an influential mode of engaging with the past.[12] If *Schindler's List* is able to demonstrate anything about the status of memory in popular film, it is perhaps that memory is never straightforwardly authentic or inauthentic. Spielberg's film was mortgaged to a notion of authenticity that relied as much upon mediated memories – notably, the ranging registers of black and white photography and the various scenes and images that evoked previous films about the Holocaust – as it did upon the use of genuine Polish film locations or the presence of living Holocaust survivors. While the film played upon the experiential chords of personal and collective memory, it also 'remembered' a line of narrative and visual representations of the Holocaust. Simply put, *Schindler's List* drew out the multiple facets of cultural memory as lived in history and experienced through the auspices of twentieth-century media.

In both national and international terms, Hollywood has become powerfully associated with the cultural politics of contemporary memory and its associated questions of taste, representation, ideology and identity. However, products of the American film industry have also become endemic to the second major focus of critical discussion associated with cultural memory: the issue of *how* (*or not*) cultures remember in a climate of accelerated technological media. If, as Andreas Huyssen suggests, 'the very structure of memory (and not just its contents) is strongly contingent upon the social formation that produces it',[13] memory has been theorised in terms of a formation where new technologies and multinational organisations of capital have engendered a culture of hyperreality and capitalist hyperdevelopment, where changing relations of space and time have produced a culture 'haunted by the explosion of temporality in the expanding synchronicity of our media world'.[14] This conditional diagnosis has been largely hatched within the critical discourses of postmodernism and has been consistently mapped onto the US as the most discreet and supposedly complete locus of late capitalist and/or postmodern energy. Specifically, the issue of amnesia has gathered conceptual momentum in significant strands of postmodern literature, refiguring the clichés of American forgetting and ahistoricism (symptomatic of a culture that has long been seen to invest, ideologically, in trajectories of the future) at a more fundamental level. The perils of postmodernism, especially as they have become associated with the US, are bound in a culture of increasing speed, space and simulacra unable to retain or engage with a meaningful sense of its own past.

For critics like Fredric Jameson, postmodernism represents a situation where 'our entire social situation has little by little begun to lose its capacity to retain its own past, has begun to live in a perpetual present and in a perpetual change that obliterates traditions of the kind which all earlier social formations have had in one way or another to preserve'.[15] Less concerned with the content of memory, the debates that figure around how (or not) the past is remembered address the prospective dissolution or potential refiguration of memory in a culture of electronic mediation and semiotic excess. If Jameson's theory of a depthless and historically impoverished culture represents the former position, a number of historians and cultural critics have challenged assumptions of postmodern amnesia, leading to discussion about the form and experience of what Andrew Hoskins has come to call 'new memory'.[16]

Defining memory in terms of a new phase or epoch brings with it the usual problems, and potential crudities, of historical periodisation. If there *is* something new or particular about the way the past is experienced in cultural life, however, this arguably turns on a heavily mediated contemporary landscape able to transmit, store, retrieve, refigure and circulate memories in very specific ways.[17] This is linked inimitably to the electronic and digital technologies that are influencing the form and development of national and transnational modes of cultural remembrance. In different ways, the notion of authentic and territorialised memory, tied to personal and collective experience, has been challenged in a media world where the past may no longer be felt or understood in any culturally specific or referential sense. It is the perceived artificiality of memory, associated with the (global) media sphere, which has led to various assumptions and theories of amnesia. However, notions of historical and memorial blockage present a limited view of modern memory practice. Crucially, they fail to address the means and possibilities for articulating the past *through* established and developing forms of technological mediation. While this will be addressed specifically in part three of *Memory and popular film*, emphasis lies throughout the volume with the presence and persistence of (American) cultural memory, rather than with the sense of loss and absence inscribed within much postmodern theory.

The concentration on contemporary culture outlined thus far should not be taken to suggest that mediated memory does not have relevance for earlier periods of history. While the relationship between memory and technological media became a central theme for critics of modernity like Walter Benjamin and Henri Bergson, memory itself has a modern history that can be examined and discursively traced. Susannah Radstone suggests that memory has developed visibility at specific historical junctures, principally as a means of expressing, and holding in balance, particular ambivalences and equivocations about identity and cultural value. While, from the nineteenth century, she suggests that these equivocations were turned towards the status of history, community, and tradition, in the late twentieth century, they focused more on fantasy, subjectivity, and fabrication.[18] These ideas are brought into focus through particular, and historically rooted, notions of memory crisis. For example, while the memory crisis of the American 1920s – which saw fears about the dilution of national purity and tradition by 'alien' elements and ideologies – was addressed in the public history films and commemoration pictures examined by Roberta E. Pearson and Heidi Kenaga in this book, *Blade Runner* (1982), *Total Recall* (1990) and *Memento* (2000) demonstrate a more contemporary concern with the unsettled boundaries between reality and simulation in the constitution of remembered identity and experience. If concerns with history, community and tradition govern the former, a preoccupation with fantasy, subjectivity and fabrication inform the latter. Of course, the distinction between history/fantasy, community/subjectivity, tradition/fabrication, can hardly be contained within set historical periods, but there is perhaps a question of emphasis here that underscores the historicity of the relationship between memory and film.

From its first beginnings, the temporal realities of early cinema – what Leo Charney equates with the shock and embodiment of modern space and time – has posed significant questions for the formation of modern memory.[19] In discursive terms, however, the contemporary period remains the key focus of concern. If a particular moment can be identified where the connections between memory and film become more tangible and self-conscious, it arguably begins in the 1970s. Discussing broad transformations in the history of American film, Robert Sklar suggests that, since the 1970s, historical memory has become the touchstone of a movie's cultural power, replacing a 'traditional rhetoric of myths and dreams'.[20] For Sklar, the identification of a shift from 'myth to memory' in the rhetorical power of mainstream American film relates to a particular dissolution of the consensus that, until the 1970s, had underpinned American liberal ideologies in the postwar period. While speculative in nature, ideological schemas of this sort do have a certain use in identifying broad historical trends and patterns in the discursive propensities of popular cinema. Sklar is one of many critics who identify the 1970s as the origin of the contemporary 'memory boom' in American life and society. In a time when it is claimed that metanarratives of history and progress have been severely undermined, and when the past has become increasingly subject to cultural mediation, textual reconfiguration, and ideological contestation in the present, memory has developed a new discursive significance. In cinema, as in other modes of cultural practice, memory has become a powerful locus for the articulation of identity in the sphere of cultural imaginings. This has been levied in rhetorical terms – Sklar's transition from the 'myths and dreams' of classical film to the 'historical memory' of more recent work – but it has also become figured in particular generic transformations and bound in regimes of industrial and institutional commercialism, such that movie memory itself has experienced a heightened cultural significance.

Hollywood has long had an obsessive fascination with the memory of its own past. From the affectionate parody of the sound era in *Singin' in the Rain* (1952) to the nostalgic atmosphere of the *Last Picture Show* (1971) and the retro sensibility of *Pulp Fiction* (1993), memory has played an instrumental part in Hollywood's strategies of production and self-promotion. In representational terms, this has been marked in recent decades by the use and reformulation of genre memory in works such as *American Graffiti* (1973), *Chinatown* (1974), *Star Wars* (1977), *Raiders of the Lost Ark* (1981), *Back to the Future III* (1989) and *Moulin Rouge* (2001). Genre memory depends less on the explicit remembering of events, characters and experiences, than on the use and appropriation of previous cinematic modes and conventions. This can involve the recreation and re-situation of motifs, music, atmosphere and feel in cinematic forms that draw from a repertoire of past styles and generic traits. In critical terms, this tendency has been levied in discussions around pastiche. Critics such as Jameson and Richard Dyer have each examined pastiche as a mode of (postmodern) cultural production, relating it in different ways to questions of historicity, authorship and cultural memory. While Jameson finds the 'nostalgia film' – his chosen label for the embodiment of postmodern pastiche – a form of evisceration or 'blank parody', Dyer holds a more positive view, suggesting a more complex cultural mode that has the potential to be critical and transgressive, but that can also suggest an awareness about the constructed nature of feelings and emotions while allowing them to be experienced and enjoyed.[21] While arriving at different conclusions about the historical antecedents and cultural value of pastiche, each critic maintains and develops the supposition that film itself has become central to the landscape and production of contemporary cultural memory.

Movie memory may be a question of representation and generic style. However, this should not prohibit or relegate the significant industrial factors that contribute to Hollywood's relationship with, and conspicuous fostering of, cultural remembering. Indeed, the development of memory since the 1970s has been linked to various aspects that are not strictly ideological or textual in nature. These include diversifying markets for memory, the growth of the heritage industry, and the proliferation of technologies of time-shifting like VCR and DVD. In various ways, these have shaped a burgeoning market for cinematic remembrance, and led to new media channels for consuming Hollywood history.

Together with the revolution in video during the 1980s, one of the most significant contemporary developments for the circulation and exhibition of Hollywood film has been the evolution of cable. The deregulation of the cable industry's pricing structure in the 1980s led to an explosion of cable channels pursuing strategies of market segmentation and niche programming. Together with the likes of MTV and CNN, some of the most successful channels to emerge have been those with rerun formats such as American Movie Classics, TV Land, and Turner Classic Movies. As Jan-Christopher Horak writes, 'the proliferation of cable networks and other new media, and the concomitant development of ever more specialized and fragmented audiences, forced distributors to turn to the collective movie past'.[22] With new outlets for movie memory, typified by cable's ability to generate audiences through the (inexpensive) replaying and recontextualising of old films and television products, a renewed interest in Hollywood heritage began to emerge in the 1980s and 1990s. While the studios' desire to collect and archive history was, according to Horak, 'driven by marketing and branding considerations, rather than any altruistic urge to preserve history',[23] investments in film memory certainly became more acute. This has, of course, developed in conjunction with the technological revolutions associated with video and DVD which have not only given film and television industries a means of repackaging their products in new commercial lines ('vintage classics', 'Hollywood legends' etc.), but that have also given the consumer more control over the way that film and television can be watched, consumed and collected. Marketing the past has, in various ways, become a lucrative by-product of the new relationship being forged in the age of video and DVD between institutions, texts and audiences.

The place of the audience is, of course, highly significant in discussions of film as a *subject* of memory. As Sarah Stubbings investigates in this book, film memory is often figured around generational nostalgia felt towards the place and purpose of cinema in specific communities. Whether this turns on particular exhibition sites, rituals and experiences, or on stars and films themselves, a growing body of work has begun to examine cultural constructions of identity produced through audience memory.[24] If what might be called a 'political economy of cinematic memory' has seen new industrial investments being figured around the form and selling of particularised film histories, appealing to fluid notions of movie classicism and various kinds of fan nostalgia, approaches within audience studies have focused on the cultural and emotional investments in cinematic memory that have been produced locally and from specific subject positions. While memory has long attached itself to the products of Hollywood, the changing status of cinema at the dawn of the twenty-first century has brought with it acute questions about the representational, institutional, and spectatorial formations of memory that inform the place and basis of film in cultural life and practice.

The broad relationship between cinema and the past has been examined in a number of recent collections, notably Robert Rosenstone's *Revisionining History*, Vivien Sobchack's *The Persistence of History* and Marcia Landy's *The Historical Film: History and Memory in Media*.[25] In different ways, these address the representation of history in film and television, applying critical questions about the status of history (encompassing issues of truth, knowledge, authenticity, and verisimilitude) to the forms of visual media that increasingly shape historical sensitivities within the public sphere. Memory is embroiled in these discussions but, frequently, the subject of memory remains a tangential issue or is rather loosely defined as history's conceptual 'other'. This volume contributes to the broad analysis of film and its representation of the past but puts memory at the *centre* of analysis; it establishes a framework for discussing issues of memory *in* film and of film *as* memory.

This does not mean to say that all methodologies of memory criticism will or could possibly be addressed. The analysis of film and memory has been developed in numerous cultural, psychoanalytic, ethnographic and formalist directions. While some critics have used memory as a means of investigating narrative techniques like that of film flashback, others have examined specific audience memories of films, stars and cinema-related experiences. Enquiries have been mapped in relation to particular kinds of remembrance, like that of the Holocaust and other cultural traumata, and with specific national contexts in mind. This collection seeks to introduce approaches to memory and film but from a position that foregrounds memory as a locus, and film as a site, for the articulation and negotiation of cultural identity. If the 'memory film' can be said to explore the means by which the past exerts a contextual bearing on contemporary life and its structures of belief, *Memory and popular film* is crucially concerned with the questions of (American) cultural identity that derive from this relationship.

The book is organised in three main sections. The first section examines the relationship between official and popular history and the constitution of memory narratives in and around the production and consumption of American cinema. The four chapters in Part I explore the status and entanglements of public history and popular memory, focused through two chapter pairings which introduce representational, industrial, audience-based and institutional contexts of study. Addressing different historical periods and using different methodological approaches, the four chapters examine the interrelations of history and memory as they apply to American cinema in the 1920s and to British memories of American cinema in the 1980s and 1990s. These contextual frames enable a focused consideration of national and international formations of the cultural and cinematic past.

The periods in question are not entirely arbitrary. Both represent moments where memory acquired currency and discursive visibility in the respective cultures at large. In the 1920s, this was linked to anxieties about the status of American identity and tradition in the face and fear of sweeping change, leading to a stake in the articulation of national history and memory. As Roberta E. Pearson and Heidi Kenaga demonstrate, this was undertaken through the auspices of cinema, and can be related to particular ideological and corporate imperatives. Examining a series of educational feature films by Yale University Press in chapter 1: 'A white man's country: Yale's *Chronicles of America*', Pearson demonstrates how the white Anglo-Saxon producers of the series made attempts to fashion the country's history and memory to make it consonant with their own cultural values. This led to an ideological project that necessitated the representation of Native Americans as 'savage savages'. Situated in a period of social turbulence and contested national identity, Pearson uses the *Chronicles of America* series to open up questions about the inscription and reformulation of the past in official and popular texts. Specifically, she suggests that, in having to appeal to a mass audience, Hollywood responded to society's contradictory discourses about Native Americans with less ideologically coherent, more polysemic texts.

Kenaga examines the same period and context but from a different perspective, exploring the industrial context within which popular commemoration films emerged in the 1920s. Her chapter, 'Civic pageantry and public memory in the silent era commemorative film: *The Pony Express* at the Diamond Jubilee', more closely examines the commercial status of the popular memory texts inferred in Pearson's essay. Specifically, Kenaga explores the means by which studios refigured lowbrow genres such as the Western historical feature into key commodities of the heritage industry, largely as a means of enabling studios such as Paramount to exploit a new position for itself as a 'legitimate' purveyor or guardian of historical memory. Together, these chapters demonstrate the adaptive and public relations potential of popular memory texts, and the means by which they are set in relation to questions of cultural and corporate legitimacy.

The second chapter pairing examines the discursive and institutional apparatus that has come to support the memory of Classic Hollywood in British cultural life. Both Sarah Stubbings and Julian Stringer examine manifestations of cinema memory in the 1980s and 1990s, a period where cultural stock and economic fortune was increasingly vested in notions of 'heritage' in British life. In '"Look behind you": memories of cinema-going in the "Golden Age" of Hollywood', Stubbings examines popular memory of cinema-going as framed through letters and articles featured in the memory narratives of a provincial city press. Refining questionnaire-based approaches to audience memory, Stubbings examines personal reminiscence of cinema-going in the public realm of the *Nottingham Evening Post*, focusing on the creation of a number of culturally sanctioned discourses figured around age, community and city identity.

Stringer is also concerned with the memory of cinema, but examines this in institutional terms. Specifically, his chapter, 'Raiding the archive: film festivals and the revival of Classic Hollywood', explores the role of the metropolitan film festival in transforming cinema history into heritage. Focusing on the circulation of old Hollywood movies at the London Film Festival between 1981 and 2001, Stringer examines the historical and preservationist agendas that lie behind the consensus about which films should be remembered and which forgotten. If the first chapter pairing examines cinema and the articulation of national memory, the second explores memories of cinema articulated in a particular national context. In each case, 'official' and 'popular' expressions of memory are set beside each other, demonstrating the frequent (con)fusion of such categories. While no pure realm of popular memory exists outside and beyond public history, public history is necessarily informed by the will and insistence of popular recall.

If Part I establishes historical and methodological case studies focusing on the tangled categories of public/popular and history/ memory, Part II examines the politics of memory in a series of chapters that take as their focus three pivotal sites of national conflict in postwar America. This includes the war in Vietnam, American race relations and the Civil Rights Movement, and the history of marginality in the geographic and cultural borderlands of the US. These sites have generated hard fought battles of memory within American historical and political identity formation. Examining specific 'memory work' within contemporary Hollywood cinema, Part II explores the specificity of film in constituting memory narratives that can function in coercive ways but that can also, alternatively, hold the potential for progressive political understanding.

The first two chapters concentrate on the former tendency. Considering cinematic articulations of the Vietnam War in Hollywood film, John Storey's 'The articulation of memory and desire: from Vietnam to the war in the Persian Gulf' establishes a series of issues that bear upon, and illuminate, the relationship between memory, culture and power. Building on Maurice Halbwachs' influential concept of collective memory – where remembering is theorised as a social process located in the present – Storey explores the articulation of Vietnam memory (and forgetting) in American cinema during the 1980s. Arguing that Hollywood produced a particular 'regime of truth' about Vietnam that was politically serviceable to President Bush in the build up to the Gulf War, Storey considers the politics of Vietnam revisionism and how 'enabling memories' were produced to legitimate subsequent political and military engagements.

In her ranging consideration of Hollywood's treatment of the Civil Rights Movement, Sharon Monteith establishes a different political context for the articulation of cinematic memory. Her chapter, 'The movie-made Movement: civil rites of passage', considers how the 'sedimented layers of civil rights preoccupations' are codified in memory films such as *Mississippi Burning* (1988), *The Long Walk Home* (1994) and *A Time to Kill* (1996). Suggesting that post-civil rights cinema frequently translates larger historical and political issues into personal histories and domestic situations, Monteith considers whether this represents a devaluation of race and rights in the present, or is, rather, a reassertion of the personal as part of the political. If Storey is concerned with the memory politics of revisionism, Monteith examines the memory politics of reconciliation as a prevailing mode of civil rights cinema. In each case, the memory work of contemporary Hollywood is seen to inflect pivotal legacies in the history of postwar America, legitimating dominant power relations and establishing potentially restrictive parameters of cultural and political thinking.

The next two chapters interpret Hollywood's memory work more positively. In 'Prosthetic memory: the ethics and politics of memory in an age of mass culture', Alison Landsberg attempts to 'imagine a

relationship to memory that forges, rather than prevents the formation of progressive political alliances and solidarities'. Developing
her provocative concept of 'prosthetic memory', Landsberg
explores the impact of mass cultural technologies and their particular ability to make memories available to those who may not have
lived or experienced them directly. Positing the radical potential of
prosthetic memory, Landsberg examines John Singleton's *Rosewood*
(1997) as a progressive and counterhegemonic text that challenges,
rather than contains, the historical politics of American race relations. She suggests that *Rosewood* invites the question of 'whether
white children – and by extension, a white audience – can take on
memories of racial oppression and in the process develop empathy
for African Americans'. While aware of the conceptual difficulties of
this position, Landsberg provides an important strategic position in
thinking through the ethical and political dimension of cultural
memory and collective identification.

In the next chapter, '"Forget the Alamo": history, legend and
memory in John Sayles' *Lone Star*', Neil Campbell provides a
detailed examination of a film deliberately concerned with various
ethnic memories (Hispanic, Anglo, African and Native American) of
those living in the southwestern border town of Frontera. Using
George Lipsitz's work on counter-memory, and set in the context of
wider redefinitions of power and identity in the US, Campbell
explores how *Lone Star* functions as a multi-layered, intertextual
film, revealing the secret histories of the New West as a contested
space where cultures collide and coexist in an uneasy, hybrid set of
relations. In its use of the past, indelibly marked by creative forgetting, Campbell suggests that *Lone Star* presents a radical, challenging revision of history and an optimistic, contested sense of the
future for a multi-ethnic America.

If 'cultural memory is a field of cultural negotiation through
which different stories vie for a place in history', Part II explores the
political stakes of cinematic discourse in its production of national
memory. While these issues are not left behind in Part III, the final
section concentrates on the issue of mediation; it explores how technological and semiotic shifts in the cultural terrain have influenced
the coding and experience of memory in contemporary cinema. Part
III considers both the presence of music and colour in nostalgia films
of the 1990s and the impact of digital and video technologies on the
representational determinants of mediated memory.

Focusing on the place and function of music in contemporary retro movies, Philip Drake considers how the past has been dealt with stylistically in films such as *Jackie Brown* (1997) and *Sleepless in Seattle* (1993). In '"Mortgaged to music": new retro movies in 1990s Hollywood cinema', Drake makes a distinction between the 'history', 'period' and 'retro' film, arguing that retro films mobilise particular codes that have come to connote a past sensibility metonymically re-remembered in the present. Music is a highly significant code in this cinematic patterning of memory, instrumental to the pleasures of 'pastness' that characterise retro's particular feel and meaning. As Drake contends, 'the language of memory in retro cinema is insistently musical as well as visual'. The consideration of music is linked in Drake's chapter to Hollywood's commercial strategies (specifically, branding considerations and the selling of film soundtracks) and to popular discourses of nostalgia as they are expressed and experienced in affective terms.

If music is a means of creating cinematic 'feel' for memory and nostalgia, so too is the use of colour (and black and white). My own chapter, 'Colouring the past: *Pleasantville* and the textuality of media memory', uses the spectacle of digital colourisation to unlock questions about the effect of postmodern technology/representation on the figuration of cultural memory. Suggesting that *Pleasantville* is an indicative memory text of the late 1990s, I locate the film in two critical contexts: within the contested field of meaning that came to debate the memory and status of the American 1960s, and in relation to the domestication of digital technology as a contemporary textual mode. Examining *Pleasantville*'s reflexive play with culture war discourse, and spectacular deployment of colourisation technique, my essay challenges theories of postmodern amnesia that suppose an evisceration of memory caused by quotational and/or technological excess.

In 'Memory, history and digital imagery in contemporary film', Robert Burgoyne deepens this concern with digital technology, providing an incisive framework for the consideration of computer generated imagery and cinematic representations of the past. Focusing on the use of documentary images, and the sense of authenticity that documentary has accrued in providing a trace of the past, Burgoyne considers the way that digital imaging has turned the (documentary) past into a site of imaginative reconstruction. Considering films such as *Forrest Gump*, *JFK* and *Wag the Dog* (1997), Burgoyne examines the 'negative and positive potential for the new kind of interweaving of fiction and history that computer generated imagery allows'. Specifically, he suggests that the destabilising of historical and referential truth may lead to a new genre of visual history that confounds, as in premodern times, the very boundaries of fantasy, fact and speculation. Returning to the relationship between history, memory and media, Burgoyne explores changes in the fundamental categories of value that underpin traditional givens of the historically remembered past: origins, authenticity and documentation.

Concluding Part III, Jeffrey Pence moves the ground of analysis to the competing forms of technology that have challenged cinema's cultural supremacy at the turn of the twentieth century and, with it, its mediation of experience and memory. In his chapter, 'Postcinema/Postmemory', Pence concentrates on postcinematic forms that have emerged through video technology, and that have been absorbed within the creative corpus of filmmakers like Atom Egoyan. Investigating questions of subjective and collective memory in a world of discrepant temporalities, Pence situates the question of memory and film in relation to new technologies of remediation and to an increasingly globalised terrain of space and time, culture and identity. While varied in approach and focus, each essay in Part III takes issue with the diagnosis in postmodern criticism (significantly, that of Jameson) that we are living in a commodified culture of historical blockage and cultural forgetting. All of the essays deal with the complex constitution, rather than mere abdication, of memory in a resolutely technologised present.

The three parts of *Memory and popular film* raise themes and questions that interpenetrate and cross each other. The popular, political and mediated status of memory, inscribed within American film, are issues that are conveyed throughout the volume. Sturken suggests that 'cultural memory is a central aspect of how American culture functions and how the nation is defined'.[26] This book explores the stakes of cultural remembering in the United States and the means by which memory has been figured through, and in relation to, Hollywood cinema. While America has been seen as a country of the future, and a land of habitual forgetting, the musical leitmotif of *Casablanca* (1943) provides this book with a final and fundamental cultural gist – 'you must remember this . . .'

Notes

1   Susannah Radstone, 'Working With Memory: An Introduction', in Susannah Radstone (ed.) *Memory and Methodology* (Oxford: Berg, 2000), pp. 1–22.

2   Popular Memory Group, 'Popular Memory: Theory, Politics, Method', in Richard Johnson, Gregor McLennan, Bill Schwarz, David Sutton (eds), *Making Histories: Studies in History and History Writing* (London: Hutchinson and the Centre for Contemporary Cultural Studies, 1982), pp. 205–52.

3   Michel Foucault, 'Film and Popular Memory', *Radical Philosophy* (1975), 28.

4   Marita Sturken, *Tangled Memories: The Vietnam War, the AIDS Epidemic, and the Politics of Remembering* (Berkeley: University of California Press, 1997), p. 1.

5   Erica Carter and Ken Hirschkop, 'Editorial', *New Formations*, Winter (1996), v–vii.

6   See Paul Grainge, *Monochrome Memories: Nostalgia and Style in Retro America* (Westport, CT and London: Praeger, 2002).

7   Robert Burgoyne, *Film Nation: Hollywood Looks at U.S. History* (Minneapolis: University of Minnesota Press, 1997).

8   Andreas Huyssen, 'Present Pasts: Media, Politics, Amnesia', in Arjun Appadurai (ed.) *Globalization* (Durham: Duke University Press, 2001), p. 69.

9   Saul Friedlander, *Reflections on Nazism: An Essay on Kitsch and Death* (Bloomington: Indiana University Press, 1993), p. 21. For a detailed consideration of the debates surrounding *Schindler's List*, see Yosefa Loshitsky (ed.), *Spielberg's Holocaust: Critical Perspectives on Schindler's List* (Bloomington: Indiana University Press, 1997).

10 Pierre Nora, 'Between Memory and History: Les Lieux de Memoire', trans. Marc Roudebush, *Representations* 26 (Spring 1989), 7–25.

11 See Hayden White, 'The Modernist Event', in Vivien Sobchack (ed.) *The Persistence of History: Cinema, Television and the Modern Event* (New York: Routledge, 1996), pp. 17–38.

12 Robert A. Rosenstone, *Visions of the Past: The Challenge of Film to our Idea of History* (Cambridge: Harvard University Press, 1995).

13 Andreas Huyssen, *Twilight Memories: Marking Time in a Culture of Amnesia* (New York: Routledge, 1995), p. 252.

14 Huyssen, *Twilight Memories*, p. 100.

15 Fredric Jameson, 'Postmodernism and Consumer Society', in E. Ann Kaplan (ed.), *Postmodernism and its Discontents* (London: Verso, 1990), p. 8. For a more extensive discussion, see Fredric Jameson, *Postmodernism, or, the Cultural Logic of Late Capitalism* (London: Verso, 1991).

16 Andrew Hoskins, 'New Memory: Mediating History', *The Historical Journal of Film, Radio and Television* 21: 4 (2001), 333–46.
17 See Grainge, *Monochrome Memories*, pp. 41–64.
18 Radstone, 'Working With Memory'. Discussing the 'divergent temporalities that distinguish nineteenth and late twentieth century understandings of and preoccupations with memory', Radstone writes: 'Whereas in the nineteenth century, it was the felt break with tradition and long dureé which constituted the temporal aspect of the memory crisis, in the late twentieth century, that crisis is inflected, rather, by the experiences of immediacy, instantaneity and simultaneity', p. 7.
19 Leo Charney, 'In a Moment: Film and the Philosophy of Modernity', in Leo Charney and Vanessa R. Schwartz (eds), *Cinema and the Invention of Modern Life* (Berkeley: University of California Press, 1995), pp. 279–94.
20 Robert Sklar, *Movie-Made America: A Cultural History of American Movies* (New York: Vintage Books, 1994), p. 357.
21 Jameson, *Postmodernism, or, The Cultural Logic of Late Capitalism*; Richard Dyer, 'The Idea of Pastiche', in Jostein Gripsrud (ed.) *The Aesthetic of Popular Art* (Kristiansand/Bergen: Høyskoleforlaget, 2001), pp. 79–91.
22 Jan-Christopher Horak, 'The Hollywood History Business', in Jon Lewis (ed.) *The End of Cinema As We Know It* (London: Pluto Press, 2001), p. 33.
23 Horak, 'The Hollywood History Business', p. 34. Horak notes that the first studio to found a fully-fledged archive was Warner Brothers in 1994.
24 See Jackie Stacey, *Star Gazing: Hollywood Cinema and Female Spectatorship* (London: Routledge, 1994); and Annette Kuhn, 'Cinema-going in Britain in the 1930s: Report of a Questionnaire Survey', *Historical Journal of Film, Radio and Television* 19 (4) 1999, 531–43.
25 Robert A. Rosenstone (ed.), *Revisioning History: Film and the Construction of a New Past* (Cambridge: Harvard University Press, 1995); Sobchack (ed.), *The Persistence of History*; Marcia Landy (ed.), *The Historical Film: History and Memory in Media* (London: The Athlone Press, 2001).
26 Sturken, *Tangled Memories*, p. 2.

I

Public history, popular memory

1

A white man's country:
Yale's *Chronicles of America*

Roberta E. Pearson

Writing in 1991, Michael Kammen stated, 'For more than a decade now, the connection between collective memory and national identity has been a matter of intense and widespread interest'.[1] Kammen's examples, ranging from Brazil to several Eastern and Western European countries, make it clear that he sees this interest as a global phenomenon, but the connection between collective memory and national identity has perhaps been most intensely debated in the historian's own country, the US. In the last two decades of the twentieth century, as identity politics gained increasing validity, 'minorities' such as African-Americans and Asian-Americans pressed claims to an 'authentic' self-representation in the country's influential signifying systems (the media, the schools, the museums and so forth). Simultaneously, a flood of immigrants from Asia and the global south sought refuge in the world's remaining super-power. Social and cultural elites (educators, state officials, public institutions and the like) reacted to identity politics and immigration with approbation or alarm: some urged a full embrace of multiculturalism while others worried about the fragmentation ensuing upon the collapse of a common culture. This elite contention echoed that of the previous century, when Southern and Eastern European immigration, African-American migration to large urban centres and the 'threat' of a rapidly expanding industrial working class had led to similar concerns about American culture and identity. These parallel circumstances, vastly different in many respects but alike enough to be instructive, suggest that issues of collective memory and national identity achieve a high profile in periods of rapid change and reconfiguration. This might account for American academics and cultural critics recently taking great interest in the representation of history and memory. Kammen's own magisterial

volume traces the formation and re-formation of American memory
from the Revolution to the end of the twentieth century. Other con-
tributions to the debate include the anthologies *Cultural Memory and
The Construction of Identity* and *History Wars*, including articles that
address topics as diverse as discourses of the past in Israeli pioneering settlement museums and the controversy over the Enola Gay
exhibit at the Smithsonian.[2] And there are many more.

My own contribution to the debate and to this volume returns to
the turn of the twentieth-century contestation over collective
memory attendant upon the decades of social turbulence beginning
in 1880 that some historians have labeled a hegemonic crisis, as
immigration, industrialisation and urbanisation rapidly altered the
country's social landscape. The immediate post-World War One
years, hailed hopefully as the 'return to normalcy', saw instead the
continuation of the crisis in the form of the upheaval of the Red
Scare and widespread labour unrest. In the face of the challenge to
national identity precipitated by rapid social and cultural change,
white Anglo-Saxon elites attempted to fashion the country's history
to make it consonant with their vision of a present and future dominated by themselves or at least their cultural values. As Michael
Wallace has suggested, 'The Haymarket affair and the great strikes
of the 1880s appear to have been the events that galvanized the
bourgeoisie into reconsidering its disregard for tradition . . . Class
struggle was transmuted into defense of "American values" against
outside agitators.'[3] The decades from the 1880s to the 1920s saw a
resurgence of interest in the colonial past as evidenced by the activities of historians, historical preservation societies, museum exhibi-
tions, and the emergence of genealogical societies such as the Sons
of the American Revolution and their higher-profile female counterparts, the Daughters of the American Revolution. These same years
were the age of historical pageants, such as 'The Pilgrim Spirit',
staged in Plymouth on the three hundredth anniversary of the
colonists' arrival, as well as of the first manifestations of the 'living
history' movement, when in 1926 John D. Rockefeller, Jr. gave
money for the Williamsburg restoration.

At a time of contested national identity, then, the colonial period
was enshrined as *the* originary moment of national identity as public
institutions and social elites constructed an official culture and official memory to shore up the hegemonic order. Might these official
texts have functioned differently than their popular counterparts?

In their fascinating study of the James Bond phenomenon, Tony Bennett and Janet Woollacott theorise that, while official culture/memory may be relatively stable, popular culture texts may act as a barometer of hegemonic reformulation.

> Periods of . . . innovation in popular fiction often coincide with those in which the ideological articulations through which hegemony was previously secured are no longer working to produce popular consent. In such moments, popular fictional forms may often prove more mobile and adaptable than more 'organic,' deeply implanted and institutionally solidified political ideologies which, owing to the longer term nature of the work they have to do, are not so conjuncturally pliable.[4]

This essay examines a group of texts that stemmed from a 'deeply implanted and institutionally solidified political' ideology, contrasting them with 'popular fictional forms' that do indeed retrospectively appear 'more mobile and adaptable'. In 1923 the Yale University Press undertook production of a series of educational feature films, the *Chronicles of America*, intended to instruct the nation's populace in their country's glorious history. The Press originally planned to make thirty-three *Chronicles of America* photoplays, taking the history of the US up to and through the Civil War, but, perhaps because of financial difficulties, ceased production in 1925 after fifteen films, most of which deal with the colonial and Revolutionary War period and several of which prominently feature Native Americans of the woodlands tribes, e.g. the Cherokee, the Shawnee and the Powhatans.[5] A statement by one of the editors chosen to supervise the project shows that the *Chronicles* producers consciously designed their texts in opposition to the historical spectacles appearing at the local Bijou.

> There must be films available that were conceived and carried out in every detail under the guidance of definite educational purposes and ideals. It seems almost obvious that films made primarily to appeal to the largest number, with little or no regard for educational values, must at best be seriously lacking as educational instruments and at worst maybe positively harmful . . . To think of using for educational purposes films designed merely to entertain would be not one whit more absurd than to think of making a set of trashy novels serve as serious textbooks.[6]

The Chronicles of America, based upon the popular fifty-volume American history series of the same title published by Yale University

Press, were sponsored by the Press, Yale's Council's Committee on Publications (the Press's editorial board) appointing three editors to supervise the project: 'Dr. Max Farrand, Professor of American History, Yale University; Dr. Frank E. Spaulding, Sterling Professor of School Administration and Head of the Department of Education at Yale; and Professor Nathaniel Wright Stephenson, formerly of the Department of History at the College of Charleston and later an exchange professor at Yale'.[7] The Council also formed a subsidiary company, the Chronicles of America Picture Corporation, headed by George Parmly Day, Treasurer of Yale and founder and president of the Yale University Press. The Corporation employed experienced Hollywood scriptwriters who wrote the scenarios in conjunction with historians, museum curators and members of various historical societies, and professional directors who oversaw the films' actual production, many of which were shot in the same locations where the historical events occurred, and at the same time of year. Before release, each film was screened and formally approved by the Council's Committee on Publications. The initial titles of each film state: 'Yale University Press presents *The Chronicles of America*. A series of photoplays based upon the fifty volumes published under the same name. The historical accuracy of this presentation of an important event in American History is guaranteed by the painstaking work of a number of distinguished historians. Approved by the Council's Committee on Publications of Yale University.' The Council intended these accurate and approved photoplays primarily for schools, colleges and other educational institutions, although response to the initial films was so positive, the publicists claimed, that the Corporation entered into an arrangement with the Pathé Exchange for a year-long theatrical distribution, apparently in the hope of ploughing profits back into production.

The *New York Times* reported that the series would not have been released to commercial cinemas if not for the desire to Americanise immigrants. 'The original plan of the Yale University Press was to show the pictures at schools and colleges but requests for a general release, to reach the foreign-born, prevailed.'[8] The producers' rhetoric was quite explicit about the series' ideological agenda. Nathaniel Stephenson, one of the three editors-in-chief of the Chronicles, reported that Yale University engaged in 'long deliberation' before granting the go-ahead for the project, persuaded by three arguments the series' proponents advanced: 'the fact that the general reader was losing interest in American history and might be recaptured by a true statement of it in pictorial form; that the great number of foreigners who read little in English except for recreation might be told the story of our country through the medium of their eyes; and that children were tired of the conventional ways of presenting history.'[9] The Press-issued pamphlet advertising the *Chronicles* series picked up on the second of these reasons, saying that the films constituted a 'powerful instrument for the stimulation of patriotism and good citizenship among native [born] Americans and foreign born citizens alike'.[10]

The perceived threat posed by the latter, the thousands of immigrants from Southern and Eastern Europe who had entered the country since the 1880s, shaped the *Chronicles*' ideological project. The panic among the country's white elites over immigration culminated in 1924, with Congressional legislation limiting the annual intake of immigrants from any country to 2 per cent of the number of that country's nationals resident in the US according to the 1890 census, a policy that favoured the British Isles, Germany and Scandinavia and restricted immigration from Southern and Eastern Europe.[11] In that same year the magazine *The World's Work*, whose publishers worried about the racial and moral degeneration of the American people and had advocated immigration laws excluding those not of British or Teutonic stock,[12] published an article about the *Chronicles of America* photoplays. Clayton Hamilton began his piece with a description of the 'immigration problem':

> For several decades, America has served not merely as a melting-pot but also as a dumping ground for aliens of many races, and it is not necessary to summon statisticians to support a general assertion that the ethnological complexion of the United States has been drastically changed within the last half-century. This drastic change is immediately noticeable in New York . . . and anybody who now travels at crowded hours in the New York subway must gather, from a gleaning of the faces within sight, an impression that our metropolis has become . . . a foreign city.[13]

Hamilton lauded the schools' effective Americanisation of the younger generation and pointed out the difficulty of reaching their non-English speaking parents. But he believed that the *Chronicles of America* photoplays could instruct even 'those polyglot multitudes in our densely populated cities that have not learned as yet to speak our common language' about 'our' common history and 'our' common values.[14] The film trade press emphasised the films' patriotic potential in slightly less xenophobic fashion, *Photoplay* asserting that the series' editors believed 'it will do much to promote good and intelligent citizenship' and *The Exhibitor's Herald* proclaiming that the films were 'a way to make better citizens'.[15]

The Chronicles' way of making better citizens was to persuade them of the virtues of Englishness and whiteness. On the title page of a draft script for *Gateway to the West* (1925) appears a telling epigram from nineteenth-century historian Francis Parkman. 'If France had preserved half of her American possessions a barrier would have been set to the spread of the English-speaking races . . .'[16] The *Chronicles of America* picture the triumphant spread of the 'English-speaking races' across the continent, all the heroes of Anglo-Saxon stock save the unavoidable Columbus, whose claims to the continent the series delegitimates in the opening title to Jamestown: 'By the 17th Century England claimed almost the whole of the present United States and most of what is now Canada'. All contesting that claim and impeding the Anglo-Saxon 'race's' manifest destiny, be they French, Spaniards or Native Americans, are the enemy, but it is always Indian 'outrages' that justify the warfare necessary to the westward march of the 'English-speaking races'. In *Vincennes* (1923) George Rogers Clark tells Patrick Henry, Governor of Virginia, that the only way to stop the Indian massacres of whites is to conquer the Northwest Territories. The two stand by the window looking out at settlers heading into the wilderness. Says Clark, 'It is always "Westward, ho!" They can't be held back, Gov. Henry, and we must make it safe for them.'

Making it safe for the settlers meant making it safe for white men (and women), as a title from the climatic sequence of *Boonestown* makes clear: 'Their tenacity has won a firm foothold on the new frontier of white colonization'. Or as the titular hero, Daniel Boone, puts it, 'If we turn and run before the Indians it will never be a white man's country.' And here's where the *Chronicles* perform a curious little ideological tap-dance. Since the *Chronicles* was aimed in part at 'the great number of foreigners who read little in English' and dependent in part upon their admissions fees for continued production, slandering potential viewers' ancestors did not make a great deal of ideological or economic sense. Yet the series' editors wanted to turn up the heat under the melting pot, not to celebrate multi-culturalism.

Hence, the *Chronicles* emphasises not simply the triumph of the 'English-speaking races' but the essential unity of all the 'white races'. Native Americans, constituting the smallest fraction of the cinema-going audience and already subject to powerful mechanisms of assimilation, perfectly filled the role of the non-white other whose negative representation conferred whiteness upon the majority of the series' viewers. The remainder of this chapter looks in more detail at the *Chronicles'* representation of Native Americans, briefly delineating the contemporary political situation that may have motivated the negativity and contrasting it with Hollywood's more positive or at the very least ambivalent portrayal.

The Puritans (1924) details the hardships encountered by some of the country's first white inhabitants: 'Privation and sorrow are the common lot during these early days in Massachusetts', declares an intertitle. The first part of the film establishes the sober, pious and self-sacrificing lifestyle of the Puritans in their Charlestown colony, the majority of the action taking place in front of Governor Winthrop's 'Great House', a half-timbered structure with leaded window panes that constantly invokes the spiritual presence of the Mother Country. In Charlestown, the country's original inhabitants are conspicuous by their absence, functioning as an unseen threat lurking in the primeval forest beyond the settlement's stockade. The first Indians appear as an intertitle shifts the setting to Merrymount, where 'flourishes a lawless trading post'. By contrast with the reassuring solidity of Governor Winthrop's residence, this settlement consists of crudely constructed lean-tos. And by contrast with the sober law and order of the Puritan community, the Indians who have come to trade scuffle playfully with their white hosts and drink liquor from large jugs. 'Thomas Morton, Master of Merrymount', has his arm around an Indian woman as she swigs from a flagon. In the next shot, two white men and two Indians bargain over the exchange of rifles for furs. Morton intervenes to expedite the proceedings then staggers off, his arm around the shoulder of one of the Indians. The sequence ends with a long shot of general revelry with Indians again swilling from jugs and staggering drunkenly. The next title tells us that 'At Charlestown, the Puritans decide to abolish the menace of Merrymount', which they do, sending an armed force, which kills many of the Indians and arrests Morton.

The Frontier Woman (1924) tells the story of the women of the Watauga settlement in Tennessee, whose men had gone to fight

the British during the Revolution. 'With every trader bringing fear-
ful tales of Indian uprisings the courageous women "carried on"
alone and refused to recall their warriors' who won a significant
victory 'that was a prelude to the defeat of Cornwallis'.[17] One of the
film's key sequences begins with the intertitle: 'Boys and old men are
the chief protection of the little stockade village against the vicious
Cherokee', followed by an exterior long shot of the gate of the
stockade village, defended by boys armed with long rifles. The following shots show women and little children in the woods, another
boy with a rifle standing guard. Margaret Johnson, the film's heroine, warns her children against straying too far, relating the cautionary tale of 'two other little girls and their mother who went into the
woods'. The film then shows us her story. A woman and two little
girls carrying baskets walk toward the camera from the rear of the
frame. Two Indians suddenly appear in the right and left foreground,
emerging from behind the boulder and bush where they had been
hiding. The women and children turn to run but other Indians leap
out in front of them and the Indians in the foreground run toward
them. The shot fades out on threatening figures with raised hatchets
surrounding the barely visible white characters, leaving the denoue-
ment to the childrens' and the viewers' imaginations. Neither the fictional children nor the film's audience should have had any difficulty
in completing the narrative, for in this scene *The Frontier Woman*
justifies the total war waged to exterminate the Indian foe by drawing upon the recurrent trope in American literature and art of white
women and children menaced by 'savages'. White women's fear of
death, and worse than death, at the hands of Indians, provided the
inspiration for the first American literary genre and the first American best-sellers, the captivity narratives, as well as for much early
American art, as in John Vanderlyn's *The Death of Jane McCrea*
(1804), John Mix Stanley's *Osage Scalp Dance* (1848) and George
Caleb Bingham's *Captured by Indians* (1848).

   The Frontier Woman's discrete fadeout spares the audience the
gruesome details, but a scene in *Vincennes* (1923) graphically alludes
to the consequences of an encounter with the hostile Indians. A
small family (mother, father, older and younger sons) sets out from
the stockaded settlement of Harrodsburg on their way west. The
father explains, 'My brother writes fer us to come, an' we're bound
fer the Ohio – Injuns or no Injuns. Somethin' keeps pulling me westward – a man can pick an' choose his acres away off yonder.' Our

hero, George Rogers Clark, says to the younger son, 'Take good care of that yellow scalp, boy'. Later, two white men arrive at Harrodsburg with an Indian captive and the white boy found with him, the older son from the previous scene. The boy reports that his younger brother may still be alive since, when Indians attacked his family, his mother told the little boy to hide. At this point one of the white men pulls a scalp from the Indian's belt. An intertitle follows: 'The scalping devil. It's the little feller's!'

The above are fairly typical examples of the *Chronicles*' representation of Native Americans as faceless, nameless lurkers in the forest, who emerge from the shadows only to kidnap, kill, scalp and, implicitly at least, rape the fair-haired Anglo-Saxons bravely establishing a new nation in the wilderness. Intertitles refer not only to 'scalping devils', a favourite descriptor, but also to 'skulking Cherokees', 'drunken Indians on a spree' and a room that 'reeks of Indian'. The few more prominent Indians, those who have names, fare no better than their unidentified brethren. The 'crafty' chief Blackfish, in *Daniel Boone*, leads his warriors against Boonestown, then retreats, convinced that 'the place is bewitched'. In *Jamestown*, Powhatan, father of Pocohontas (perhaps the only unproblematically 'good Indian' in the *Chronicles*), first sends spies to the colony to ascertain the state of its defences and then refrains from attack only because Gov. Dale has wisely taken his daughter hostage. The *Chronicles* represented its Indian villains as superstitious, credulous and easily intimidated, in short as in all ways inferior to any and all white men. In *Daniel Boone*, the shrewd woodsman time and again easily outwits his Indian foes. In one scene, walking alone through the forest, he instinctively knows that two Indians hide in waiting to pounce upon him. He stops, leans his rifle against a tree, takes out his knife, pantomimes hunger, pretends to swallow his weapon and then resumes his journey. One of the Indians says to the other, 'No kill – that man Boone swallow knife – him great paleface medicine man'. The *Chronicles*' Indians are so dull-witted that they cannot even wage war on their own, but must be lead by Spaniards, Frenchmen, and later Englishmen, who incite them to fight the colonists. As Daniel Boone says when the Indians try to tunnel into his settlement, 'More of the Frenchman's doings – those scalping devils would never think of it themselves!' But in the Revolutionary War period films, British officers leading the Indians against their fellow English-speakers pose an ideological contradiction for the

Anglophiliac *Chronicles* that a scene in *Vincennes* attempts to resolve. Henry Hamilton orders his Indian allies to make war on the colonists, but a British officer warns him, 'If you let loose these devils upon the rebels, the whole country will rise to drive you out!' Hamilton says to the Indian chief, 'Tell your braves there is to be no war against women and children – remember!' French officers issue no such injunctions.

The incidents omitted by the *Chronicles of America* from its 'accurate' and 'authorised' history of the US are perhaps even more revelatory of the producers' ideological stance. *The Frontier Woman* ceases its chronicle well before the forcible removal of those 'vicious' Cherokee from the land that had been theirs for generations. *Columbus* (1923) culminates with the arrival of the titular hero and his men in the 'new world'. The film shows the native peoples only in long shot, their backs to the camera as they cower behind foliage and watch a row boat approach the shore, and, then, rather sensibly, run away when the white men disembark. No natives watch as Columbus proclaims, 'In the name of Holy Church and in the name of their joint Majesties, Isabella, Queen of Castile, and Ferdinand, King of Aragon, I claim dominion over this new empire!' The film ends here, before Columbus and his successors enslave and murder the native populations. Perhaps even more curious than the omission of the white man's mistreatment of the Indian is the omission of the Indian's generous treatment of the white man, often the only factor saving the early colonists from starvation during harsh New England winters. *The Pilgrims* emphasises the threat posed by the Indians but not the aid offered. After the burial of a small child, Miles Standish orders the grave leveled. 'No trace of graves may be left; otherwise the watchful Indians might learn how pestilence is weakening us!' Then he directs that the colony's one cannon be prominently placed to impress the Indians. The film ends not, as one would expect, with the scene known to every American schoolchild of Pilgrims and Indians celebrating the first Thanksgiving, but rather with the Mayflower, the last link to home, departing for England.

The Chronicles' extremely negative representation of Native Americans can be seen as a displacement of fears stemming from the US's contemporary imperialistic responsibilities and from the domestic disturbances that resulted from industrial unrest and the Red Scare. After the closing of the western frontier, officially declared by Frederick Jackson Turner in 1893, the triumphant march of the white race across the nation had been extended on a global scale. As Richard Slotkin shows in *Gunfighter Nation*, many involved in advancing and in reporting the country's turn-of-the-century imperialist adventures used the frontier warfare analogy to cast indigenous peoples in the role of the hostile Indians and thus justify savage warfare in the service of white civilisation. For example, Slotkin quotes an article by Marion Wilcox on 'Philippine Ethnology' in which the author argues that 'that some of our present hostiles are blood-relations to the poor foes of the Pilgrims and the Puritans'.[18] This analogy still held in the 1920s, as demonstrated by the fact that a conference on 'Indians and Other Dependent Peoples' was held every fall at Lake Mohonk in New York State.[19] By showing how earlier generations had defeated and assumed administration over the 'primitive' Indians, the *Chronicles of America* could instruct the nation's youth, even those not descended from the 'English-speaking races', in the spirit of imperialism, a particularly important lesson in light of the prominent position among nation-states assumed by the country in the aftermath of the very recent World War One. As Frank E. Spaulding, one of the *Chronicles*' three co-editors, pointed out, '[The schools] must ever be mindful that the content and method of instruction is serving, and should be consciously made to serve, not merely to give adequate understanding of the past, and that as a guide to the future, but to shape the ideals and attitudes and to stimulate the resolutions of pupils who are bound to become large factors in determining the content of the historical stream as it flows on.'[20]

Just as the *Chronicles*' representation of Native Americans may well have resonated with the culture's discourses about imperialism and other 'dependent' peoples, it may also have resonated with discourses about the mobs and machinations of Reds, or Bolsheviks, or anarchists, or strikers that were said to be menacing the Republic. The perceived threat to national values escalated during the immediate post-World War One years, the years of high profile industrial disputes and the Red Scare, responded to by elites in government and industry with both violence and the violation of civil rights. Labour supported the government's war efforts, but as inflation hit hard after the victory, workers demanded higher wages. Management resisted these demands, causing great industrial unrest. Strikes became prevalent; in 1919 there were 3600 strikes involving more than 4 million workers and affecting key sectors, including the police and the steel and coal industries.[21] Industry leaders attempted to equate an anti-labour stance with 'Americanism'; for example, the president of the National Association of Manufacturers said in 1923, 'I can't conceive of any principle that is more purely American, that comes nearer representing the very essence of all those traditions and institutions that are dearest to us than the open shop principle.' In defense of those dear traditions, industry leaders adopted what they referred to as the American plan, which involved the hiring of strike-breakers and the use of gas and machine guns against strikers, the latter often stockpiled in anticipation of a strike.[22]

The conflation of Americanism and anti-unionism entailed forging links between labour and socialism or Bolshevism or anarchy, distinct political positions collectively labeled 'Reds' or 'radicals'. Despite the fact that many labour leaders, such as Samuel Gompers, supported capitalism and opposed collectivist schemes, the press and government officials attempted to fuse labour and radicalism in the public mind, amplifying fears of the possibility of a communist revolution in the US similar to that which occurred in Russia in 1917. In 1919, for example, the influential *Literary Digest* ran articles entitled 'American Labour and Bolshevisim' and 'Red Threat of a Revolution'. Senator Miles Poindexter, writing in the leading journal *Outlook* in 1920, claimed:

> There is no doubt whatever . . . that the majority of those strikes have been fomented by radical agitators, who are not concerned merely with demands for increase of wages or reduction of hours . . . but whose avowed purpose is to 'abolish the wage system'. By this, they mean communism. Strikes and sabotage, murder and assassination, are regarded by many [labour] leaders as legitimate means of bringing about [communism].[23]

To be fair, the fear of radicals was not entirely unfounded for in June 1919, anarchists mailed bombs to eighteen government officials and industry leaders. But the government responded with the most massive violation of civil rights in US history, the Justice Department rounding up six thousand supposed radicals, Bolsheviks and anarchists and deporting several hundred.

Hollywood produced several films that contributed to this fevered atmosphere of fear and suspicion: *Bolshevism On Trial* (1919), *The Burning Question* (1919), *The Right to Happiness* (1919), *The Undercurrent* (1919) and *Dangerous Hours* (1920). In many of these films, the generic 'Red' or 'radical' villains fomented worker unrest that led to strikes and riots. The armed intervention of the heroic US military suppressed the dangerous and violent mobs that threatened the very fabric of the Republic.[24] The cycle of explicitly anti-Red films ended as the high tide of the Red Scare receded but these films, together with other propaganda, established the stereotype of the 'Red' 'with wild eyes, bushy and unkempt hair and tattered clothes, holding a smoking bomb in his hands'.[25] A picture perfect example of this wild-eyed Red appears in Buster Keaton's *Cops* (1920), hurling a bomb into a police parade.

The *Chronicles of America* photoplays, of course, feature no 'Reds', for the producers never intended to extend their history beyond the Civil War, perhaps precisely because they feared dealing with contemporary and controversial topics such as labour unrest. But they clearly saw their chronicling of the country's early history as having relevance to the present. Writing about the *Chronicles* photoplays for his fellow educators, Frank Spaulding, Dean of Yale's School of Education and co-editor of the series, asserted, 'Recent world events and present conditions are stimulating us as never before to try to get our bearings with respect to the past, that we may proceed into the future more intelligently. Facts . . . of course remain forever unchanged but the interpretation of facts and the understanding of the significance of facts are subject to continuous change'.[26] Let us consider *The Puritans* again in the context of immediate post-war history and Spaulding's comments. Might not the mob of drunken and unruly Indians, with their illicitly obtained weapons, have been intended by the *Chronicles*' producers to serve as surrogates for the mobs of strikers and 'Reds' who had so recently rioted in America's cities? By comparison to the well-turned out Puritans they are as unkempt and wild-eyed as any 'Red' or anarchist. They are the threatening other, the dangerous mob, opposing the American values of the sober and hard working Puritans, just as 'Reds' and 'radicals' opposed the 'Americanism' of many government officials and industry leaders. Armed suppression of the transgressive inhabitants of Merrymount and their Indian friends may have recalled the similar violence meted out to strikers and 'Bolsheviks' during the immediate post war years with the same avowed intention of saving the sober and virtuous Republic.

In *The Puritans*, as in all the other *Chronicles* films in which they appear, Native Americans serve as stand-ins for the collective bogey men of the white American psyche: Bolsheviks; labour agitators; the

non-white races and so forth. This displacement permits the broad-
ening of that dominant white psyche to include those viewers who
under other circumstances may not have been granted the accolade
of whiteness: the Irish, Jews, Southern and Eastern Europeans. But
appealing to the whiteness of these viewers necessitated an unremit-
ting portrayal of Native Americans as savages. In this regard, the
Chronicles were in sympathy with many official histories that predi-
cated the country's foundation upon the subjugation of the Native
American, justifying their extinction by portraying them as
unreedemably savage. As Jon Sensbach, of the Institute of Early
American History and Culture, said in a response to an earlier version of this essay, 'It was crucial to demonstrate that despite the white
man's best intentions and efforts, the Indians' inherent barbarism
made them unfit for peaceful coexistence, unfit for redemption and
assimilation, unfit indeed for anything but conquest and confinement
on reservations'.[27]

Yet the official perspective represented in the *Chronicles* was but
one side of the two contrasting representations of Native Americans
that dated back several centuries. From the moment of the first
encounter, Europeans had oscillated between describing native peoples as 'savage savages', fit only for extermination, or 'noble savages', at one with nature in a manner that eluded Europeans
corrupted by 'civilisation'. Both representations served to justify the
eradication of native peoples and their cultures but did so in slightly
different ways. The 'savage savage' depiction sanctioned the genoci-
dal policies that mandated the forcible removal to the reservations
and the military suppression of those who resisted. The 'noble
savage' depiction was easily deployed in the rhetoric of nineteenth-
century scientific racism: admirable in many ways, Native Americans
were still lower on the evolutionary scale than Europeans and the
process of natural selection would ensure their ultimate disappearance. By the 1920s this disappearance seemed well under way and
the 'noble savage', also known as the 'Vanishing American',
appeared throughout the culture, from anthropological studies to
major Hollywood features. During the silent film era, 1894–1927,
Native Americans featured in countless films.[28] Although many of
these were run-of-the-mill Westerns in which Indians served only as
moving targets, a fair number featured sympathetically drawn
Indian protagonists. For the sake of brevity, then, let us look at two
of the silent period's historical epics, *The Last of the Mohicans*

(1920) and *The Vanishing American* (1925), films that feature good examples of the 'noble savage' trope so prevalent in the 1920s and so conspicuously absent from *The Chronicles of America*.

The Last of the Mohicans, directed by Maurice Tourneur, features two Indian protagonists: Magua, so savage that he 'does not kill his prisoners. He tortures them', and Uncas, the titular last of his race, so noble that the film permits a romance between him and the white heroine, Cora. The film here follows its literary source, but, unlike the novel, does not establish that Cora herself is of mixed racial heritage, a device Cooper used to justify the attraction between Uncas and Cora to his early nineteenth-century readers. In the film, a key scene between the two shows Cora watching Uncas silhouetted against the mouth of the cave where they hide from the hostile Indians pursuing them. An intertitle guardedly alludes to the racial difference, stressing their disparity rather than their common link of 'non-white' blood. 'The bond of a common danger – drawing together these two, so widely separated by the mystery of birth'. Uncas comes to sit by Cora, points at the rising moon and talks. The next intertitle deliberately distinguishes this prince of the wilderness from your common or garden variety savage. 'Simple words of a savage – yet revealing depths of thought and imagination'. Of course, Uncas is not only noble but doomed and dies fighting the wicked Magua. The film's final scene shows Uncas' father standing beside his son's burial scaffold on a lonely crag at sunset. He proclaims, 'Woe, for the race of red men! In the morning of Life I saw the sons of my forefathers happy and strong – and before nightfall I have seen the passing of the last of the Mohicans.'

Despite its sympathy for its titular character, *The Last of the Mohicans* features an extensive massacre of white men, women and children by the hostile Indians and thus might be said implicitly to support savage warfare against the Maguas if not the Uncases, who will conveniently manage their own disappearance. *The Vanishing American*, based on Zane Grey's 1925 novel of the same name, takes a more 'scientific' view of the Native American, a prologue added for the film mounting a Spencerian argument about the natural succession of stronger races over weaker. The film begins with a quote from Herbert Spencer's 'First Principles': 'We have unmistakable proof that throughout all past time there has been a ceaseless devouring of the weak by the strong . . . a survival of the fittest.' The film then shows a series of 'races' – cavemen, basket makers, slab-house people, cliff dwellers, 'the first of the race we now call "Indians"', the Spanish and finally the white man, in the person of Kit Carson and the US Cavalry, all claiming dominion over the same southwest valley, each ousting the previous residents. Kit Carson promises that the Indians will dwell forever in their valley, but an intertitle tells us,

> To those who followed him, the Indians were but encumbrances to the soil, to be cleared away with the sage brush and the cactus. By the opening of the twentieth century, the Indians had been forced backward, into a desert country called by courtesy, a 'reservation' – with one narrow strip of fertile fields, barely sufficient to provide corn for the winter. In the shade of great trees, and with flowing water murmuring by, the white man had laid out – for his own use – the town of Mesa, headquarters of the Indian Agent.

The film's present-day story, set before, during and immediately after World War One, echoes contemporary events that revealed among white Americans of the 1920s a widespread sympathy for the Native American. The exploitation of Southwest tribes, such as the Pimas of Arizona, by whites eager for their land and natural resources had been much in the news, as had the efforts of various progressive reform organisations to aid the Indians. In 1924, in that great bastion of middle-American sentiment, *The Saturday Evening Post*, Herbert Work, the current Secretary of the Interior, condemned those who would defraud his Indian wards as 'beyond the pale of public respect and impervious to the promptings of humane motives'.[29] *The Vanishing American* took much this view of its white villains, the assistant Indian agent and his minions, who throughout the film plot and scheme to steal the Indians' horses, water and land. While the white characters are savage, the Indian characters are all thoroughly noble, the most noble of all being Nophaie, descendant of the brave warriors who fought the Spanish and the Americans. Upon his departure for the war he tells the white school teacher whom he loves, and who reciprocates his feelings, 'Since we are Americans, we go fight. Maybe if we fight . . . maybe if we die . . . our country will deal fairly with our people'.[30] But like Uncas, his literary and cinematic predecessor, Nophaie too dies by the film's end, and although his death coincides with the defeat of the evil white men, he becomes yet another in a long line of noble but doomed savages.

Both Uncas and Nophaie belong to the race of 'Vanishing Americans', established as a powerful metaphor early in the nineteenth century by Cooper among others, and a prevalent trope by the late nineteenth and early twentieth centuries, appearing in paintings, sculptures, novels, photographs and scholarly treatises.[31] But these sympathetic 'vanishing Americans' did not appear in Yale's *Chronicles of America*, which were much more negative and monolithic in their representation of the Native American than much popular culture of the 1920s. Intended to meet fairly clear cut ideological goals, the *Chronicles* exhibits none of the inconsistencies and contradictions that mark films such as *The Last of the Mohicans* and *The Vanishing American*. The producers of popular culture, having to appeal to a mass audience, seem to have responded to the society's contradictory discourses about Native Americans with less ideologically coherent, more potentially polysemic texts. In the case of the *Chronicles of America*, at least, 'popular fictional forms' do indeed seem to have been 'more mobile and adaptable than more "organic", deeply implanted and institutionally solidified political ideologies'.

Notes

1   Michael Kammen, *Mystic Chords of Memory: The Transformation of Tradition in Amerian Culture* (New York: Vintage Books, 1993), p. 3.
2   Dan Ben-Amos and Liliane Weissberg (eds), *Cultural Memory and the Construction of Identity* (Detroit: Wayne State University Press, 1999); Edward T. Linenthal and Tom Engelhardt (eds), *History Wars: The Enola Gay and Other Battles for the American Past* (New York: Henry Holt and Co., 1996).
3   Michael Wallace, 'Visiting the Past: History Museums in the United States', *Radical History Review* 25 (1981), 66.
4   Tony Bennett and Janet Wollacott, *Bond and Beyond: The Political Career of a Popular Hero* (London: Macmillan, 1987), p. 281.
5   The fifteen films in production, not historical, order were: *The Frontier Woman* (1923); *Vincennes* (1923); *Daniel Boone* (1923); *Columbus* (1923); *Jamestown* (1923); *The Declaration of Independence* (1924); *Dixie* (1924); *Alexander Hamilton* (1924); *Peter Stuyvesant* (1924); *The Pilgrims* (1924); *The Eve of the Revolution* (1924); *Wolfe and Montcalm* (1924); *Yorktown* (1924); *The Puritans* (1925) and *Gateway to the West* (1925). The Motion Picture Division of the Library of Congress has viewing copies of all fifteen, although some are incomplete, and I understand that Yale University also has a set in its film archives.

While financial difficulties most likely caused the cessation of production, it might also have been the case that the post-Civil War period, dealing with events a mere half-century in the past, might have proved too contentious for filming.

6 Frank E. Spaulding, 'America's History Vitalized', *The Journal of the National Education Association* 14 (June 1925), 175.
7 'The Chronicles of America Photoplays' (New Haven: Yale University Press, n.d.), p. 10.
8 'Yale Shows "Columbus"', *New York Times*, 5 October 1923, p. 2.
9 Nathaniel W. Stephenson, 'Yale Historical Films', *National Education Association, Proceedings and Addresses* 62 (1924), 982.
10 'The Chronicles of America Photoplays', p. 2.
11 Irving Bernstein, *The Lean Years: A History of The American Worker, 1920–1933* (Boston: Houghton Mifflin Co., 1960), p. 50.
12 Richard Slotkin, *Gunfighter Nation: The Myth of the Frontier in Twentieth-Century America* (New York: Atheneum, 1992), p. 159.
13 Clayton Hamilton, 'American History on the Screen', *The World's Work* (August 1924), p. 525.
14 Hamilton, 'American History', p. 526.
15 'Filming the History of America at Yale', *Photoplay*, December 1923, p. 89 and *The Exhibitor's Herald* quoted in 'The Chronicles of America Photoplays', p. 2.
16 Draft script for *Gateway to the West*, Folder VII, Box 1 (Photoplay Scenarios), Nathaniel W. Stephenson Collection, Manuscripts Division, Library of Congress.
17 'The Chronicles of America Photoplays', p. 57.
18 Marrion Wilcox, 'Phillipine Ethnology', *Harper's Weekly* (13 May 1899), pp. 485, 487, quoted in Slotkin, *Gunfighter Nation*, p. 110.
19 See 'America and Its Dependent Peoples', *The Outlook* (28 October 1914), p. 441.
20 Spaulding, 'America's History Vitalized', p. 175.
21 Robert K. Murray, *Red Scare: A Study in National Hysteria, 1919–1920* (Minneapolis: University of Minnesota Press, 1955), pp. 8–9.
22 Bernstein, *The Lean Years*, pp. 89, 147, 151.
23 'Labour and the Open Shop', *Outlook* (5 May 1920), p. 324.
24 Kevin Brownlow, *Behind the Mask of Innocence* (Berkeley: University of California Press, 1990), pp. 442–55.
25 Murray, *Red Scare*, p. 68.
26 Spaulding, 'America's History Vitalized', p. 175.
27 Jon Sensbach, 'Comment on Roberta E. Pearson, "A White man's country!" *The Chronicles of America Photoplays*', at the conference 'Possible Pasts: Critical Encounters in Early America', Philadelphia, 1994.

28 Since the majority of silent films no longer survive (due to the chemical instability of the film stock), it is impressive that the Library of Congress has issued a forty-eight page filmography of pre-sound films concerning the American Indian in its collection alone. See Karen C. Lund, *American Indians in Silent Film: Motion Pictures in the Library of Congress* (Washington, DC: Library of Congress, n.d.).

29 Herbert Work, 'Our American Indians', *The Saturday Evening Post* (31 May 1924), p. 27.

30 In fact, Indians were granted citizenship in 1924, following arguments that those who were allowed to die for their country should be allowed to vote.

31 For information on the social and cultural position of Native Americans during this period see Brian W. Dippie, *The Vanishing American: White Attitudes and U.S. Indian Policy* (Lawrence: University of Kansas Press, 1982) and Robert F. Berkhofer, Jr., *The White Man's Indian: Images of the American Indian From Columbus to the Present* (New York: Alfred A. Knopf, 1978).

2

Civic pageantry and public memory in the silent era commemorative film: *The Pony Express* at the Diamond Jubilee

Heidi Kenaga

> 'The Pony Express' is one of the group of pictures we planned to make that would tell, in dramatic form, the absorbing story of this country's growth. 'The Covered Wagon' told the story of the pioneers' trek· across the prairies. 'The Pony Express' will depict the hardships, the trials and the victories of the men who maintained communication with the outposts of civilization which those pioneers established in the Far West.
>
> (Jesse Lasky, Paramount head of production, 1925)

> [W. H. Fuller, chief counsel to the Federal Trade Commission, acknowledged] that under the public interest angle . . . pictures as a whole have been admitted to be a greater influence than the public schools upon the youth of the nation. The contrast was made, however, that the purpose of the schools was to build good citizens while pictures are shown for but one purpose – to build dividend.
>
> (*Variety* story on the anti-trust proceedings, 1925)[1]

Paramount's historical Western, *The Pony Express* (1925), was one of a cycle of popular frontier epics released in the late silent era.[2] Capitalising on the tremendous success of Paramount's *The Covered Wagon* (1923), several American producers released similar prestige features, including among others Fox's *The Iron Horse* (1924), Paramount's *The Vanishing American* (1925) and a Goldwyn production distributed by United Artists, *The Winning of Barbara Worth* (1926). Despite their popularity and central position in the studios' production strategies during the mid-1920s, these movies remain underexamined in film studies literature.[3] George Fenin and William Everson, for example, argue that *The Pony Express* was 'ignored by the public', achieving neither the huge box office returns nor the long-term impact of *The Covered Wagon*. Yet the film was considered one of 1925's top moneymakers, and it also made the 'Ten Best' list in many trade journals as well as periodicals and newspapers.[4] Other historians have simply substantiated producers' own claims that such movies were the first to present the West 'authentically', or suggest that they presage the 1950s' superwesterns in their appeal to adult audiences.[5] These accounts fail to explain why the Western subject became so broadly popular as well as culturally sanctioned during the postwar era, nor do they fully account for the industry's avid promotion of the prestige frontier feature during this time.

In this chapter, I will discuss how American producers (especially Paramount) cultivated this cycle with a view toward exploiting its public relations utility. By transforming the erstwhile materials of dime novels into 'authentic' documents of national culture, the studios sought to legitimise their market dominance and burgeoning social power. As such, I argue that these films should be reconceptualised as key commodities of the heritage industry – what I call 'commemorative films' – during the period of New Era corporatism. Paramount carefully developed and marketed these movies in order to construct a new position for itself as a 'legitimate' purveyor and even guardian of historical memory. Other studios followed suit, hoping to sanction their product as an authoritative voice in the arena of historical representation. As Roberta Pearson notes in the preceding chapter, this was a much-contested domain during the early decades of the twentieth century, when racial nativist movements sought to control popular expressions of the nation's primogeniture. Here I take a case-study approach to understanding this process of mediation and negotiation by focusing on the postwar industrial and cultural contexts of *The Pony Express*, which premiered at California's Diamond Jubilee in 1925.

Initiatives by social and civic elites during the early 1920s to regulate the dominant form of entertainment in American life reveal the extent to which movies had become a site of struggle over who could legitimately circulate types of knowledge (for example, historical knowledge) that were invested with cultural power. Postwar xenophobia, on the ascent in domestic policies, often helped fuel such elites' anxieties about the putative control of the studios by 'nonnatives'. Further, the Federal Trade Commission was investigating Paramount's alleged monopolistic practices, viewed as undemocratic and 'alien' to the American free-market system. In response, the producers (largely under Paramount's leadership) established the Motion Picture Producers and Distributors of America

(MPPDA). While its public mandate addressed concerns expressed by cultural custodians about transgressive movie content, the MPPDA primarily sought to deflect criticism of the industry by adopting the strategies of the emergent public relations trade.[6] As Richard Maltby has persuasively argued, discourses on censorship during this period were less about eliminating offensive material than about struggles to delineate 'the cultural function of entertainment and the possession of cultural power'.[7] Always ready to adopt modern business practices, the studios realised that their skillful marketing apparatus needed to encompass not just product, but producer; in the New Era, successful companies had to be refigured as both 'economically efficient and socially beneficial . . . the economic realities of the industrial society [threatened by the instability of market forces] encouraged the use of specialists and auxiliaries, including publicity men'. Wartime experiences had shown how useful trade associations could be in securing not just economic stability but something equally valuable, public approval and endorsement.[8] Consequently, under the MPPDA's aegis, Paramount proactively targeted an adaptation of a wholesome frontier story, *The Covered Wagon*, for prestige treatment. For an imperiled mass-culture industry, upgrading the noncontroversial 'horse opera' to the status of national epics – commemorations in episodes in the American frontier metanarrative – was an opportune solution. As *Exhibitors' Trade Review* noted,

> [T]he biggest thing about [*The Covered Wagon*] is not its entertainment value, though that factor is absolutely certain and points the way to extraordinary box-office success. The biggest of all the big things about 'The Covered Wagon' is its emphatic Americanism. The picture gives this industry a push forward because it shows that the American story can be just as dramatic . . . than 9/10 of all the other kinds of stories, American or foreign . . . every person in the country should see it. It's a prosperity picture, and the prosperity will not consist wholly of financial return. The bigger prosperity it will bring . . . will be in the form of a good-will check upon the greatest of all banks – the Bank of Public Opinion.[9]

Hoping to cash in on that 'good-will check' again, Paramount tried a variant of the formula in *The Pony Express*, which visualised historical events while interpolating fictional characters whose actions affect the course of nationhood. The film depicts the machinations of California Senator McDougal Glen (Albert Hart) to control the

Pony Express circuit. His alliance with the pro-slavery movement as well as a drive for personal power leads to covert strategies to rend California from the Union. By delaying the swiftest transmission of the results of the Lincoln election in November by the express riders, Glen hopes to foment a secessionist movement in the state which would result in the creation of a Republic of California. His plans are foiled by Frisco Jack Weston (Ricardo Cortez), a gambler who secretly learns of Glen's plans and joins the express service to make sure the message gets through to 'save California for the Union'. Stationed in Julesburg, Colorado, with his friend 'Rhode Island Red' (Wallace Beery), Jack falls in love with Molly Jones (Betty Compson), daughter of local religious fanatic Abraham 'Ascension' Jones (Ernest Torrence). Julesburg's de facto mayor, Overland Express agent Jack Slade (George Bancroft), is conspiring with Glen to subvert the election results. Slade's henchman, Charlie Bent, is a 'half-breed' scout who leads Sioux raiding parties against covered wagon trains moving westward, later splitting the proceeds with his boss. But just as the Pony Express rider arrives with news of Lincoln's election, Bent tires of Slade's manipulation and conspires with the Sioux to destroy the town. Frisco Jack manages to get the election results through while the army arrives to quell the Sioux attack. Slade dismisses Weston from the Pony Express service on a technicality, and despite his actions to subvert its purposes, Slade is promoted by the company for 'his honesty, loyalty and bravery', getting public credit for Jack's efforts. As the nation prepares for the outbreak of war, Jack and Molly marry.[10]

Like its predecessors, *The Pony Express* places a white couple at the forefront of this historical trajectory. Jack Slade's privileging of self-interest and acquisition over national commitment takes on an explicitly racial cast in the film. His opportunistic collaboration with the Indians to raid passing covered wagon trains functions as a local analogue to his anti-nationalist alliance with Senator Glen. Although he treats his 'half-breed' henchman with disdain, his enlistment of Charlie Bent – whose name suggests his racial sympathies are also out of alignment – implies their kinship rather than their difference. It is thus Slade's inability to respect the hegemonic relationship between whites and Others which is associated with the erosion of national unification.

At the same time, Slade is linked with Jack Weston; not only do they share a first name, both are aligned with national figures (Glen and

Lincoln), both are pursuing Molly Jones, and both have a 'secret mission' regarding the Pony Express. This paired structure in the classical Hollywood narrative is common, of course, but the ending of *The Pony Express* is not. Slade's public promotion contrasts starkly with his unpatriotic actions in obstructing the course of national unification, whereas Jack's efforts to 'save California for the Union' go unrecognised. In this way, the film offers spectators an object lesson in the motive power of a single individual's national sentiment. If Slade was the historical beneficiary of Jack's actions, *The Pony Express* offered contemporary spectators a more laudable Western progenitor committed to sovereignty of nation rather than pragmatic racial accommodation and economic opportunism. And by obscuring the Pony Express' historical origin as a business venture in favour of its role in ensuring Lincoln's mandate, the narrative motivates the emergence of the transcontinental connection not in commercial, but rather national, interests.

It is clear that Paramount designed this narrative as another statement of its commitment to Americanism; such films could help the studio refigure its position within public discourse as a legitimate purveyor of historical memory, with less interest in building 'dividend' than in creating 'good citizens'. While the director of *The Covered Wagon*, James Cruze, had achieved a solid reputation as a deft visualiser of historical chronicle, Paramount understood the importance of linking authorship with those elites who had participated in the debates over movies' social power. Consequently, they hired Henry James Forman, a Harvard-educated fiction writer and literary critic who had worked at several upscale magazines and was editor of *Collier's* during the war. While Forman may have been brought on the project for his research skills, or his ability to build a compelling story around the historical familiar of a racing express rider, it is likely that his class position as well as his 'white' racial identity were most appealing to the studio. Further, Forman was no doubt willing to participate in the 'cinema uplift policy' championed by the MPPDA; he is probably best known as the author of the 1933 summary of the Payne Fund research, *Our Movie-Made Children*, which reveal his opinions about the responsibilities of the industry to maximise the tutorial possibilities of the moving image. *The Covered Wagon*, he claimed, 'thrill[ed] audiences with pride in the courage and fearlessness of their forefathers, in the irresistible conquest of obstacles'. Writing a sequel to this cinematic document offered Forman an opportunity to educate viewers about the historical foundations of national growth as a means to garner civic commitment. In turn, Paramount's cultivation of this writer for *The Pony Express* story demonstrated their commitment to avoiding 'unsuitable' stories for the screen, often the subject of controversy within public discourse.[11]

Repeating the strategies of their promotional campaign for *The Covered Wagon*, Paramount's publicity narratives about the preparation of *The Pony Express* focused on the accuracy of the story. One such narrative, published in *Sunset*, a magazine about California history, offered readers a detailed account of the production circumstances. This piece is an artefact of studio-generated public relations, epitomising Paramount's tactic to maximise the 'authenticity' of their new cycle of historical Westerns. Subtitled 'Old-Timers May View Pony Express Thriller Without Being Outraged by "Things That Ain't So"', it was written (or ghost-written) by H. C. Peterson, 'an authority on the old West' hired by Cruze to ensure the production's accuracy in costume and setting. In a sense, Peterson constitutes a de facto 'witness' for readers to the history being (re)created on screen, endorsing Forman's efforts to 'thrill audiences with the fearlessness of their forefathers'. The article asserts the film's firm foundation in the historical record by asking a rhetorical question that implies the cinema's emergent position as a purveyor of historical memory: 'Is the motion picture public yet ready to accept a technically correct historical film, one showing events as they actually happened, or must it show them as the movie fan would prefer they should have happened?' In the course of his research, *Sunset* reports, Forman had discovered that 'documentary evidence on the story of the Pony Express was notoriously scarce, that the books on the subject left much to be desired, and that practically every man connected with that early mail service was dead'. His work on behalf of the film project therefore continued, in a transcontinental journey taking him from the Library of Congress and archives in New York through repositories in St. Joseph, Missouri; Cheyenne, Wyoming; Denver, Colorado; and Reno, Nevada. Then officials of the Wells Fargo Bank heard of the project. 'For old times' sake' – the Wells Fargo express company had purchased the original pony express franchise – the bank directed Forman toward Sacramento's California collection, the 'largest and rarest collection of pony express data in existence, data which made it possible for him to complete his story'. Here the publicity narrative paralleled the filmic one: culled from sources all over the country, Forman's story could only be completed when he 'arrived' in California, just as the pony express riders had to 'make it' to Sacramento to create a transcontinental link.[12]

Paramount's drive to authenticate *The Pony Express'* historical mise-en-scène optimally served the goals of national chronicle, providing movie patrons with knowledge not readily available in the traditional literature on the West. The story of the pony express 'with its fearless riders [provided] a most fascinating possibility for the motion picture', and moreover cinema could restore this forgotten story to the public.[13] The documents of visual culture, especially motion pictures, challenged the hegemony of the written word as the authoritative repository of historical memory. In fact, in the case of *The Pony Express*, the usual process of fiction-to-film adaptation is reversed: Forman's historical novel, *The Pony Express: A Romance*, derived from his research for the film, was published after the movie's premiere.[14] Demonstrating the studio's disavowal of any economic imperative behind the prestige frontier feature, this text helped reinforce Paramount's promotional claims that their films offered patrons a viewing experience constructed as socially and culturally remedial. At the conclusion of the book's prologue, Forman asserts the tutorial value of this nearly forgotten struggle for contemporary America, especially its youth: 'To the youngsters today, after the Great War, the business of slavery and anti-slavery, secession and unionism, things that tore a nation asunder, are dead words read in a history book . . . who now thinks of that epic of American growth, the overland pony express, that did so much in saving both California and the Union'.[15]

This feature also distinguishes *The Pony Express*, film and novel, from the contemporary tradition of commemorative films: both texts strongly express a link between 'saving' California and the preservation of the Union. As historian David Glassberg has commented, the state has often viewed as lacking the strong sense of the past found in other regions of the country, such as New England or the South. 'For much of American history', he notes, 'California has represented a land of new opportunities, a place where Americans move to escape the past, not to find it . . . the California landscape appears to have sprung up yesterday, the material expression of a people rootless, placeless, always in flux'.[16] Since the 1920s' nativist movements commonly constructed the American historical legacy as edifying, capable of producing better citizens, the documents of that legacy were given greater cultural power. Not surprisingly, therefore, Hollywood's film producers – and Paramount in particular – had much at stake in cultivating in cinematic form a shared public memory of California's participation in the foundations of the modern nation. Correspondingly, the studio designed *The Pony Express*, from earliest conception to its premiere event, to revise the American movie patron's historical amnesia about the state. My comparison of preproduction materials with the extant print of *The Pony Express* suggests that, for Paramount, serving the interests of industry public relations was likely more important than that of 'authentic' historical chronicle. Despite Forman's extensive research on the 'lost' Pony Express story, he shared screenplay credit with the head of Paramount's scenario department, Walter Woods. Moreover, director James Cruze – described in one contemporary biographical sketch as having 'a corporation and not an artistic conscience' – contributed significantly to the script.[17] Perhaps the most salient result of this collaborative effort was the addition of many more explanatory intertitles detailing how the Pony Express 'did so much in saving both California and the Union' – that is, how Jack's selfless actions served Lincoln's national mandate – offering regular reinforcements of the film's didactic function to commemorate the state's history.

Ultimately, however, the success of *The Covered Wagon* had demonstrated to Paramount the importance of controlling the publicity narratives about their commemorative films, more so than the specific features of the story itself. Principal photography on *The Pony Express* only took about six weeks, during which time the studio's exploitation apparatus worked overtime to create national interest in the production. One key tactic involved broad press coverage of trips by political figures and Western writers to the location filming, 'such was the attraction of the historical production of a famous story'. California Senator Samuel Shortridge watched the activities on the four rebuilt blocks of the old capital, while 'old-timers' from Salt Lake, Denver, and Montana as well as writers and historians such as Arthur Chapman and Rufus Steele visited the Cheyenne location. Attempting to generate patron interest in the 'Far West' theme, Paramount invited 'forty-two editors of Utah and Colorado', who observed the production and reported on its progress for state papers.[18]

However, the most noteworthy event, covered in both the trades and the popular press, was Vice President Charles Dawes' July visit to 'Camp Cruze', who by lucky coincidence was en route to San Francisco for the Diamond Jubilee celebration. Cruze even offered the Vice President the chance to turn the crank 'on one of the most important scenes'. Having seen when the 'wild West was still wild' during his boyhood in western Nebraska, Dawes commented, he could offer his sanction of the film's authenticity: 'I think you are trying to do a tremendous thing in making pictorial history. Today you can still make pictures which show the old West in accurate form. Fifty or one hundred years from now it will be impossible to do it.' Just as there had been a special screening of *The Covered Wagon* for Warren Harding at the White House during the summer of 1923, Dawes suggested a similar event be scheduled for President Coolidge when *The Pony Express* was completed. By 1925, Paramount had succeeded in achieving a position as an 'authoritative' national chronicler to the extent that they could secure endorsement by a *civic paterfamilias* of their heritage films prior to release, rather than after distribution and critical response.[19]

Of greatest importance to Paramount's goal to invite consumption of *The Pony Express* as an historical document of the nation's reunification was the selection of the premiere site. The studio's carefully orchestrated debut of *The Covered Wagon* in New York had proven how the controlled exhibition event could have tremendous returns, both financially and from the 'Bank of Public Opinion'. My research suggests that in fact the studio may well have designed the production to optimally fit the premiere setting: California's Diamond Jubilee celebration of the state's 1850 admission to the Union. Held in San Francisco in early September, the Jubilee had been widely publicised across the state since early in the year, and the boosters of the event had contacted Los Angeles' Chamber of Commerce in April to elicit their support of 'California's Jubilee Year'. The state's larger theatres had already been partially enlisted in the effort; ushers wore new uniforms in Jubilee colours during the summer and fall of 1925, and beginning in August managers set up brief radio talks about the Jubilee before showings.[20] In a move than seems more than coincidental, Paramount had recently acquired the 1,400–seat Imperial theatre, the city's leading extended-run venue, as part of their purchase of the Rothchild chain.[21] Debuting *The Pony Express* during the Diamond Jubilee would help the studio

build fruitful associations (both short and long-term) between cinematic text and historical pageantry, offering patrons a suitable commemorative document as well as evidence of their commitment to
Americanism. At the same time, the cultural work performed by the
film – a onetime 'lowbrow' product now refigured within its premiere setting as document of public memory – camouflaged the
studio's continuing acquisition of exhibition outlets as a means to
secure market hegemony.

Held from 5–12 September 1925, California's Diamond Jubilee
was probably the most extravagant statewide celebration of the
decade. 9 September was Admission Day, 'a holiday originated by
the Pioneer societies to commemorate the anniversary of California
statehood . . . [and] the occasion for ever more elaborate celebrations'.[22] Over one and a half million people attended the Jubilee, at
a time when the total population of California was four million.
Multiple commercial and civic interests determined its features,
designed to surpass previous state centennials by imitating the scope
and ambition of the world's fairs and expositions. Important early
supporters included San Francisco's Down Town Association and
prominent editors and publishers of San Francisco newspapers,
especially the *Chronicle*. From its inception, the Jubilee was clearly
conceived as a vehicle of state boosterism, 'directed toward [making
the Jubilee] the cynosure of the eyes, not only of California, but of
the world', reported the official commemorative monograph.[23] Like
the earlier expositions, the Jubilee's primary *raison d'être* was to
chart a specific historical trajectory for broad public consumption
via interpretive staging, made particularly pressing by growing concerns about the economic and social power of 'non-natives'. The
Jubilee commemorative monograph is dedicated to three hereditary
organisations who had sponsored the festival's pageantry: 'the Society of California Pioneers, the Native Sons of the Golden West and
the Native Daughters of the Golden West'.[24]

The dissemination of 'authentic' historical episodes in the state's
past was considered an essential function of the exposition, both in
terms of public commemoration and civic education. Its centrepiece
was the Admission Day march, the preparation for which required
'absolute authenticity in detail, with reasonable allowances for col-
orful presentation'.[25] With over fifty-five thousand marchers and one
hundred floats, the parade depicted incidents across four centuries of
settlement in California, beginning with the 'legendary period' and

the successive depiction of Indian, Spanish and Mexican cultures. But all of these eras were simply prelude to the greatness to come, the 'American period', during which time there arrived in California 'the brave, the dauntless, the men of great hope and vision, with strong arm and clear head, relying upon individual exertion and native ability to conquer all hardships and dangers and build a nation'. Correspondingly, floats depicting these hardships of the American period constituted about one-half of the entire parade.[26] According to historian John Bodnar, such a design was common in historical commemorations during the 1920s. The patriotic campaigns of World War One and 'Americanisation' drives greatly influenced the expression of ethnic ancestry during the 1920s, resulting in 'colourful' but depoliticised representations of music or costume that 'neatly fitted into the larger pageant of American history [which] told of an inevitable and painless transformation of diverse folk cultures into a unified American culture'.[27]

One observer's firsthand account of the parade illustrates well the ideological function of the Admission Day parade. Writing for *The Outlook*, Hugh A. Studdert Kennedy describes his experience this way:

> From far and near men and women had come with their wonderful moving tableaux, designed to show how man's inventive genius, courage, and patience had here found their typical American expression . . . in San Francisco and throughout the State in Diamond Jubilee week . . .

> And so for one glorious week [the San Franciscan] spent himself in telling himself and his neighbors and all the world how great things the idea that is California, that is America, that is, in the last test, the ideal of Anglo-Saxon thought and hope, had done for him and his . . . In all this last western movement of our race, which began three centuries ago, no greater barrier to progress was ever interposed than that which lay between the East and West in the days of the covered wagon . . . Thousands died on those weary marches – died of hardships and toil, starvation and cold. Many of those who rode or walked in the parades through the city or looked on along the route could tell of fathers and mothers who had 'crossed the plains'.[28]

The Jubilee committee's selection of the Native Sons and Daughters to sponsor the Admission Day parade, rather than one of the many nationally known directors of such pageantry at the time, demonstrates the extent to which nativist views inflected the forms of mass-produced historical representation during the decade. As John Higham has shown, the 'Americanisation' initiatives had strong patrons in the hereditary societies, founded in large part upon hostility toward foreign cultures and anxieties about immigrant 'swamping'.[29] Correspondingly, during this time the Native Sons and Daughters were much concerned that 'the glories of California's heroic period might be submerged by traditions of other men and places unless some organisation existed to keep alive the historic memories and preserve the spirit of California'.[30] They actively elicited the government's assistance in maintaining racial hegemony by demanding it 'enforce restrictions which will not only prevent California from being swamped by an influx of ineligible aliens but will put an end to the constant friction which unavoidably arises when the White race clashes with races of other colors'. As David Glassberg argues, '[h]istorical space in California of the 1920s was . . . white space, echoing the increasingly strident nativism of the Native Sons of the Golden West'.[31]

It would be hard to imagine, therefore, a more apt choice for the premiere of *The Pony Express*, Paramount's commemorative document of California history. But rather than develop alliances with the Jubilee committee, or any of the pioneer or hereditary societies, instead the studio publicised its collaboration with Wells Fargo, the financial institution headquartered in San Francisco, in developing the pony express project. The bank had provided the filmmakers with historical information in the interests of 'authencity'. Yet such patriotic interest cloaks the studio's more pragmatic motivations: 'there was a decidedly practical angle', *Moving Picture World* commented, 'to [Paramount's eliciting] the bank's cooperation as well as the moral effect of the interest of this still powerful institution'.[32] Securing Wells Fargo's patronage helped the studio market *The Pony Express* as 'authentic' in its publicity narratives by co-opting folk knowledge about the bank's role in developing the West and its connection to the frontier past. In turn, the film operated as a kind of public service announcement for the bank. Ultimately, Paramount had the most to gain in marketing this cinematic commemorative text; it visualised for Jubilee spectators the Pony Express' contribution to national unification, thus sanctioning California's subsequent rise as a commercial power in the present and, by extension, the film industry's new role as a de facto 'guardian' of historical memory.

Cover of *San Francisco Chronicle* Sunday Magazine, 6 September 1925

Working with Wells Fargo, Paramount developed an array of exploitation tactics for circulating *The Pony Express* under the Jubilee banner. Much of the publicity foregrounded the figure of the dedicated pony express rider as an emblematic California character, like the gold miner or the stalwart covered-wagon pioneer, whose efforts in the region had national import. The bank 'planted stories in the financial publications' while ensuring that the studio secured extra space in the local newspapers. The *Chronicle*'s Sunday Magazine, entirely devoted to Jubilee festivities, featured on its cover a pony express rider, just about to pull up in front of the Wells Fargo & Co. office (see illustration above). Throughout September, the bank used similar iconography in its display ads, foregrounding accounts of Wells Fargo's commercial heritage framed in explicitly nationalist terms: 'Saint Joe to Sacramento – over plains and mountains, through storms, blizzards and hostile Indian country – to the Union's newest state from her sisters 2000 miles away rode the Pony Express, linking California to civilization'. Early in the Admission Day parade, Wells Fargo arranged for a rider to race madly all the way from Embarcadero to Market Street to hand-deliver a letter to Vice President Dawes on the reviewing stand. As the 'surviving unit' of the express company, Wells Fargo assumed control over the commodification of its historical properties, recirculating the 'relics' used in the location shoot for use in thirty Bay area store windows. The bank also built a 'reproduction of a frontier town in the days of the pony express' for the front of the Imperial theatre. The connections between *The Pony Express* and the Jubilee were made most concrete when, under the auspices of Wells Fargo, the film was named 'the official Diamond Jubilee picture' after a preview by the Jubilee committee.[33]

As if to inaugurate the upcoming festivities, the studio arranged a gala premiere on the evening of 4 September, just before Jubilee week. Paramount carefully selected the Imperial for the opening, considered the city's finest extended-run theatre. Most importantly, the theatre was located at Market between 6th and 7th Streets, guaranteeing maximum marquee exposure since this spot was closest to the reviewing stand in front of the Civic Centre and City Hall, the heart of the festivities.[34] The premiere itself was equally orchestrated: 'society leaders, city officials, and prominent citizens in finance' and publishing were given gratis invitations to an event billed as a 'Hollywood-style' opening, complete with klieg lights, throngs of movie fans, and red-carpet arrivals of stars. Descriptions of that evening's program offer evidence of *The Pony Express*'s niche as both historic document and public relations vehicle for the studio. Rather than the usual atmospheric prologue, a featurette of scenes taken during the making of the film preceded the feature, with Senator Samuel Shortridge testifying to the movie's veracity. The premiere screening went very well, *Variety* later reported, noting that the Imperial had its 'best week in eight months'. Interest in the film was so high that additional screenings were scheduled, an almost predictable result of the studio's meticulous efforts to constantly connect the movie with Jubilee themes.[35]

If the historical pageantry of the Jubilee maximised the appeal of Paramount's latest epic for movie patrons, it is also clear that the industry's commodification of frontier imagery in the epics provided attendees with similarly powerful symbols of popular memory. During the festivities, earlier methods of staging the mise-en-scène of historical commemoration (the pageant, the parade, the tableaux) negotiated a hegemonic alliance with the competing representational form of the modern era, motion pictures. Witness the Jubilee's Covered Wagon Babies Revue, a string of automobiles that carried forty-five women and men who had been born in or under a covered wagon.[36] The Covered Wagon Babies were escorted to a screening at the Imperial, where decorated boxes in the theatre awaited them. Such an event parallels Paramount's previous efforts to substantiate the authenticity of their frontier epics by publicising the 'real-life' analogues to the fictional characters portrayed, in an effort to establish the film's provenance in the experiences of local residents. The *Chronicle* speculated that 'to younger San Francisco the "covered wagon babies" in particular provoked the thought that here were living, breathing men and women whose brave forebears spanned the continent in prairie schooners to take up their lives in the Golden State'.[37] As such, *The Pony Express'* position with respect to the Jubilee's pageantry was carefully mediated so that it served the interests of the hereditary societies in the 1920s: The cultural expressions of historical memory should be both nativist and tutorial. In turn, Paramount exploited the exhibition setting to challenge the social meanings attached to attending 'a Western', previously considered a lowbrow, mass-produced form. Spectatorship was transformed into an educational experience, consumption refigured as a patriotic, even civic duty. In the course of Jubilee events, the setting of the

Imperial itself became a preeminently 'historical space', and a 'white space' as well.

The critical response to *The Pony Express* in San Francisco city papers no doubt met the studio's expectations. Typical is George Warren's comment in the *Chronicle* that the film was a 'worthy successor' to *The Covered Wagon*, 'carry[ing] on splendidly the history of the planting of civilization in the Far West'. In the *Examiner*, Idwal Jones concurred while acknowledging the timeliness of the topic and the studio's strategy to elevate the 'lowbrow' product: '"The Pony Express" fans the local-patriotic mood of these days. It looks as if James Cruze is starting out to screen the "Taming of the West". The first installment was "The Covered Wagon". This is the second, and . . . it bears up excellently [and] is more exciting'. Curran Swint of the *News* thought it a 'great picture historically, with true epic sweep against which is set a moving, thrilling, humorous and emotional story', and the *Call* and *Daily Herald* reviewers pointed similarly to the story's educational value: discerning patrons, they claimed, should not miss this 'truly constructive picture', a 'lesson in visualized history'.[38] Such notices in city papers further piqued Jubilee spectators' interest in the film, offering a more fully narrativised version of the static tableaux comprising the pageant-parade.

As the studio had anticipated, the reviews of the film in the New York papers were generally good. Although several writers thought the movie fell short of the exemplary *The Covered Wagon*, many articulated the studio's 'preferred' reading by foregrounding the text's authenticity and nativist value as well as commending the producers' contribution to 'elevating' the cinema. In his influential review in the *New York Times*, Mordaunt Hall commented that

> [t]his pictorial document, which causes one's heart to throb with delight, is another chapter in American history which is bound, as was the case with 'The Covered Wagon' . . . to stir all audiences to a state of intense pride for the achievements of the men of yore . . . Motion picture producers come in for their share of blame for unworthy films, and it is only just that they should receive full marks when they make such a sterling story as 'The Pony Express', which incidentally was produced by the Famous Players-Lasky Corporation.[39]

Other major city papers broadly assumed the film's merit, largely on the basis of the premiere's success, although Paramount's success in disseminating its publicity narrative was also clear. A long article in the *World* described the origins and conditions of the production, quoting Wyoming Senator Warren's sanction of the film as 'an accurate picture of my own country and my own time' while situating his response in relation to public discourse about the 'authenticity' of frontier narratives. The writer also described Forman's archival research and the careful reconstructions of Old Sacramento and Julesburg.[40] As *The Pony Express* opened across the country in the fall and winter of 1925, reviewers in newspaper and mass-market periodicals responded in similar ways, and apparently movie audiences did as well.[41] By this time, it would appear that the combination of Paramount, James Cruze, and 'historical Western' were becoming trade labels for 'painless history', offering movie patrons not just prestige entertainment but lessons in the foundation of contemporary national growth and development.

At least one reviewer, however, offered what might be described as a 'resisting' reading of *The Pony Express*, wryly noting that '[i]t is rumored that there are some people who will be antagonized by the men this photoplay intends to glorify, upon being presented with the information, via a subtitle, that "The riders of the pony express saved California for the Union". But such persons, of course, are under the suspicion of being unfriendly to that cultural capital, Hollywood'.[42] This comment, albeit tongue-in-cheek, implies an awareness of how public discourse about that 'cultural capital' might be shaped by the specific projects the studios chose to cultivate. In the case of *The Pony Express*, Paramount clearly worked with the exploitation possibilities of the Jubilee historical pageant in mind. Such a selective distribution had multiple advantages: it was economically efficient, since the studio would not have to finance a marketing campaign but rather co-opt the Jubilee committee's months of advertising and promotion in California. Essentially, Paramount could reap all the benefits of the controlled exhibition setting while incurring little of the cost.

At the same time, the studio had complex motivations in marketing the epic Western cycle during the 1920s. The work of cultural historians like John Bodnar and David Glassberg can help film scholars understand not only why Paramount chose the Diamond Jubilee debut setting, but also the cultural origins of and economic contexts within which emergent New Era corporations like motion picture companies promoted 'authentic' historical memory in the guise of popular film.[43] In *Remaking America*, a study of the relationship between national industries and historical commemoration during the twentieth century, Bodnar argues that such events were devised by 'a rising industrial elite' of entrepreneurs, business owners, professionals, and civic leaders during the late nineteenth century who sought to regulate the forms of public memory available for broad consumption as a means to legitimate economic ventures in the present.[44] Both Bodnar and Glassberg point to the 1876 American Centennial as a widely imitated template: politicians 'employed narratives of local community development alongside the religious rhetoric of nationalism to forge a united community of believers out of residents with diverse ethnic, class, and regional backgrounds'.[45] However, by the turn of the century, industrial and professional elites emerged as the boosters of such events. Accordingly, these festivals often charted the 'progress' of American capitalist enterprise. But in international fairs as well as smaller state centennials, organisers also fomented specific interpretations of the past as a key tactic to justify their economic achievements in the present. In particular, the first two decades of the century saw a proliferation of historical pageants throughout the country, where thousands of Americans enacted varieties of dramatic public rituals that presented, usually in tableaux style, chronicles of local and state historical development. Such pageantry combined the 'patriotic and religious themes of the historical oration, revised for an age of mass spectacle, with a growing interest in the past as a source of communal traditions that could offer emotional respite from the consequences of modern progress'.[46]

Placed within these contexts, Paramount's selection of the Jubilee as the debut site for *The Pony Express* reflects the complexity of the industry's incentives to produce and disseminate documents of historical memory during the 1920s. Constructed as a chronicle of both California's ascendancy in the West and the nation's eventually-victorious struggle to reunify, the film offers in cinematic form pageantry's use of historical episodes to commemorate the legacies of the frontier past for a contemporary industrial society. But, as Bodnar has argued, forms of public memory always emerge discursively, within existing structures of social and cultural power that negotiate struggles for expression among multiple rivals.[47] This explains why Paramount chose to work with Wells Fargo, since the alliance would help deflect potential criticism by the hereditary

groups governing the pageant that the studio – most prominent
within public discourse as controlled by 'nonnatives' – was an
inappropriate, and possibly inauthentic source of historical knowledge. Further, as Paramount expanded during the late teens and early
1920s, acquiring theatre chains across the country and developing
the distribution networks needed to keep them profitable, the studio
sought to legitimise this coast-to-coast access by cloaking their product within pageantry's rhetoric of national unity. Like the business
and civic leaders of the corporate age who became involved 'in the
sponsorship and coordination of activities designed to shape and
promulgate versions of the past for mass consumption', Paramount's
cycle of epic frontier features helped 'foster specific interpretation
of powerful historical symbols'[48] – in this case, the artefacts of California historical memory – for those 'under suspicion of being
unfriendly to that cultural capital, Hollywood'. As such, *The Pony
Express* was part of the studio's long-term strategy to align itself with
those industrial elites who produced and regulated public forms of
historical memory as a means to sanction their pursuit of a national
market, as well as garner prosocial rewards.

Notes

1 The quote by Lasky is from 'Cruze's Next for Paramount Will be "The
   Pony Express"', *Moving Picture World* (4 April 1925), p. 484; Fuller's
   comment appeared in 'Line of Famous Defense in Government Hearing', *Variety* (25 November 1925), 28.
2 At the time of *The Covered Wagon*'s release (early 1923), Paramount's
   corporate name was Famous Players-Lasky. For simplicity's sake, I will
   refer to the producer as 'Paramount', although the name was officially
   changed in mid-1925, when *The Pony Express* was in production.
3 One difficulty is that many of the epic Westerns produced during the
   1920s are considered lost or exist only as incomplete versions, most
   notably *The Covered Wagon*. According to *Classic Film Collector*,
   'Only the re-edited versions of these films exist, for they were con-
   densed by Kodascope many years ago and the original complete neg-
   atives disappeared' (Spring 1976), 19. Contemporary reviews of *The
   Pony Express* indicate that the film ran about 110 minutes (ten reels),
   whereas the present version available from video vendors is a little
   over an hour long. Since in this chapter I am interested in a reception
   analysis which encompasses the institutional and economic dimensions of consumption, how the industry solicited and constructed

patrons for its products, and an account of the exhibition as a social space, lack of access to a complete print does not substantially impact my argument.

4   G. N. Fenin and W. K. Everson, *The Western From Silents to the Seventies* (New York, Grossman, 1973), pp. 135–6; 'Ten Best Pictures of 1925', *1926 Film Daily Yearbook*, pp. 417–25.

5   See K. Brownlow, *The War, the West, and the Wilderness* (New York: Knopf, 1979), p. 223; R. Koszarski, *An Evening's Entertainment: The Age of the Silent Feature Picture, 1915–1928* (Berkeley: University of California Press, 1990), p. 248.

6   For a detailed discussion of these issues, see chapter 1 of my dissertation, 'The West Before the Cinema Invaded It: Famous Players-Lasky's "Epic" Westerns, 1923–1925' (University of Wisconsin-Madison, 1999).

7   R. Maltby, 'The Production Code and the Hays Office', in T. Balio (ed.) *Grand Design: Hollywood as a Modern Business Enterprise* (Berkeley: University of California Press, 1993), p. 41.

8   A. Raucher, *Public Relations and Business, 1900–1929* (Baltimore: Johns Hopkins University Press, 1968), pp. 65–6.

9   Editorial, 'A Big Achievement', *Exhibitors' Trade Review* (31 March 1923), p. 878; see other trade editorials in *Moving Picture World* (24 March 1923), p. 401, 'Some Inside Stuff', *Film Daily* (20 May 1923), p. 2.

10 Paramount selected the players for *The Pony Express* carefully. For example, casting Ricardo Cortez (formerly 'Jacob Krantz', born in Vienna) may well have been designed as a 'concession' to California's Spanish heritage.

11 See Forman obituary in the *New York Times* (4 January 1966), p. 27; entry in *Who's Who in America* (Chicago: Marquis, 1939), p. 925; also Henry James Forman, *Our Movie-Made Children* (New York: MacMillan, 1933), pp. 2, 31, 53.

12 H. C. Peterson, 'Filming a Real "Western": Old-Timers May View Pony Express Thriller Without Being Outraged by "Things That Ain't So"', *Sunset* (November 1925), pp. 37–9, 97–9.

13 Peterson, 'Filming a Real "Western"', p. 38.

14 H. J. Forman, *The Pony Express: A Romance* (New York: Grosset & Dunlap, 1925). According to the Paramount script files for *The Pony Express* (Herrick Library, Academy of Motion Picture Arts and Sciences, Los Angeles) Forman was paid the substantial sum of $33,500 for his work. In comparison, Emerson Hough received $8,500 for the rights to *The Covered Wagon*. This indicates how valuable (in all senses of the word) the frontier-themed prestige picture had become to the studio.

15 Forman, *The Pony Express*, pp. 9–10.

16   D. Glassberg, *Sense of History: The Place of the Past in American Life* (Amherst: University of Massachusetts Press, 2001), pp. 168–9.

17   J. Tully, 'James Cruze', *Vanity Fair* (December 1927), p. 116.

18   'Vice-President Charles G. Dawes Watches James Cruze, Directing "The Pony Express"', *Moving Picture World* (15 August 1925), p. 751; 'Dawes Helps Direct Movie in Wyoming', *New York Times* (25 July 1925), p. 6; 'National Affairs', *Time* (3 August 1925), p. 7.

19   Dawes' reference to a screening at the White House also suggests at least the possibility of an informal arrangement between Paramount and MPPDA head Will Hays – a former member of the Harding cabinet and still active in national Republican politics – in regard to promoting *The Pony Express*. At Hays' behest, Warren Harding had engaged in similar activities for *The Covered Wagon* during 1923.

20   *California's Diamond Jubilee* (San Francisco: E.C. Brown, 1927), pp. 16, 18, 56.

21   'More for Famous', *Film Daily* (30 June 1925), p. 1.

22   Glassberg, *Sense of History*, p. 181.

23   *California's Diamond Jubilee*, p. 9.

24   *California's Diamond Jubilee*, p. 7

25   *California's Diamond Jubilee*, pp. 19, 26.

26   *California's Diamond Jubilee*, pp. 24, 80.

27   J. Bodnar, *Remaking America: Public Memory, Commemoration, and Patriotism in the Twentieth Century* (Princeton: Princeton University Press, 1992), p. 71.

28   H. A. Studdert Kennedy, 'California and Her Diamond Jubilee', *The Outlook* (23 September 1925), pp. 114–15.

29   J. Higham, *Strangers in the Land: Patterns of American Nativism, 1860–1925*, 2nd edn (New Brunswick: Rutgers University Press, 1992), pp. 236–7.

30   E. J. Lynch, 'Native Sons Vital Factor in State's Progress', *San Francisco Examiner* (5 September 1925), p. 9.

31   Lynch, 'Native Sons', p. 11; F. Cutler, 'The Order of Native Sons of the Golden West', *Official Program of the 1925 Diamond Jubilee*, p. 26 (located in California Historical Society's San Francisco ephemera collection, 'Admission Day – 1925'); Glassberg, *Sense of History*, p. 193.

32   '"Pony Express" Another Big Western Hit', *Variety* (9 September 1925), p. 23; 'Tied Pony Express to California Fete', *Moving Picture World* (10 October 1925), p. 478.

33   See, for example, the Wells Fargo ad in the *San Francisco Examiner* (5 September 1925), p. 2; for a description of the publicity tactics, see '"Pony Express" Has Great World Premiere in 'Frisco', *Moving Picture World* (26 September 1925), p. 346; 'Story of Old West Fits in With Jubilee', *San Francisco Chronicle* (4 September 1925), p. 13.

34   The parade route began at the Embarcadero and moved down Market Street, turning west on Fulton toward the City Hall/Civic Center quadrangle. The Imperial was located on Market at Jones, just before the curve onto Fulton.

35   See for example in the *San Francisco Examiner*, 'Formal Opening for "Express"' (1 September 1925), p. 15; '"Pony Express" Film to be Jubilee Feature' (4 September 1925), p. 5; 'Huge Crowd Sees Premiere of New Film' (5 September 1925), p. 3; I. Jones, 'Pony Express Proves to be Historical Melodrama' (5 September 1925), p. 14. In the *San Francisco Chronicle*, see G. Warren, '"Pony Express" Stirring, Appropriate Jubilee Feature, Imperial Stages Realistic Bit of the Old Wild West' (5 September 1925), p. 4; 'Imperial Enjoys Crowded Houses for New Film' (7 September 1925), p. 9; '"Pony Express" on Long Run' (11 September 1925), p. 13; '"Pony Express" Makes Big Hit' (12 September 1925), p. 9; 'Early Days of Stage Coach Story Told' (19 September 1925), p. 7. For the box office results for *The Pony Express*, see *Variety* (16 September–7 October 1925); Senator Shortridge's speech is excerpted in '"Pony Express" Has Great World Premiere in 'Frisco', *Moving Picture World* (26 September 1925), p. 346.

36   Both *The Covered Wagon* and *The Pony Express* had focused on the strategic significance of a wagon train's 'cargo' of infants. In the first film, an aged man, while cooing over a newborn, comments to the pioneers that it is 'more important to get these babies across than it is the grown folks – they're the real Empire Builders'. And later, an actual birth in a wagon is implied. In *The Pony Express*, a female toddler named 'Baby' is the lone survivor of one of Charlie Bent's raids on a passing wagon train. She later identifies him as the perpetrator when she sees him in Indian dress. Molly and Jack take her to Sacramento, forming a familial unit that brings a future 'Empire Builder' to the farthest reaches of the West, and the state's capital.

37   See '"Covered Wagon Babies" Revue', in *California's Diamond Jubilee*, pp. 77–8; also 'Dinner Tonight for ''49 Babies', *San Francisco Examiner* (8 September 1925), p. 4; 'Covered Wagon Babies Meet', *San Francisco Examiner* (9 September 1925), p. 2; '"Wagon Babies" Will be Feted', *San Francisco Chronicle* (8 September 1925), p. 5; 'Pioneers Live to See Glories They Wrought', *San Francisco Chronicle* (10 September 1925), p. 7.

38   G. Warren, '"Pony Express" Stirring, Appropriate Jubilee Feature', *San Francisco Chronicle* (5 September 1925), p. 4; I. Jones, '"Pony Express" Proves to be Historical Melodrama', *San Francisco Examiner* (5 September 1925), p. 14; capsule reviews in 'San Francisco First to Applaud Cruze's "The Pony Express"', *Exhibitors' Trade Review* (19 September 1925), p. 18.

39   M. Hall, 'A Smiling Villain', *New York Times* (14 September 1925), p. 16.

40   A. S., 'Dancer on Horseback', *New York World* (20 September 1925), 3M; see excerpts from other New York dailies in *Film Daily* (22 September 1925), p. 6.

41   See, for example, reviews in Chicago dailies: P. Wood, 'Cruze Makes "Pony Express"', *Herald and Examiner* (28 September 1925), p. 9; 'New Phase of West's Growth Shown in Good Movie', *Evening American* (30 September 1925), p. 27; 'If You Don't See This One It's Your Loss', *Chicago Tribune* (29 September 1925), p. 33; see also the brief summary of other Chicago dailies' response in *Film Daily* (18 October 1925), p. 13.

42   Anonymous *Theatre* review (December 1925), p. 32.

43   Bodnar, *Remaking America*, especially chapters 1–2; D. Glassberg, *American Historical Pageantry: The Uses of Tradition in the Early Twentieth Century* (Chapel Hill: University of North Carolina Press, 1990).

44   Bodnar, *Remaking America*, pp. 28–30.

45   Glassberg, *American Historical Pageantry*, p. 14.

46   Glassberg, *American Historical Pageantry*, p. 283.

47   Bodnar, *Remaking America*, pp. 13–20, 245–53.

48   Bodnar, *Remaking America*, p. 114.

3

'Look behind you!': memories of cinema-going in the 'Golden Age' of Hollywood

Sarah Stubbings

Roger Bromley, in his study of British memory in the inter-war period, has written that: 'Memory is not simply the property of individuals, nor just a matter of psychological processes, but a complex cultural and historical phenomenon constantly subject to revision, amplification and "forgetting".'[1] This perspective reverberates through the conceptual underpinnings of this book. While personality and personal history affect the content, intensity and emotional tone of a memory, the social and cultural context of memory also exerts a substantial influence on its form and experience. This chapter explores formations of memory in a contemporary British context, specifically as it relates to memories of cinema-going that have been reproduced in local newspapers. Based on research into the memory narratives of a particular local city press, the study argues that personal memory of cinema is socially constructed by its context to create certain culturally sanctioned discourses, in this case figured around age, community, and city identity.

If the last two chapters raised issues of history and memory through particular historical and commemorative texts and events in the 1920s, this chapter moves the focus of concern to popular reminiscence for early cinema in the 1990s. Rather than consider the memory of particular films, it concentrates on the memory of cinema-going itself. This has become increasingly significant within forms of oral and questionnaire-based analysis. Annette Kuhn's questionnaire and interview-based study of the memory of cinema-going in the 1930s, for example, found that films were markedly less important to her respondents than the activity of going to the cinema.[2] Kuhn's work is part of a small but growing field investigating the personal memory of cinema-going, including work by Jackie Stacey, who is concerned extensively with women's recollections of female stars.[3] In contrast with the questionnaire-based methodologies of Stacey and Kuhn, utilising newspapers as source material directs research towards patterns of memory within media discourse rather than towards the solicitation and interpretation of memories from sample participants. This more closely examines how private memories are figured within recurrent themes and images of a sub-genre of memory narrative that has become increasingly significant within local newspapers. In broad terms, this methodology facilitates analysis of particular (generational) memories but also, and significantly, the role of the press in fostering, formulating and structuring these memories within the context of local discourse and in terms of particular commercial imperatives.

The examples of memory narratives discussed in this chapter are all taken from the local press of Nottingham and concentrate on generational memories of cinema-going in what has been discursively construed as the 'Golden Age' of cinema, a period figured around the Hollywood studio era of the 1930s and 1940s. As a medium-sized English city, Nottingham's cinema fans of the 1930s and 1940s could choose from over fifty cinemas and the city's current population includes a substantial number who remember trips to Nottingham's cinemas in their youth. Memory narratives relating to local cinema experience have been developed most significantly within the city's only daily newspaper, the *Nottingham Evening Post*. This trend began in the 1980s, when the memory or heritage imperative in British cultural life, described by critics such as Raphael Samuel and Robert Hewison, became acute.[4] A significant additional source of local media memory, however, has been the occasional supplement of the *Evening Post,* called *Bygones.* As the name suggests, this supplement examines various elements of the city's past, and has, on a number of occasions, taken cinema as its focal point. The memory narratives contained in the *Nottingham Evening Post* and in *Bygones* are in the form of articles and letters based upon personal cinema reminiscence. These memories are of experiences between the 1920s and the 1950s, with those of the 1930s and 1940s forming the vast majority. Overwhelmingly, the period is remembered fondly, a 'Golden Age' where popular cinema and cinema-going were seen to be at their pinnacle.

While some memories of cinema in Nottingham's local press are generated in response to a particular news item, such as the closure or demolition of a specific cinema, as many are stand-alone items.

The memories that emerge in the letters and articles that I examine cover four main themes: identity, community, morality and decline. While there is necessarily some overlap between them, this chapter will examine these four areas in order to draw out their significance in terms of the process of framing memory in cultural terms. These themes all have a powerful social resonance, which partly explains their prominence and serviceability within the press. Not only do they provide the kind of human interest stories that James Curran and Jean Seaton[5] suggest has become instrumental to British local press since the early 1930s, memory narratives are also strategic in commercial terms. Significantly, they have the function of appealing to an important sub-section of media readership in that of the elderly, the demographic audience towards whom the memory narratives are substantially geared. Additionally, however, memory narratives are cost-effective in terms of news production. According to Rod Pilling, the local press is 'largely staffed at reporter level by trainees' who 'typically undertake the greater part of that work in the office'[6] due to low staffing levels. Articles comprising memories sent in by readers are ideal in this context for they are less labour-intensive than stories and features requiring active or investigative research.

Stacey's study of female fans in the 1940s and 1950s makes reference to 'the negotiation of "public" discourses and "private" narratives'.[7] This sense of negotiation between the public and the private has direct bearing for memory narratives as they are used, framed, and published in local newspapers. Not least, individualised memories form, as they themselves are informed by, a sense of iconic recall. Visual and written memories of Nottingham cinema-going frequently coalesce into a hardened set of impressions: of cinema queues snaking down the street, of the respective merits of the flea pit and the picture palace, of the connotations of the back row. What might be called a 'genre of memory' is developed in the local press, a structured set of themes that work to include certain issues and that can frequently marginalise others. Aspects of cinema-going that are rarely discussed in Nottingham press narratives include, to name just a few, cinema smells, smoking, the unwanted advances from strangers (that fuelled moralists' opposition to cinema in the 1930s and 1940s) and the possibilities of sex and coupling enabled by the dark 'privacy' of the cinema.[8] As referred to earlier, films and film stars are generally, although not exclusively, presented as a secondary part of the

experience. While all of this may not constitute a deliberate fore-
closure of memory, a form of sanctioned reminiscence does emerge,
based upon organising themes, images and memory topics.

In his book, *How Societies Remember*, Paul Connerton offers a
persuasive account of the ways in which societal frameworks mould
not only the form but also the content of social memory.[9] The case
of personal cinema memory, situated in the public realm of the local
press, foregrounds a number of issues about the constitution of
memory and identity for particular social groups. At one level, it can
provide insights into the operations of memory and nostalgia as they
are figured around the lived experience of cinema and the city. At the
same time, memory narratives in the local press raise issues about
the ways in which these forms of reminiscence are figured discursively. That is to say, the way they join, or are seen to inflect, contemporary debates in the present about issues such as criminality or
the perception of declining moral standards. This chapter will now
go on to consider the interconnection of personal and public
memory as it relates to four key themes in the sub-genre of memory
narrative heretofore described. To reiterate, these are identity, community, morality, and decline.

Identity and community

The psychologist Joseph Fitzgerald has argued that 'personal identity is a culturally and historically specific notion', which he locates
within modern Western society. He relates the development of personal identity to the narrative mode used in literature, something
that is 'used extensively in the socialization process by which new
members are taught the underlying themes and values of the group
through "true" stories, fables and allegories'.[10] I would suggest that
film, as a dominant cultural medium, also offers a valuable means of
studying identity formation or, in this case, memories of the process.
Fitzgerald's 1988 study of reminiscence found that, for all age
groups, those surveyed reported that their greatest number of vivid
memories (which he terms flash-bulb memories) were of events
between the ages of sixteen and twenty-five – the period which is
crucially important to adult identity formation.[11] This is also the age
when cinema attendance is generally at its highest and the age that
recurs most frequently in newspaper accounts dealing with Nottingham cinema memory. This section examines the causal connection

between memory, cinema and identity formation, measured through the lens of nostalgia. As sociologist Fred Davis comments, nostalgia is 'one of the means . . . we employ in the never ending work of constructing, maintaining, and reconstructing our identities'.[12]

An important element of cinema nostalgia, foregrounded in newspaper accounts, is the fondly remembered imitation of film stars. This is specifically measured in terms of clothing, manner and hairstyles. So Margaret Corkill relates how she and her friends followed film stars closely and 'tried to imitate their hairstyles and make-up'.[13] This theme is important to the fascinating and highly detailed reminiscences of Bill Cross in the *Nottingham Evening Post*. He recollects he and his friends 'worshipping' and copying the style of film stars as teenagers in the 1930s, particularly stars of gangster films such as James Cagney. For Bill, this even led to being able to recreate film star lifestyle at the cinema with a girl: 'You in your James Cagney outfit, she in her Joan Blondell dress, you were the stars of the screen for the night.'[14] The surroundings were crucial to his depiction of reliving film star lifestyle at the cinema – he recounts dating as a young man at the plush, luxurious cinemas in Nottingham, the Adelphi and the Ritz, in contrast to his childhood haunt the Palace that 'had another name, the Flea Pit'.[15] He clearly presents this development in terms of the lifecycle in which dating at a luxury cinema symbolises both adulthood and a rise in social status as a whole. So inside the Ritz, 'After the hard-up times as a boy you were a young man, nice clothes, money in your pocket and a lovely girl on your arm.'[16]

Many memories of cinema-going in local press accounts focus on cinema's role in key aspects of the lifecycle and key moments of identity formation, particularly in terms of courtship. For many, a trip to the cinema was their first date, and one couple even recalled getting engaged in the cinema.[17] For girls, a date at the cinema also indicated the level of a boy's regard; if he really liked her he would arrange to meet outside and pay, otherwise the arrangement would be to meet inside so the girl paid her own way.[18] For Audrey Booth, writing in the *Nottingham Evening Post*, her first date was at the cinema and the boy met her outside and asked her to give him the money as he didn't like girls to pay for themselves![19] This recollection is also significant with regard to the effect of nostalgia on the emotional tone of her memory, resulting in a rather humiliating experience being transmuted over time into something that she 'has had many a laugh about since'.[20]

The same process is evident in Mrs Whittaker's defining memory
of a Nottingham cinema, the Futurist. A film had been made at the
factory where she worked, which included some footage of herself
and a friend. On its release they excitedly went to see it, their anticipation piqued by the prospect of seeing themselves on screen. However, they found that they had been edited out. Mrs Whittaker
claims 'We were so disappointed, but I often think back'.[21] The
implication of the 'but' is that her perspective has since altered, and
this inference is borne out by the title of the piece, 'Happy memories of the Futurist'. The original disappointment has subsequently
become wrought into nostalgia for the time as a whole, a sentimental memory of youth. As she describes, 'we were just 14 years of
age!'[22] Mrs Whittaker's remembered eagerness, hope and enthusiasm as a fourteen-year-old emerge as the key memory, the event at
the Futurist a tangible means of accessing that former self and locating it within a specific time and milieu. The telling exclamation mark
suggests an incredulity that she could ever have been so young and
naïve. This indicates both a perception of her former identity and a
nostalgic sense of how that identity has changed over time. As Davis
claims, an important element of nostalgia is that it fosters the belief
that 'we have in the interim "grown" and "matured" and are now
better equipped to confront the considerably more challenging
demands of the present'.[23]

The further significance of this item is Mrs Whittaker's call to
her friend and co-worker, and to other readers, 'do you remember?'[24]
This indicates that personal memories are linked to ideas of collective
experience and to the notion of community. Indeed, the invocation of
community is central to many memory narratives in the local press
and this functions on two levels. Firstly, there is an attempt to recreate a (lost) community of those who remember, as Mrs Whittaker aims
to achieve. Secondly, there is an infusion of historical nostalgia in the
recall of community life; memories of a shared leisure practice are
often contrasted implicitly or explicitly with the individualistic ten-
dencies of contemporary culture. Andrew Hoskins states that societies
'turn to the past, in an attempt to find some kind of anchor in the
characteristically fragmented experience of modern life'.[25] Cinema
memory invests in, and enables, a sense of community that frequently
plays against the perception of social diffusion in the present.

This sense of community is expedient to the local press. Indeed,
one of the key functions of the local press is in fostering communal

identities. For Pilling, local newspapers are successful when they make their readers feel part of a community.[26] As such, they will frequently instigate campaigns about issues such as transport systems, shopping facilities or social problems as a means of furthering the perception of the city as 'our' city. More importantly in terms of the commercial imperatives of the press, developing an imagined community at the local level provides a means of securing readership loyalty to 'our' local paper. In this way, city identity and press identity are inter-linked.

As a means of achieving this highly productive mutual dependence between city and press identity, many retrospective accounts of cinema-going in the local press close with an invitation for readers to write in and share their memories. In *Bygones* there is a special text box inviting readers to send 'any memories or photographs you want to share'.[27] This technique fulfils the important role of strengthening readers' loyalty by asking them to participate in the process and formation of city memory. On a wider level, the technique helps to foster a sense of ownership among the readers, a feeling that this is 'their' newspaper appealing to 'their' generation and interest group. The following quote from the *Nottingham Herald,* a rival city newspaper to the *Evening Post,* is typical in this respect. 'Do you remember the old Nottingham picture houses or have fond memories or experiences of a night at the flicks? If so, write to us'.[28] In this example, the newspaper clearly signals the type of anecdote it will print. Rather than memories of moral scandal or economic want, cinema-going is associated with all things fond, nostalgic and quintessentially communitarian.

Cinema-going from the 1920s to the 1950s is almost decidedly remembered as a collective experience. One of the activities that audiences frequently shared, and that is duly recalled, was that of singing along with the musical interludes. Vocal participation in Nottingham's Ritz cinema is especially remembered due to its well-respected and nationally broadcast organist in the 1930s and 40s, Jack Helyer. Kath Price recounts 'Memories of Jack Helyer and our sing-songs during the interval when he came up through the floor of the stage on that wonderful Wurlitzer organ and we sang from the song sheet hanging down from the ceiling'.[29] The organist was both a spectacle (his appearing through the floor with its resonance of a magical apparition and the splendour of the organ itself) and a symbol of audience participation, giving everybody the opportunity to sing together. Indeed, a letter in the Nottinghamshire Archives states that Helyer's 'forte was singalong medleys' which 'created the special atmosphere that is unique to community singing'.[30]

The place of community within the activity and process of cultural recall has been taken up by theorists of memory and nostalgia. Davis suggests a generational sense of community in his discussion of 'the powerful generation-delineating properties to which nostalgia lends itself so easily'. For Davis, 'images from our past . . . seem to iconically bestow an age-graded distinctiveness'.[31] And for Robyn Fivush, Catherine Haden and Elaine Reese, 'joint remembering, or reminiscing, serves a very special purpose, that of creating interpersonal bonds based on a sense of shared history'.[32] Raymond Williams refers to generational identity in his theory about structures of feeling. In writing of the social links that produce emotions, Williams suggests that 'what we are defining is a particular quality of social experience and relationship, historically distinct from other particular qualities, which gives the sense of a generation or of a period'.[33] Cinema in its Golden Age, the time of its largest audience base, is a valuable means of illustrating such structures of feeling at work. For those who remember cinema through the local press, reminiscence is a discursive means of community-building. While any city newspaper will have different readership constituencies with potentially competing investments in the idea of community, memory narratives are a means of courting and displaying a generational sense of community that, in a wider capacity, can enrich a broad-based notion of the city's lived experience.

Some articles and letters about cinema's past offer a strong sense that going to the cinema was instrumental in forging, and not simply hosting, community sensibilities. An article in the *Nottingham Evening Post* comprising a selection of readers' memories about cinema in their youth states that 'local cinemas played such a vital part in bringing communities together'.[34] A factor in this is that many cinemas between the 1930s and 1950s were in residential areas around the city. These, rather than cinemas located in the city centre, feature most in readers' memories in the local press, unless the coverage relates to a specific city centre event. For the large number of suburbs built in the 1930s, a cinema tended to be the only leisure or community facility. In Nottingham there were few pubs in these suburbs as most of the housing built in Nottingham in the period comprised council estates that were almost always refused that provision. There is some evidence, then, that for those who moved to a new estate in the period, going to the local cinema was the only way of mingling socially with others of that new community. This included children, enticed by the popular children's clubs that began in the 1930s, where 'millions of youngsters spent their Saturday mornings marvelling at the wonders on screen in their local picture palace'.[35]

The fact that cinema was a dominant mass medium in the 1930s also bears upon the centrality of community in many memory narratives. As the *Nottingham Evening Post* makes clear, 'going to the pictures was very much a shared experience' which offered 'the sheer pleasure of roaring with laughter amidst a thousand others'.[36] In all of these ways, cinema is often remembered as the place where the cinema-goer met others from his or her neighbourhood, where s/he belonged in a club as a child, where s/he sang along with the accompaniments, shouted advice to the stars, and shared all the powerful emotions that films of the 'Golden Age' could invoke. Cinema-going is invariably linked with powerful impressions of community in the memory narratives of the local press, a sense of remembrance that not only helps foster and secure a particular readership but that also plays off and within contemporary figurations of city identity and cultural value. In the following section, I will examine questions of value as they relate specifically to narratives of morality and decline.

Morality and decline

In the memory narratives of *Bygones* and the *Nottingham Evening Post,* films of the Golden Age are remembered as being fervently moral in nature. This morality is recalled fondly as a secure touchstone. As a respondent to an oral history interview in Nottingham so effectively phrased it, 'In those days films were black and white both in terms of colour and their morality'.[37] As in particular memories of community, the overriding sense amongst the elderly generation is that morality has declined since their youth. For many respondents, the morality on screen in the Golden Age was evidence of values in the society as a whole, values that have subsequently declined.

The morality evinced by films of the Golden Age is taken by many readers to explain the widespread level of audience participation. So, according to an article of cinema reminiscence in one Nottingham

paper: 'to the hero we shouted in unison "Look behind yer!" or if he
hesitated to shoot, "Shoot! Shoot!" we chanted'.[38] This type of reminiscence evokes the sense that good and evil were clearly differenti-
ated on film as in life; no memories recall any grey or uncertain
characters or plots onscreen. The audience as a whole, we are told
retrospectively, felt the same, so 'Good always triumphed over evil
and there is no doubt whose side we were on'.[39] In the memory of
audience response, there is an insistence that everyone felt the same
and responded in the same way, reflecting a broader set of shared
values (as well as cinematic expectations). This implied sense of a
strong moral compass amongst Nottingham cinema-goers of the
1930s and 1940s is particularly significant in the context of the
1990s, where issues of morality were frequently discussed in relation
to urban criminality. In a time where crime waves were being seized
upon in local news coverage – largely provoked by Nottingham's
higher than average crime-rate, made conspicuous by national sur-
veys rating crime such as burglary, car theft and mugging[40] – the inclusion of personal memories helped generate perspectives about city
identity in the past and for the future. More specifically, memory
became a news strategy for maintaining the stake and readership of
the elderly as it responded to community dramas in the present day.

Memory of cinema's inherent morality in the Golden Age
extends from the films to the experience of cinema-going itself. The
role of authority in the Golden Age and the attitude of cinema-
going children and young people are central to this form of recall.
The commissionaire and doorman are remembered as the repre-
sentatives of cinema's vociferous policing of behaviour: they were
the people who disciplined any rowdy children in the Saturday children's clubs. Their smart uniforms are especially remembered as
central to their unarguable authority. Hence the following quotes
are representative: 'the commissionaire was in control in his peaked
hat, his smart uniform in gold braid, military style' and 'the commissionaire or doorman would keep us all in order . . . very smart
in his uniform adorned with gold braid'.[41] Another respondent
remembers 'commissionaires in military-style uniforms . . . controlling the queues' and adds the interesting personal reflection that
'I was always rather disappointed when I saw these power wielding
people out in their ordinary clothes – they didn't look at all important then'.[42] If the increasingly militarised 1930s and 1940s were a
period where uniforms became a powerful signature of authority, a

sense of regimental discipline carried forth into the cinema clubs inhabited by Nottingham's children.

While the behaviour of children at the cinema is often remembered to be rowdy and noisy – some letters even refer to children as hooligans – there is an overwhelming sense that behaviour was never a serious threat or danger. One respondent recalls that after eating bananas, pranks would begin. He writes: 'you see we were hooligans in those days as we slung the skins over the balcony!'[43] And another that 'When one of us had no money to get in we all kept guard while he or she sneaked in, but we always got caught. Oh such criminals!'[44] Both of the exclamation marks that end these reminiscences and their overall tone are typical of this group of memories. The recollected 'hooliganism' and 'criminality' are seen more as high spirits or as minor misdemeanours. Either way, such infringements were always dealt with effectively by the uniformed cinema staff or by parents, and those reminiscing seem pleased that order was maintained. The memories are comic rather than threatening or frightening; none of the memories tell of any violence, vandalism or danger inflicted by Golden Age audiences. Who would dare? As local cinema historian, Rick Wilde, recalls, boisterous children were dealt with firmly, 'law and order was enforced with a rod of iron'.[45]

For the press, this type of memory is often utilised to fuel debate about youth and criminality in the present day, inflecting a discourse of social change, especially as it bears upon manners of behaviour and levels of youth discipline. For those who proffer memories of cinema-going in the local press, a picture of decline frequently emerges, set in relation to relaxed expectations of personal probity and against a more aggressive and materialistic contemporary milieu. These rather clichéd notions of social decline are not uncommon within structures of personal and cultural nostalgia. As Davis claims about nostalgic reminiscence: 'present circumstances and condition . . . compared to the past are invariably felt to be . . . more bleak, grim, wretched'.[46] However, certain incidents and events can mobilise a focused sense of decline, related to particular news issues that may invoke youth (mis)behaviour, or that may relate more broadly to manifestations of corporate infiltration in the city sphere.

The announcement that the city centre Odeon (Britain's first split-screen cinema) was to close in January 2001 is a marked example of the latter, inspiring letters to the *Nottingham Evening Post* mourning what one writer saw as a general decline in the city's sense of heritage and identity. She wrote: 'We know changes to our city centre are inevitable through the years but are they really for the better?'[47] Another letter by a man who used to work at the Odeon commented that 'I was very upset to hear about its closure. It was *the* cinema in Nottingham.'[48] These comments are part of a wide sense among older generations that the city centre is being devalued. Significantly, this can be set in relation to new forms of city investment, most notably an inner-city urban entertainment complex that emerged in 2001 that combined brand bars and restaurants with a fifteen-screen Warner Village.[49] While the opening of the complex was met with considerable news fanfare, especially honed for the young professional and middle-aged target users, elderly respondents often saw it as a white elephant. As one letter stated: 'who is going to fill the many bars and cinemas during the week?'[50] To many elderly respondents, the mall-like complex was further evidence of Nottingham's perceived decline, and was contrasted with the individual splendour of the Ritz in the 1930s.

For many, the Odeon functioned as a signifier of certain standards and values, and has been mourned in the same way as the demise of Nottingham's high-class shops, such as Pearson's department store and Burton's food shop. In addition, the closure of the Odeon, along with that of the original *Evening Post* Building and the long-standing Co-operative store, is seen by some to mark a deterioration of the city's architectural heritage. A further letter on the subject of the Odeon's closure wrote: 'It has tried to compete with the noisy monsters that now go under the name of cinemas where there is no personal service any more.'[51] A cinema's closure and the re-use or demolition of the building can make people protective of their memories. In this case, local press narratives are infused with characteristic phrases such as 'they can't take my memories away'. While Davis claims that for the elderly there is 'the apparent *unquestioned* belief that the past was better, that one's belief to that effect is a true reflection of *real* change in the world',[52] memories can often function discursively in response to tangible change, in certain cases bearing upon the restructuring of the city's public space and leisure culture.

Either stated or inferred, the past is constantly referred to as superior to the present. So Margaret Corkill remembers people eating fish suppers, pork pies and oranges in the cinema but 'Curiously enough I don't remember these old cinemas being grubby or littered'.[53] Interestingly, for some, in tandem with recollections of the palatial grandeur of the old cinemas go recollections of them being flea-ridden and of the usherettes going down the aisle spraying air freshener. Any sense of tension between these two perceptions is invariably absent. For the elderly, today's cinemas have far less atmosphere than the ones that live on in memory. For one man, 'One can only look back and marvel at the wonderful entertainment these movie palaces gave us'.[54] For most, the films too have declined since their heyday: 'The films are not as good now . . . we never come away saying we'd enjoyed because we'd had a good cry!'[55] Equally, the expense of recent trips to the cinema is often resented, especially as the price is for just one film, whereas in the Golden Age there would be two full-length films, plus a supporting short film.

This notion of decline is further represented by a recurrent sense that the past had a vigour and vividness, in contrast with the present's bureaucratic and staid character. In large part, this observation bears upon the age of those reminiscing. For the elderly, health problems and a general 'slowing down' often restrict activity and liveliness and, therefore, the relative perception of vigour. In general terms, many kinds of reminiscence state that past times were 'good old days'. This not only forms a sense of the superiority of the past over the present, but also helps cement generational commonalities in belief, experience and attitude. Such discussion of the past is beneficial to the local press for it encourages readers to write in with their views, and can lead to in-depth features on the state of the city. While notions of decline may be endemic to the experience of nostalgia, and to memories of cinema-going in particular, these can be used to enrich and democratise news discourse as it negotiates issues of city life for, and in response to, its various demographic constituencies.

Conclusion

The cinema-going past lives on in the local press. This chapter has tried to present various patterns of memory that emerge in a specific city context, suggesting that the relationship between memory and popular film is just as much about social activity as it is about specific movies. For *The Nottingham Evening Post* and its supplement publication *Bygones,* memory narratives are one of the ways in which members of the ageing population are maintained among its readers. All the memories of cinema reproduced in the local press evince a very positive attitude to that past experience, often locating it as one of the activities that helped people through 'hard times'. There are no examples of memories that live on as unpleasant reminders. Again, this bias may be attributable to the memories being situated in, and sanctioned by, the public realm of the press – both the city of Nottingham and the individuals concerned are placed in a favourable light. The press needs to build up a positive image of the city (to which it is inescapably linked) and memory narratives are a key means of highlighting the history and heritage of city life, even as these memories may contribute discursively to ideas of contemporary decline. Memories have the social function of affirming, in a public forum, themes and issues such as community, city building, leisure practice, and social behaviour, and bring together those who reminisce about emotions and experiences that may have receded into the past. The press benefits substantially from each of these, both in raising perspectives that inform local city debate (memory as news) and in securing the readership of a growing sector of the population (memory as niche-market).

Notes

1   Roger Bromley, *Lost Narratives, Popular Fictions, Politics and Recent History* (London: Routledge, 1988), p. 1.
2   Annette Kuhn, 'Cinema-going in Britain in the 1930s: Report of a Questionnaire Survey', *Historical Journal of Film, Radio and Television*, 19: 4 (1999), 531–43.
3   Jackie Stacey, *Star Gazing, Hollywood Cinema and Female Spectatorship* (London: New York, Routledge, 1994).
4   See Raphael Samuel, *Theatres of Memory* (London: Verso, 1994) and Robert Hewison, *The Heritage Industry* (London: Methuen, 1987). Samuel offers a detailed and wide-ranging study of some of the ways in which memory is preserved in British society, arguing that 'the last thirty years have witnessed an extraordinary and, it seems, ever growing enthusiasm for the recovery of the national past' (p. 139). Hewison argues that the heritage industry has developed in the United Kingdom in response to the widespread perception that the nation is in decline. This perceived decline is evidenced in both the economy (with the heritage industry functioning as a substitute for the manufacturing industry) and across society as a whole. He believes that when studying the past we should ask 'what kind of past we have chosen to preserve, and what that has done to our present' (p. 47).
5   James Curran and Jean Seaton, *Power Without Responsibility: The Press and Broadcasting in Britain* (London: Methuen, 1985), p. 49.

6 Rod Pilling, 'The Changing Role of the Local Journalist: From Faithful Chronicler of the Parish Pump to Multiskilled Compiler of an Electronic Database', in Bob Franklin and David Murphy (eds), *Making the Local News: Local Journalism in Context* (London: Routledge, 1998), pp. 184–5.

7 Stacey, *Star Gazing*, p. 63.

8 An article by Alan Bennett on his memories of cinema offers an interesting variation on the fare provided by the local press. He recounts a man groping his leg in the cinema when he was a child and his realisation that: 'this must be what Mam's mysterious warnings had been about'. I would suggest that while this theme may be acceptable for a well-known and well-respected figure in a literary journal, it is not common or generally favoured by local newspapers. See Alan Bennett, 'Seeing Stars', *London Review of Books* (3 January 2002), 12–14.

9 Paul Connerton, *How Societies Remember* (Cambridge: Cambridge University Press, 1989).

10 Joseph Fitzgerald, 'Reminiscence in Adult Development', in David C. Rubin (ed.) *Remembering Our Past: Studies in Autobiographical Memory* (Cambridge: Cambridge University Press, 1995), p. 370.

11 Fitzgerald, 'Reminiscence in Adult Development', pp. 367–9.

12 Fred Davis, *Yearning For Yesterday: A Sociology of Nostalgia* (New York: Free Press, 1979), p. 31.

13 'Double Seats and Savoury Snacks', *Nottingham Observer* (March 1984).

14 'Guys and Molls in Back Row', in *Bygones* supplement to *Nottingham Evening Post* (7 February 1998).

15 'Guys and Molls in Back Row'.

16 *Ibid.*

17 Nottingham City Library newspaper holdings.

18 Evidence from oral history research project, February 2000.

19 *Bygones*, 7 February 1998.

20 *Ibid.*

21 'Happy Memories of the Futurist', *Basford Bystander*, 34 (Nov–Dec 1991).

22 *Ibid.*

23 Davis, *Yearning For Yesterday*, p. 45.

24 'Happy Memories of the Futurist', *Basford Bystander*, 34 (Nov–Dec 1991).

25 Andrew Hoskins, 'New memory: mediating history', *Historical Journal of Film, Radio and Television* 21: 4 (2001), 333–47.

26 Pilling, 'The Changing Role of the Local Journalist', pp. 187–8.

27 *Bygones*, 7 February 1998.

28 *Nottingham Herald*, 18 July 1996.

29   Nottingham City Library newspaper holdings.
30   Nottinghamshire Archives, DD 2117/4/4.
31   Davis, *Yearning For Yesterday*, p. 102.
32   Robyn Fivush, Catherine Haden and Elaine Reese, 'Remembering, Recounting, and Reminiscing: The Development of Autobiographical Memory in Social Context', in Rubin (ed.) *Remembring Our Past*, p. 341.
33   Raymond Williams, *Marxism and Literature* (Oxford: Oxford University Press, 1977), p. 131.
34   *Nottingham Evening Post,* 6 March 1996.
35   *Nottingham Evening Post,* 10 April 1993.
36   *Bygones,*7 February 1998.
37   Interview for Nottingham oral history project, February 2000.
38   *Basford Bystander*, November 1989.
39   *Ibid.*
40   For the most recent figures see, for example, www.guardian.co.uk/graphic/0,5812,344426,00.html
41   *Bygones*, 7 February 1998.
42   *Nottingham Observer*, March 1984.
43   *Nottingham Evening Post*, 6 August 1996.
44   *Bygones*, 7 February 1998.
45   *Nottingham Evening Post*, 10 April 1993.
46   Davis, *Yearning For Yesterday*, p. 15.
47   *Nottingham Evening Post*, 14 November 2000.
48   *Ibid.*
49   For a discussion of the possible impact of the Warner Village on Nottingham's city centre, see Mark Jancovich and Lucy Faire with Sarah Stubbings, *The Place of the Audience: Cultural Geographies of Film Consumption* (London: BFI, forthcoming).
50   Nottingham City Library newspaper holdings.
51   *Nottingham Evening Post*, 27 October 2000.
52   Davis, *Yearning For Yesterday*, p. 64. Italics in original.
53   *Nottingham Observer*, March 1984.
54   *Bygones*, 7 February 1998.
55   *Ibid.*

4

Raiding the archive: film festivals and the revival of Classic Hollywood

Julian Stringer

> History becomes heritage in various ways. Artifacts become appropriated by particular historical agendas, by particular ideologies of preservation, by specific versions of public history, and by particular values about exhibition, design, and display.
>
> (Arjun Appadurai and Carol A. Breckenridge)[1]

Film Studies has to date paid too little attention to the role cultural institutions play in the transformation of cinema history into heritage. At the dawn of cinema's second century, a range of organisational bodies – including museums and art galleries, the publicity and promotion industries, film journalism and publishing, as well as the academy – work to activate and commodify memory narratives concerning the movies' own glorious and fondly recalled past. Such bodies serve different kinds of agendas, broadly identifiable as the commercial, the cultural and the educational (or a combination thereof). However, all help determine the specific shape of current thinking regarding cinema's past, present and future.

At a time when more films than ever before are being exhibited on a greater number of different kinds of screens than ever before, the cumulative effect of all this institutional activity is to create consensus around which films should be remembered and which forgotten. With so many 'old' and contemporary titles jockeying for position at the multiplex and the art cinema, on television and cable, video, DVD and the Internet, as well as in the classroom, the relatively small number of titles eventually sold, projected, written about, taught or revived, will be largely confined to those legitimised for one reason or another by these different kinds of organisational bodies. In order for a film to stand the test of time, it needs to be 'voted' as worthy of preservation. If this does not happen, the movie concerned is in danger of slipping from public consciousness.

The institution of the film festival has over recent years provided a key location for the advancement of such historical and preservationist agendas. Major events like those held annually in Berlin, Cannes, Hong Kong, New York, Pusan, Toronto and Venice act as lynchpins around which a diverse range of cultural activities rotate. As Kenneth Turan's *Sundance to Saravejo: Film Festivals and the World They Made* has most recently confirmed, such events have developed a number of key roles and functions.[2] Filmmakers, producers and industry personnel, scholars and journalists, archivists and 'ordinary fans', among others, constitute the 'festival publics' who invest differently in diverse aspects of the jamboree atmosphere facilitated by such events. In attracting such a broad spread of participants and audiences, the ever-expanding globalised film festival circuit proves that cinephilia is alive and well and living in the international marketplace.

As news media reports habitually demonstrate, festivals can make or break new films. Certainly, many of the larger events act as launching pads for foreign (i.e. non-US), marginal or 'difficult' movies, and as such constitute an alternative distribution network for contemporary world cinema. In this sense, festivals have an important forward-looking sensibility, providing a vital arena for the emergence of the culturally 'new'.[3]

At the same time, however, it has been less widely acknowledged that many festivals also embody a backward-looking sensibility. Over recent years some festivals have come to function as veritable museums of audio-visual culture. The international festival circuit now plays a significant role in the re-circulation and re-commodification of 'old' and 'classic' movies. Taking the form of revivals, retrospectives, special gala screenings, and archive-driven events, the contemporary exhibition of such historical artefacts provides a powerful means of extending cinephilia into the second century of cinema through a process that Grant McCracken has identified as the 'displaced meaning strategy':

> Confronted with the recognition that reality is impervious to cultural ideals, a community may displace these ideals. It will remove them from daily life and transport them to another cultural universe, there to be kept within reach but out of danger. The displaced meaning strategy allows a culture to remove its ideals from harm's way.[4]

It is the institutional nature of the film festival which creates the conditions necessary for the existence of this particular cultural arrangement. As with the process of labelling that happens at museums and art galleries, any movie shown at a film festival needs to be positioned for public display, and this is achieved through acts of classification and identification. At its moment of reception by a festival audience, a title will be made sense of, in part, through the weight of the interpretative frames provided at and around such events. When this happens, the classification identity and cultural status of old movies is likely to undergo change. In Steve Neale's terminology, titles initially produced as 'generically modelled films' (i.e. gangster films, musicals, and so on) are re-circulated as 'generically marked films'[5]: i.e. as 'festival films' (here understood for purposes of convenience simply as films shown at festivals). This exhibition and classificatory process works to secure the importance of some titles rather than others within the memory narratives of institutionalised culture.

One topic of particular significance for Film Studies is the revival at international film festivals of movies made during the heyday of the Hollywood studio system – that is to say, the recirculation of those films most commonly held to represent the popular memory of commercial cinema itself. In this chapter, I want to explore this subject by considering briefly the circulation of old Hollywood movies – especially, but not exclusively, those produced between 1910 and 1960 – at the London Film Festival during the years 1981–2001. I have chosen to focus on this particular festival and specific time period for largely practical reasons. On the one hand, London is a festival with which I have some familiarity. I have lived in the city and attended the event, worked in film distribution and on the fringes of the festival in the late 1980s, and have access to its relevant publications (i.e. the festival catalogues themselves; such materials constituting a major, if still largely untapped, source of information for film history scholars).

On the other hand, this concentration on a two-decade period in the life of one of the UK's most visible annual cinematic events provides a convenient point of historical comparison. In 1981, the London Film Festival's parent organisation, the British Film Institute, published *Water Under the Bridge*, a dossier on the history of the festival's first twenty-five years, from its founding in 1957 to that date. One of the most valuable aspects of this publication is that it includes a list of all the films screened by the festival during those years.[6] As such, this chapter provides a means of revisiting and updating some of the information contained in that dossier – in other words, to consider the screening of some of the festival's films in the twenty-year period since 1981. I am not concerned at the present time with the exhibition of new or contemporary movies at the London Film Festival. What I am interested in, though, is the question of how the revival of old Hollywood films serves distinct institutional interests.

Few old movies of any kind appear to have been screened at the London Film Festival prior to 1981. According to *Water Under the Bridge*, the first non-contemporary title to be exhibited was the Jean Renoir French classic *The Rules of The Game*, which was produced in 1938 but screened at the 1960 event. The first Hollywood title to be unspooled was Buster Keaton's *Seven Chances* (1925) in 1965. 1967 saw the revival of another Renoir classic from France, *La Marseillaise* (1937), while *The Movies That Made Us*, a Warner Bros. compilation film, was screened in 1973, and *Spite Marriage* (1929) in 1976. The start of the decade of the 1980s saw a watershed, however. *Twinkletoes* (1926), *Chang* (1927), *The Crowd* (1928) and the UK title *Elstree Calling* (1930) were all screened in 1981, and the initiation soon after of Thames Television's annual showcase – 'Thames Silent Classics' (revived silent movies with full orchestral accompaniment, later shown on British free-to-air television) – helped set in motion the fad for revivalism which has intensified markedly in subsequent years.

The Thames Silent Classics series established a useful baseline for examining the revival of classic Hollywood cinema at the London festival for two key reasons. First, such revivals immediately created a sense of rarefied distinction by activating the displaced meaning strategy around, on the one hand, aesthetics factors, and on the other, 'special' modes of public presentation. In short, these Thames titles, these examples of classic cinema, are both inherently worthy and worthy of being preserved. (Typically, they are presented as being among the most noteworthy of their time (e.g. the most expensive or most spectacular movies of the silent era).) Second, they also allow new varieties of cinephilia to be generated through the reproduction of original film viewing pleasures.

For example, the revival of *The Thief of Bagdad* (1924) in 1984 is presented as akin to a 1920s roadshow presentation of a silent 'superspecial', with an orchestral score 'specially composed by Carl Davis who will conduct the Philharmonia Orchestra at each performance', and variable ticket prices (£5, £7, £10) 'available only from the Dominion, Tottenham Court Rd, London W1, until the period 9–29 November when a limited selection will be on sale at the NFT Box Office'.[7] These forms of product differentiation – special musical accompaniment, prestige exhibition at a prestige venue and in prestige seats, exclusivity of exhibition dates and times – are meant to both recall the classic tradition of first-run presentation of Hollywood features, and also recreate it. Indeed, this has been a constant attraction at the London Film Festival during this twenty-year period. It characterises, for example, screenings of the following selected list of silent classics, all of which were showcased through such rarefied modes of public presentation: *The Big Parade* (1925; screened at the 1985 event), *Greed* (1924; screened in 1985), *Ben-Hur* (1925 [1987]), *Intolerance* (1916 [1988]), *Sign of the Cross* (1932 [1989]) and *Wings* (1927 [1993]). Many of these films were shown at venues like the London Palladium, rather than the festival's regular institutional home, the National Film Theatre.

Such revivals also helped to set in motion two specific memory narratives which the London festival has activated in diverse kinds of ways across this twenty-year period. On the one hand, the Thames events very often fetishised industrial and technological innovations, or 'firsts'. On the other hand, they promoted fairly traditional conceptions of authorship.

Use of the first of these two narratives is fairly widespread. At the simplest possible level, this means that the London festival has on occasion worked to underscore the most conservative storylines regarding the 'great moments' of cinema history. The tale being told here admittedly does extend beyond Hollywood. For example, the pioneering German silent classics *The Cabinet of Dr Caligari* (1919), *Metropolis* (1927) and *Nosferatu: A Symphony of Terror* (1921) were revived in 1985, 1984 and 1995, respectively, and the Soviet milestone *October* (USSR, 1927–28) was shown in 1988 after Alan Fearon had 'reconstructed the massive score using original research by musicologist David Kershaw'.[8] However, these are all safe, stellar attractions from the global film canon which have in effect already been voted as worthy of preservation by international film culture.

Hollywood titles are often revived through the foregrounding of a sense of technological presence. Focusing on the soundtrack, for example, easily allows for discussion of path-breaking industrial developments. *Gold Diggers of Broadway* (1929) was revived in 1987 as 'one spectacular reel' from this 'long lost 2–strip Techni-colour musical . . . recently discovered and restored by the National Film Archive with its music track transferred from the original 16' discs by the National Sound Archive'.[9] Similarly, the 1988 event included a MOMI Vitaphone – A Tribute show emphasising the rare, and hence special, nature of this particular festival presentation. 'Many of these films from the late 20s were considered either totally lost or, if they did survive, existed in picture form with no sound.' As if to compensate for the festival audience's lack of familiarity with such films, though, other novel aspects are then emphasised: 'Tonight's selection opens with the first Vitaphone short seen by the general public, an address by Will Hays, which was filmed in June 1926.' Furthermore, the presence of familiar named actors helps obviate the perceived 'primitive' nature of the technology put on show. These Vitaphone titles act 'as a testing ground for new acting talent, as evidenced by Spencer Tracy in *The Hard Guy* (1930) and Pat O'Brien in *Crimes Square* (1930)' (68).

The appeal to notions of authorship similarly provides a com-pelling way of presenting and recreating Hollywood pleasures. The screening in 1986 of the hour-long *Directed by William Wyler* (1986) was supported by the twenty-minute short, *It's All True* (1942, directed by Orson Welles) – the only evident connection between these two films being the fact that the London festival has institutionally identified and framed them as auteur titles. In addi-tion, an important component of the cinephiliac nostalgia for clas-sic Hollywood demonstrated across the years at London is the frequent presentation of documentary films about old Hollywood. These contemporary movies often provide new knowledge and so present new ways of remembering films past. Again, however, they tend to tell fairly standard stories concerning the great and the good of film history. Such films include the following (unless stated other-wise, production date corresponds to screening date): *Marlene* (West Germany, 1984 – on Marlene), *The Thrill of Genius* (Italy, 1985 – on Hitchcock), *Making of a Legend: Gone With the Wind* (US, 1988, but screened in 1989), *Preston Sturges: The Rise and Fall of an American Dreamer* (US, 1990), *Jack L. Warner: The Last Mogul* (US, 1993), *Music for the Movies: The Hollywood Sound* (US, 1995), *Wild Bill: A Hollywood Maverick* (US, 1995 – on William Wellman) and

Carmen Miranda: Bananas is my Business (US/Brazil, 1994, but screened in 1995).

With the exhibition of these kinds of movies, the archive is 'raided' so as to revive key moments of cinema history via appropriate modes of big-screen audio-visual presentation. Such a method of promoting the highbrow and rarefied atmosphere of 'authentic' Hollywood pleasures works to separate public film festival screenings from the more private pleasures associated with home video spectatorship.

As the 1980s wore on, the London event evidenced a growing self-consciousness concerning the potentially problematic relationship between the popularity, or lowbrow nature, of classic Hollywood, and the highbrow or rarefied nature of the festival's own museum aesthetic. The sense that here is a festival which reproduces the official line on film history while not really wanting to can be seen most bizarrely in a catalogue description for the 1989 screening of *Safety Last* (1923). 'The still of Harold Lloyd hanging from the clock is an icon of silent comedy', write Kevin Brownlow and David Gill. 'Sadly, it's all most people know of Harold Lloyd. The most neglected of the great comedians, his films work best on the big screen. You have to see *Safety Last* with an audience to realise what a brilliantly funny piece of work it is.'[10] The contradiction here is clear. On the one hand, this festival audience is learning nothing more than prior viewers of Lloyd's films – it is *Safety Last* which is once again being revived in showcase form, not other titles. On the other hand, while concentrating on the special circumstances of a 'big screen' and prestigious festival revival of this particular classic, the two writers evidently feel under no obligation to inform readers of the titles of the 'two short films from Harold Lloyd' (102) which accompany their revival of an already more-than-famous main attraction.

There is, then, a slight instability in the title of the 1995 restoration and revival season – 'Saved! Restorations From the Archives'.[11] Sure, by being preserved and screened at the London festival, such movies are being saved from obscurity and old age. Equally, though, the exhibition of canonic titles such as *Cabinet of Dr Caligari*, *October*, and *Safety Last* suggests that what is being saved are those films already well-known and available within the postmodern audio-visual archive. In short, the London Film Festival has on occasion given pride of place to those films which are already widely known, which do not technically *need* to be saved.

In fact, the picture is more complicated than this. Among the US titles presented through archive events at the festival are some intriguing selections. To take one example, *Paramount on Parade* (1930) – restored by UCLA (University of California at Los Angeles) Film and Television Archive, 'in cooperation with Universal Pictures' – seemingly has nothing in particular going for it: 'Some of the musical numbers were filmed in two-colour Technicolor. Unfortunately, all that remains of these segments is a faded, deteriorating work print, with no soundtrack; excerpts of these segments will be shown, to give an idea of the original staging' (103). By contrast, there is a conscious attempt to rewrite history with a series of 'Warner Bros. Second Vitaphone Programme, October 7 1926' and 'Jazz Age Vitaphone Shorts' (USA, 1927–29). The former includes Al Jolson in *A Plantation Act* (1926); 'a full year before his triumph in *The Jazz Singer* . . . Withdrawn by Warner Bros., this short had been considered lost until the Library of Congress found the picture, and the Vitaphone Project located the only surviving copy of the Vitaphone disc – broken into four pieces and badly glued together. Thanks to perseverance and the marvels of modern technology, we are pleased to present the first public screening of this landmark Al Jolson short in almost 70 years' (105). Here, the London festival is itself presented as making cinema history by innovating a different and new kind of 'first'.

Given the proliferation of examples such as these, it appears as if the two core memory narratives I have identified above were refocused throughout the 1990s. Technological innovation and notions of authorship were retained in festival descriptions of archive-based events. However, these became framed slightly differently, and in a manner that exposes the specific institutional interests served by London's preservationist agendas.

As a way of beginning to explain this phenomenon, consider the 'Treasures from the Archive' presentation of 1997. This series includes a short season on Frank Capra 'in his centenary year'.[12] The three titles presented here are instructive in terms of the different ways in which 'one of the greatest directors of Hollywood's Golden Age' (58) is being re-positioned for contemporary audiences. Readers are first told that this particular director 'enjoyed complete creative freedom, producing evergreen comedies and warm morality fables such as *It Happened One Night*, *Mr Deeds Goes to Town*, and *Arsenic and Old Lace*'. Next, three separate screenings are then introduced. First, a new documentary, *Frank Capra's American Dream* (1997), creates updated specialised knowledge by 'inducing fresh admiration for Capra's seldom celebrated flair for crowd and action sequences, editing innovation and moody visual nuances'. Second, a print of the early Capra comedy, *The Matinee Idol* (1928), is unspooled; 'long thought lost, [it] was recently rediscovered in a foreign vault belonging to the Cinematheque Francaise. Newly restored under the auspices of the Academy of Motion Pictures Arts and Sciences and Sony Pictures, it is sure to charm and delight audiences anew'. (It is notable that what is being emphasised here is not just rarity and exclusivity, but the ambiguous status of the institutions involved – one is foreign, the other from the US, the former independent of Hollywood ownership, the latter part of the corporate system.) Finally, the 1997 festival is 'delighted to present the re-release of one of cinema's most enduringly popular titles, in memory of its star James Stewart' – namely, *It's a Wonderful Life* (58). The evocation of this re-release along the lines of it being 'in memory' of star Stewart is perhaps slightly disingenuous – after all, the film was about to be recirculated on commercial DVD. The festival's appeal to Stewart's cherished memory thus hides a clear commercial logic.

In short, these three Capra screenings present different aspects of the gradual refocusing of notions of innovation and authorship that occurs across the 1990s: the production of new knowledge concerning the Hollywood film industry; the promotion of rare and exclusive attractions; and the investment in tried and trusted pleasures (or the consolidation of the reputation of those films which have already been 'voted' as worthy of preservation in popular memory).

As conceptions of technological development and authorship began to change, the links established between the various relevant cultural institutions became easier to see. Consider the fact that the description of the 1987 screening of *The Big Trail* (1930), a film 'more often quoted than seen', is presented courtesy of 'the New York Museum of Modern Art Film Department's remarkable reconstruction' (23). (The same holds true for the 1997 screening of *Orphans of the Storm* [1921]). FIAF (the International Federation of Film Archives) reveals itself to be another important organisation. The 1988 festival celebrates FIAF's fiftieth anniversary by screening two restorations (including John Ford's *She Wore a Yellow Ribbon* [1949]) carried out by the UCLA Film and Television Archive, 'with the cooperation of RKO Pictures and Turner Entertainment

Company and sponsored by the David and Lucile Packard Foundation and AFI/NEA'. Moreover, an extra degree of specialness is
secured in this particular case through knowledge that 'this restored
print was much acclaimed at the Berlin festival' (68): success at one
globalised film festival now justifies success at another. Other institutional activities include restorations from the National Film and
Television Archive in 1993, such as *The Glorious Adventure* (1922),
Under Capricorn (1949) and the 'lush Technicolor spectacle' (28) of
Jungle Book (1942).[13] Similarly, the year 2000 brought the showcasing of George Eastman House's restoration work on *When a Man
Loves* (1927).[14]

Crucially, a key form of institutional involvement in the London
Film Festival involves the presence of the Hollywood studios themselves. They appear to facilitate the restoration and re-presentation
process at every opportunity, demonstrating that when it comes to
turning Hollywood history into heritage, the studios are the most
adept of all. As these examples are too numerous to note, just one
should suffice: *Four Horsemen of the Apocalypse* (1921) was
restored for exhibition in 1992 by Photoplay Productions based on
a negative presented by MGM.

More interesting, perhaps, is the convergence of the studios'
interests with those of related institutions. 1992 also saw the public
arrival of the Champagne Piper-Heidsieck Classic Film Collection of
the British Film Institute. According to Project Manager, Erich
Sargeant, this 'is the first international project of its kind and
involves the cooperation of rights holders [i.e. the studios], film
organisations and archives throughout the world. Over the next
four years the BFI will be assembling 200 pristine prints of classic
films programmed into imaginative seasons. These seasons will tour
worldwide and feature in many prestigious arts and film festivals as
well as at a number of cinemateques'.[15] In emphasising the prestigious nature of both festivals and cinemateques, this description
once again plays down the humdrum availability of these same films
for domestic consumption. The studios' home video and DVD
releases of these same titles constitute the commercial Other of rarefied film festival screenings.

The 1993 'Gala screening' of *The Searchers* also forms part of the
Champagne Piper-Heidsieck Classic Film Collection's promotional
activities. Once again, this re-release '[has] featured at festivals
throughout Europe' (117). Moreover, the 'second season, Early

Hitchcock, has just completed a successful American tour and is currently to be seen at venues in Belgium' (117). Along these same lines, further 'Special Events' at London across the years have included a 1999 screening of *Annie Laurie* (1927), a work 'greatly admired' upon its 're-launch' at the 1998 Pordenone Film Festival, and now presented as one of 'the incomparable Lillian Gish's lesser-known, late silent starring vehicles'. This is announced as a 'collector's piece which will be complemented by a special lecture presentation on Lillian Gish's career by her former personal manager, James Frasher'.[16] The notion of a collector's piece is highly significant. Such language refers not to an available material object which may be acquired (such as a video or reel of celluloid), but to the more intangible 'collection' of a rare and distinct event – namely, a special film festival exhibition and presentation. According to the London Film Festival, it is enough simply to have been there; if you attended the event that day, you 'collected' a unique and 'lesser-known' film viewing experience. (Even if the festival public at Pordenone had already enjoyed a similar kind of experience.)

Re-launches often take the form of anniversary events. The fiftieth anniversary of the National Film Archive was occasioned in 1985 by the showcase presentation of *The Toll of the Sea* (1922) and *Becky Sharp* (1935). But for the studios, anniversaries represent a new window of opportunity where old films can be recommodified under the guise of celebrating this or that particular attraction. *The Apartment* (1960) was presented in 2000 'to commemorate the 40th anniversary of its release' (60) and *Rear Window* (1954) in 1999 as conclusion to 'the BFI's year of Hitchcock Centenary celebrations' (56). Moreover, *Elvis – That's the Way It Is* (1970–2000), shown in 2000 to 'coincide with the 30th anniversary of the release of this documentary and accompanying album', was enabled because 'Turner Classic Movies have undertaken comprehensive re-editing and digital restoration' (61). This latter example suggests both an underlying commercial motivation, and that the definition of 'old' and 'classic' movies is now moving out of the studio period (i.e. into the 1960s and beyond). This is another highly significant development. Simply put, it is one thing to 'save' canonic and endangered old films so as to preserve their memory. But it is quite another to digitally update a work from the much more recent past so as to reclassify it as a must-see movie classic.

As the above examples suggest, the London Film Festival appears to hold a special place in its heart for film archive-friendly people. Without wishing to take anything away from the extremely good work that such professionals undoubtedly do, it is also worth mentioning that archivists can easily become enlisted in the recommodification process. A primary reason for the studios to re-circulate films in the contemporary era is to make profit from new DVD releases. Indeed, DVD technology draws monies through promoting a patina of cultural distinction, for example, on those occasions when a DVD re-release becomes culturally sanctioned because the film concerned has already been revived at highbrow festivals.

In 1999, the festival screening of *How Green Was My Valley* (1941) was advertised as a 'chance to see another of the impeccable restorations of classic American films (this one with crucially renovated sound) to come out of the Academy Film Archive in Beverly Hills' (54). More than this, it 'is also an opportunity to pay tribute to the memory of one of its stars, the British-born Roddy McDowell – a friend and benefactor of film archives in the United States – who died this year' (54). The specific connotations being advanced here – of the work of other institutions, the appropriateness of having a 'British-born' actor spotlighted at a London event, and of once more 'paying tribute' to the 'memory' of a star's work – all disguise the fact that what we have here is another commercial re-release in the making. The DVD of *How Green Was My Valley* became available in UK high street shops shortly thereafter.

Furthermore, as the London festival itself acknowledged in its description in 2000 of *In Cold Blood* (1967), 'even the more recent classic movies need restoration. Legendary cameraman Conrad Hall [*American Beauty*] collaborated with Grover Crisp of Sony Pictures to bring his own timeless (and very topical) stunning black and white widescreen images to atmospheric life' (63). Here, cinemagoers and fans now have the very welcome opportunity to see an important title from the recent past in excellent and enjoyable exhibition circumstances. On the other hand, the opportunities for future exploitation are revealed through this particular occasion to be enormous. Just think of all the collaborations that could potentially be made between contemporary creative workers and huge conglomerates such as Sony Pictures. Films currently on release could always be enlisted in the marketing of an 'old' movie tangentially linked to it in some way. (The latter may well appear 'timeless' if claimed to be enough times.) In other words, what is now beginning to happen at festivals such as London is the construction of an institutionalised memory for relatively recent, not to say contemporary Hollywood titles.

At the time of writing, the most recent London Film Festival, held in 2001, gives some interesting indications of what may be expected in the near future. With this event, the refocusing of technological developments and firsts, and the concomitant shifts in conceptualisations of authorship, come full-circle. Its 'Treasures from the Archives' season is now clearly 'Sponsored by Turner Classic Movies', thus solidifying the link between festivals and studios. Beyond this, though, three of the films presented at this particular event are worth commenting upon in more specific detail.

First, *The Big Heat* (1953) is explicitly introduced through a new kind of auteurism – namely, the craft of the preservationist him/her self: 'This has been a remarkable year for Sony Pictures' knowledgeable preservationist Grover Crisp (see also *Funny Girl* and *Ride Lonesome*), but nothing exemplifies the perfectionism in his craft better than this restoration of Fritz Lang's *noir* masterpiece'.[17] Fittingly, perhaps, the preservationist has now become the very centre of attention.

Second, *The Sin of Nora Moran* (1933) constitutes an interesting attempt to shift the focus of attention around ever-more obscure, rather than simply canonic or rare material. This movie is described as a 'bizarre, fast-moving, bold, "avant-garde" B movie from the early 30s, about a victimised woman accused of murder', and as 'rapidly achieving cult status. Described as "neither classic nor camp, but a unique melange of both" . . . [it] is (in the words of UCLA's 2000 Festival of Preservation brochure), "haunting, hallucinatory, artistic, exploitative . . . maybe the best Hollywood B-movie of the 1930s"' (65). Clearly, the festival is making appeals here both to the cultish nature of connoiseurship and cinephilia and to the interest of B-film production. This provides a further sense of product differentiation within the cultural remit of preservation work. Tellingly, in a novel spin on the self-perpetuating cycle of festivals supporting and promoting each other, a preservation company's own festival is now referenced and quoted with approval by its peers.

This awareness of the vogue-ish nature of contemporary memory work around old Hollywood movies is to be found in a final description from the 2001 catalogue. A collection of 'Warner Brothers Shorts from the Turner Film Library' is introduced thus: 'With the current fashion for restoring great classics, "lost" masterpieces and director's cuts, it is easy to forget the true orphans of the cinema – the bread-and-butter movies, especially those from and about Hollywood, which supported the main feature and made up the cinema pro-grammes of the past.' This leads into a series of restored two-reelers from the 1930s and 1940s, restored by 'Richard May, in charge of preservation at Warner Bros.' (65), linked together once more by tech-nological novelty – here, the fact that all were shot in Technicolor.

Two points are worth emphasising about this most recent devel-opment. First, the shift in focus around more obscure material is jus-tified by the claim that these B movie titles are the 'true' orphans of cinema history. Second, it is also justified through the attempt to recreate what was felt to have once been a common type of movie experience, and so to experience a time – the 1930s and 1940s – now fading from lived experience: 'From Dick May's recommenda-tions we have compiled this sampling of newly-restored Warner sub-jects – all Technicolor – of the kind which made pre-television era moviegoers happy as they waited for the big picture' (65).

As this final example suggests, notions of historical authenticity played an important role in the revival of Hollywood cinema at the 2001 London Film Festival. Yet while some movies may or may not be 'lost', some revivals are certainly more 'true' than others. Symp-tomatically, even a modern classic like *The Exorcist – The Director's Cut* (aka The Version You've Never Seen) (1973–2000, and shown at the London Film Festival in 2000) epitomises this same trend. This movie is indeed part of a current 'fashion' – it is a restored 'great classic', a film that audiences have 'never seen before' – but it is in no sense 'lost' since *The Exorcist* has been widely available for years on video in a slightly different version. Against this, the titles exhibited as part of the Warner Brothers Shorts series wear their obscurity like a badge of honour: examples include *Romance of Robert Burns* ('as it says (expect the worst), with Owen King, 1937' [65]) and *Hollywood Wonderland* ('Fritz Feld . . . as a Michael Curtiz-style director conducting a musical tour of the Warner Studio, 1946' [65]).

As the above discussion has hopefully demonstrated, there is much at stake in the revival of these kinds of films at these kinds of events. At London between 1981–2001, the emphasis on technological developments and firsts, as well as on authorship, has mutated over time into a celebration of the act of preservation itself: the artistry and the tools of archival memory work, as well as the skills of those who preserve Hollywood's fondly recalled past, have now taken centre stage. However, the process of reviving Hollywood films at this particular festival arguably still emphasises the logic of the commercial agenda over cultural and educational agendas.

Yet one of the most intriguing aspects of the growth of the international film festival circuit is the possibility it opens for a more de-centred and de-territorialised view of Hollywood's reception history. If at London old Hollywood films are revived within familiar contexts – technological developments and firsts, special modes of public presentation, traditional conceptions of authorship and opportunities for recommodification – they may be screened elsewhere around different preservationist concerns.

To give just one example, the Universal horror classics *Frankenstein* (1931) and *The Mummy* (1932) were revived at the Puchon International Fantastic Film Festival, South Korea, in 2001, within the context of a desire to explore knowledge around this particular genre.[18] To be sure, there was a 'reason', a justification, for such revivals – the appearance of the 1999 Hollywood blockbuster *The Mummy*. However, history has here become heritage in very different ways. These particular Hollywood artefacts have become appropriated by different kinds of historical agendas, by differing ideologies of preservation, by other versions of public history, and around alternative values about exhibition, design, and display. (Certainly, all of this is dependent on the existence at Puchon of a different set of festival publics.) Such will also be the case at the multifarious other festivals around the world where the Hollywood archive is being raided in order to advance specific institutional interests. However, this process always happens in conjunction with, or under the watchful eye of, the Hollywood studios and archives themselves.

Notes

1   Arjun Appadurai and Carol A. Breckenridge, 'Museums Are Good to Think: Heritage on View in India', in Ivan Karp, Christine Mullen Kreamer and Steven D. Kavine (eds), *Museums and Communities: The Politics of Public Culture* (Washington and London: Smithsonian Institution Press, 1992), pp. 36–7.

2 Kenneth Turan, *Sundance to Saravejo: Film Festivals and the World They Made* (Berkeley: University of California Press, 2002).

3 For a discussion of some of the specific ways in which 'new-ness' signifies on the festival circuit, see Bill Nichols, 'Discovering Form, Inferring Meaning: New Cinemas and the Film Festival Circuit', *Film Quarterly* 47: 3 (1994), 16–30.

4 Grant McCracken, *Culture and Consumption: New Approaches to the Symbolic Character of Consumer Goods and Activities* (Bloomington: Indiana University Press, 1990), p. 106.

5 Steve Neale, *Genre and Hollywood* (London: Routledge, 2000), p. 28.

6 Martyn Auty and Gillian Hartnoll (eds), *Water Under the Bridge: 25 Years of the London Film Festival* (London: British Film Institute, 1981).

7 28th London Film Festival, National Film Theatre, 15 November–2 December 1984, programme booklet, 78.

8 32nd London Film Festival, National Film Theatre, 10–27 November 1988, programme booklet, 21. Hereafter cited in text.

9 31st London Film Festival, National Film Theatre, 11–29 November 1987, programme booklet, 23.

10 33rd London Film Festival, National Film Theatre, 10–26 November 1989, programme booklet, 102.

11 39th London Film Festival, National Film Theatre, 2–19 November 1995, programme booklet, 103. Hereafter cited in text.

12 41st London Film Festival, National Film Theatre, 6–23 November 1997, programme booklet, 58. Hereafter cited in text.

13 37th London Film Festival, National Film Theatre, 4–21 November 1993, programme booklet, 29, 26, 28.

14 44th Regus London Film Festival, National Film Theatre, 1–16 November 2000, programme booklet, 64.

15 36th London Film Festival, National Film Theatre, 1992, programme booklet, 122.

16 43rd London Film Festival, National Film Theatre, 3–18 November 1999, programme booklet, 54.

17 45th Regus London Film Festival, National Film Theatre, 7–22 November 2001, programme booklet, 62. Herafter cited in text.

18 The 5th Puchon International Fantastic Film Festival, 12–20 July 2001, programme brochure, 51.

II

The politics of memory

5

The articulation of memory and desire: from Vietnam to the war in the Persian Gulf

John Storey

In this chapter I want to explore, within a context of culture and power, the complex relations between memory and desire.[1] More specifically, I want to connect 1980s Hollywood representations of America's war in Vietnam (what I will call 'Hollywood's Vietnam') with George Bush's campaign, in late 1990 and early 1991, to win support for US involvement in what became the Gulf War. My argument is that Hollywood produced a particular 'regime of truth'[2] about America's war in Vietnam and that this body of 'knowledge' was 'articulated'[3] by George Bush as an enabling 'memory' in the build up to the Gulf War.

Vietnam revisionism and the Gulf War

In the weeks leading up to the Gulf War, *Newsweek* featured a cover showing a photograph of a serious-looking George Bush. Above the photograph was the banner headline, 'This will not be another Vietnam'. The headline was taken from a speech made by Bush in which he said, 'In our country, I know that there are fears of another Vietnam. Let me assure you . . . this will not be another Vietnam.'[4] In another speech, Bush again assured his American audience that, 'This will not be another Vietnam . . . Our troops will have the best possible support in the entire world. They will not be asked to fight with one hand tied behind their backs.'[5] Bush was seeking to put to rest a spectre that had come to haunt America's political and military self-image, what Richard Nixon and others had called the 'Vietnam Syndrome'.[6] The debate over American foreign policy had, according to Nixon, been 'grotesquely distorted' by an unwillingness 'to use power to defend national interests'.[7] Fear of another Vietnam, had made America 'ashamed of . . . [its] power, guilty about being strong'.[8]

In the two Bush speeches from which I have quoted, and in many other similar speeches, Bush was articulating what many powerful American voices throughout the 1980s had sought to make *the* dominant meaning of the war: 'the Vietnam War as a noble cause betrayed – an American tragedy'. For example, in the 1980 presidential campaign Ronald Reagan declared, in an attempt to put an end to the Vietnam Syndrome, 'It is time we recognized that ours was, in truth, a noble cause.'[9] Moreover, Reagan insisted, 'Let us tell those who fought in that war that we will never again ask young men to fight and possibly die in a war our government is afraid to let us win.'[10] In 1982 (almost a decade after the last US combat troops left Vietnam), the Vietnam Veterans' memorial was unveiled in Washington. Reagan observed that Americans were 'beginning to appreciate that [the Vietnam War] was a just cause'.[11] In 1984 (eleven years after the last US combat troops left Vietnam) the Unknown Vietnam Soldier was buried; at the ceremony President Reagan claimed, 'An American hero has returned home . . . He accepted his mission and did his duty. And his honest patriotism overwhelms us.'[12] In 1985 New York staged the first of the 'Welcome Home' parades for Vietnam veterans. In this powerful mix of political rhetoric and national events, there is a clear attempt to put in place a new 'consensus' about the meaning of America's war in Vietnam. It begins in 1980 in Reagan's successful presidential campaign and ends in 1991 with the triumphalism of Bush after victory in the Gulf War.

The political and historical revisionism of the 1980s produced a mythology about why the US had been defeated in Vietnam. Moreover, it was a mythology that had more to do with preparing for the future than it ever had to do with explaining the past. As Reagan had stated, in his 1980 presidential campaign, '[The United States has] an inescapable duty to act as tutor and protector of the free world . . . [To fulfil this duty] we must first rid ourselves of the Vietnam Syndrome'.[13] In this sense, 1980s revisionism was an enabling discourse; its aim was to enable the US to once again take up the role of 'tutor and protector of the Free World'. To achieve these aims, Bush (and Reagan before him) had to both acknowledge and limit the meaning of Vietnam. In this task of mixing memory and desire, Bush (and Reagan before him) received significant support (I will argue) from Hollywood's Vietnam. Films such as *Cutter's Way* (1981), *First Blood* (1982), *Uncommon Valor* (1983), *Missing In Action* (1984), *Missing In Action II – The Beginning* (1985),

Rambo: First Blood Part II (1985), *Platoon* (1986), *POW: The Escape* (1986), *The Hanoi Hilton* (1987), *Braddock: Missing In Action III* (1988), *Casualties of War* (1989), *Born on the Fourth of July* (1989) and others, helped to create a memory of the war, and a desire to win the war retrospectively, that enabled Bush to say, with some credibility and conviction, that the Gulf War would not be another Vietnam.

The difficulty, of course, is in connecting Hollywood films to people's thinking on Vietnam and the war in the Persian Gulf. For some film critics the influence of Hollywood is self-evident. Robert Burgoyne, for example, points to what he calls 'the preeminent role that film has assumed in interpreting the past for contemporary [US] society'.[14] He also refers to 'the central role that the cinema plays in the imaging of the nation'.[15] Similarly, Robert Brent Toplin claims, without offering much in the way of evidence, that 'Historical films help shape the thinking of millions. Often the depictions seen on the screen influence the public's view of historical subjects much more than books do.'[16] In a discussion of French cinema in the 1970s Michel Foucault argued that recent French films (featuring the French Resistance) were engaged in 'a battle . . . to reprogramme . . . the "popular memory"; and . . . to . . . impose on people a frame-work in which to interpret the present . . . So people are shown not what they were, but what they must remember having been.'[17] Although I reject Foucault's rather crude notion that films can 'reprogramme . . . popular memory', I do like the idea that memory is one of the sites where culture and power may become entangled. To explore the relations between memory, culture and power, I will build my analysis on an 'appropriation' of the work of French sociologist Maurice Halbwachs.[18] In particular, I will deploy his concept of 'the collective memory'.

Memories are made of this

Halbwachs makes four overlapping claims about what he calls 'collective memory'. First, memory is as much collective as individual. Halbwachs explains this in two ways. Firstly, like Sigmund Freud,[19] Halbwachs recognised that memories are often fragmented and incomplete. But whereas Freud searched for completion in the unconscious, Halbwachs argued that completion should be sought in the social world outside the individual. In other words, what is provisional in our own memories is confirmed by the memories of others. As he explains,

> We appeal to witnesses to corroborate or invalidate as well as supplement what we somehow know already about an event . . . . Our confidence in the accuracy of our [memory] . . . increases . . . if it can be supported by others' remembrances . . . Don't we believe that we relive the past more fully because we no longer represent it alone . . . but through the eyes of another as well?[20]

This is not to deny that individuals have memories, which are their own, but to point to the ways in which individual memories and collective memories intermingle. As he explains, 'the individual memory, in order to corroborate and make precise and even to cover the gaps in its remembrances, relies upon, relocates itself within, momentarily merges with, the collective memory'.[21] Think of what happens when a photograph album is produced at a family gathering. As the photographs are passed around, particular photographs cue memories for one family member, which are then either supported, elaborated or challenged by other members of the family. The discussions which ensue seek collectively to fix specific memories to particular photographs. In this way, family histories are rehearsed, elaborated and (temporarily) 'fixed'.

Memory is also collective in another way. We often remember with others what we did not ourselves experience firsthand. Halbwachs explains it like this,

> During my life, my national society has been a theater for a number of events that I say I 'remember', events that I know about only from newspapers or the testimony of those directly involved . . . In recalling them, I must rely entirely upon the memory of others, a memory that comes, not as corroborator or completer of my own, but as the very source of what I wish to repeat. I often know such events no better nor in any other manner than I know historical events that occurred before I was born. I carry a baggage load of historical remembrances that I can increase through conversation and reading.[22]

In an argument similar to Halbwachs', Alison Landsberg has coined the term 'prosthetic memory' to describe the ways in which mass media (especially cinema) enable people to experience as memories what they did not themselves live. As she explains,

> Because the mass media fundamentally alter our notion of what counts as experience, they might be a privileged arena for the production and

circulation of prosthetic memories. The cinema, in particular, as an institution which makes available images for mass consumption, has long been aware of its ability to generate experiences and to install memories of them – memories which become experiences that film consumers both possess and feel possessed by.[23]

Moreover, she claims that 'What individuals see might affect them so significantly that the images actually become part of their own personal archive of experience'.[24]

Halbwachs' second claim about memory is to point to how remembering is not a process in which we resurrect a 'pure' past; memories are not veridical reports of past events; remembering is always an act of reconstruction and representation. In a study of eye-witness testimony, Elisabeth Loftus[25] shows how a person's memory for an event that they had witnessed can be influenced and altered. Loftus argues that if witnesses are exposed to additional information during the period between witnessing an event and recounting the event, the 'post-event information' can have the effect of modifying, changing or supplementing the original memory. This results from a process social psychologists call 'destructive updating',[26] in which what was originally remembered is displaced, transformed and sometimes lost. What is true of eyewitness testimony is also true of memory in everyday life. What we remember does not stay the same; memories are forgotten, revised, reorganised, updated, as they undergo rehearsal, interpretation and retelling. Moreover, the more important the event remembered, the more it is vulnerable to reconstruction, as it will be more frequently rehearsed, interpreted and retold.

Halbwachs' third point is to argue that remembering is always present-situated; memories do not take us into 'the past', rather they bring 'the past' into the present; remembering involves what psychologist Frederic Bartlett calls an 'effort after meaning'.[27] In other words, remembering is about making meaning in the present and in response to the present. That is, in order for our memories to remain meaningful to us, they have to make sense in the context of the present. As Bartlett explains, memories 'live with our interests and with them they change'.[28] Put simply, our memories change as we change. As Halbwachs explains, 'a remembrance is in very large measure a reconstruction of the past achieved with data borrowed from the present'.[29] To study memory, therefore, is not to study the past, but the past as it exists in the present (a past-present dialectic).

Moreover, it is the play of the past in the present which makes memory, and appeals to memory, always potentially political.

Halbwachs' final point is that collective memory is embodied in mnemonic artefacts, forms of commemoration such as shrines, statues, war memorials and so on – what French historian Pierre Nora calls 'sites of memory'.[30] I think we can add to Halbwachs' list of mnemonic artefacts what I will call the 'memory industries', that part of the culture industries concerned with articulating the past. Heritage sites and museums are obvious examples, but we should also include the mass media (including cinema). The memory industries, like the culture industries of which they form a part, produce representations ('cultural memorials'), with which we are invited to think, feel and recognise the past. But these representations do not embody memory as such, they embody the materials for memory; they provide the materials from which 'collective memory' can be made. The process is not of course monolithic or uncontested; there is always in circulation and potential contestation both dominant and subordinate memories and traditions and mythologies. It is my claim, however, that Hollywood in the 1980s produced compelling materials out of which could be made memories of the Vietnam War. As Marita Sturken observes,

> survivors of traumatic historical events often relate that as time goes by, they have difficulty distinguishing their personal memories from those of popular culture. For many World War II veterans, Holly-wood's World War II movies have subsumed their individual memories into a general script.[31]

Again, as Sturken notes (more specifically related to my argument), 'Some Vietnam veterans say they have forgotten where some of their memories came from – their own experiences, documentary photographs, or Hollywood movies?'[32] For example, Vietnam veteran William Adams makes this telling point,

> When *Platoon* was first released, a number of people asked me, 'Was the war really like that?' I never found an answer, in part because, no matter how graphic and realistic, a movie is after all a movie, and war is only like itself. But I also failed to find an answer because what 'really' happened is now so thoroughly mixed up in my mind with what has been said about what happened that the pure experience is no longer there. This is odd, even painful, in some ways. But it is also testimony to the way our memories work. The Vietnam War is no

longer a definite event so much as it is a collective and mobile script in which we continue to scrawl, erase, rewrite our conflicting and changing view of ourselves.[33]

History lessons: you must remember this

Memories do not just consist of what is remembered but also of what has been forgotten. The memory industries, therefore, do not just circulate things to remember, they also, and significantly, fail to articulate that which might also be remembered. I want to consider briefly four examples of what Hollywood 'forgot' about America's war in Vietnam.

Forgetting Vietnam

Nowhere in Hollywood's discourse on Vietnam are we informed about the extent of the resistance to the war. The counterculture, and the anti-war movement in general, has been given little visual space in Hollywood representations of the war. Yet, according to US Justice Department figures, between 1966 and 1973, 191,840 men refused to be drafted.[34] This has never been represented. One can of course respond by pointing out that these are war films, and therefore the anti-war movement is peripheral to their narrative project. To a certain extent this is of course true. But can the same argument be used to exclude representations of the opposition to the war which existed within the American armed forces? Between 1966 and 1973, 503,926 members of the US armed forces engaged in what the US Defense Department described as 'incidents of desertion'.[35] The extent of the problem is made clear by the fact that 28,661 deserters were still at large in 1974.[36] By 1970, according to Pentagon sources, there were 209 verified 'fraggings' (killing of officers by their own men) in Vietnam. Michael Klein suggests that 'the death toll from fragging by soldiers disaffected with the war may be as high as 5 per cent of the total loss of life in combat sustained by the US armed forces during the war'.[37] There is also the known instances of mutinies. Perhaps the most famous example is the mutiny of marines at Da Nang in 1968. Finally, to counter the optimism and propaganda of the very official newspaper *Stars and Stripes*, it has been estimated that something like 144 alternative newspapers were in circulation on American bases in Vietnam.[38]

Hollywood also 'forgets' the details of the gender and ethnicity of those Americans who fought in Vietnam. Between 1965 and 1972, the US sent between ten and fifteen thousand[39] women to the war in Vietnam; 75 per cent of whom were exposed to combat and hostile fire. Watching only Hollywood representations of the war, one would get no sense of this at all. African-Americans have suffered a similar exclusion. As Wallace Terry points out,

> black soldiers were dying at a greater rate, proportionately, than American soldiers of other races. In the early years of the fighting, blacks made up 23% of the fatalities . . . [In 1969] [b]lack combat fatalities had dropped to 14%, still proportionately higher than the 11% which blacks represented in the American population.[40]

Similarly, once drafted and in Vietnam, the likelihood of seeing heavy combat makes interesting reading when related to ethnicity: white Americans 29 per cent, African-Americans 34 per cent, Hispanic-Americans 41 per cent.[41] Again, relying only on Hollywood representations of Vietnam, one would get no sense of the extent to which African-American and Hispanic-American soldiers were fighting and dying in the war.

Hollywood also 'forgets' the extent of US firepower deployed in Vietnam. Put simply, the US deployed in Vietnam the most intensive firepower the world had ever witnessed. Hollywood narratives do not feature the deliberate defoliation of large areas of Vietnam, the napalm strikes, the search-and-destroy missions, the use of Free Fire Zones, the mass bombing. For example, during the 'Christmas bombing' campaign of 1972, the US 'dropped more tonnage of bombs on Hanoi and Haiphong than Germany dropped on Great Britain from 1940 to 1945'.[42] In total, the US dropped three times the number of bombs on Vietnam as had been dropped anywhere during the whole of the World War Two.[43] In a memorandum to President Johnson in 1967, Secretary of Defense Robert McNamara wrote '[the] picture of the world's greatest superpower killing or seriously injuring 1,000 noncombatants a week [his estimate of the human cost of the US bombing campaign], while trying to pound a tiny backward nation into submission on an issue whose merits are hotly disputed, is not pretty'.[44] The bombing only intensified as the war continued for another six years. Daniel Ellsberg, who worked for McNamara, was equally damning about US involvement in Vietnam. He described America's war in Vietnam as a 'crime . . . a brutal

fraud, a lawless imperial adventure'.[45] The destructive power and
the perverse logic of the war is captured perfectly by a US officer's
comment on the destruction of Ben Tre: 'It was necessary to destroy
the town in order to save it.'[46] The documented American atrocities
(My Lai being the most reported example) committed during the
course of the war tend to be presented (when presented at all) as
isolated moments of understandable madness or as individual acts of
sadism, and never as the inevitable result of the logic of America's
prosecution of the war.

Hollywood also 'forgets' the human costs of the war. If our
knowledge of the war was derived solely from Hollywood's Vietnam, we would be forgiven for thinking that America suffered an
enormous number of both casualties and fatalities in Vietnam.
58,191 dead is the figure recorded on the Vietnam Veterans' Memorial ('The Wall'). Without wishing to diminish the suffering that this
number represents, it has to be placed in the context of a figure of at
least two million Vietnamese dead.

Remembering Vietnam

I want now to examine the other side of memory. That is, what
Hollywood 'remembers' about America's war in Vietnam. To see
Hollywood's power as not (or not only) about forgetting but also as
about remembering differently, I take as my guide Foucault's work
on 'power'.[47] From the perspective of a Foucauldian reading of Hollywood's Vietnam, it does not really matter whether Hollywood's
representations are 'true' or 'false' (historically accurate or not),
what matters is the 'regime of truth' they put into circulation. From
this perspective, Hollywood's power is not a negative force, something which denies, represses, negates. On the contrary, Hollywood's power is productive. Foucault's general point about power
is also true with regard to Hollywood's power: 'We must cease once
and for all to describe the effects of power in negative terms: it
"excludes", it "represses", it "censors", it "abstracts", it "masks", it
"conceals". In fact, power produces; it produces reality; it produces
domains of objects and rituals of truth.'[48]

I want now to briefly describe three narrative paradigms, or 'rituals of truth', that feature strongly in Hollywood's Vietnam in the
1980s. I have chosen these particular 'rituals of truth' because of the
way they inform and underpin the comments made by Bush in the
political and military build up to the war in the Gulf.

The first of my chosen narrative paradigms is 'the war as betrayal'. This is first of all a discourse about bad leaders. In *Uncommon Valor, Missing In Action I, Missing In Action II – The Beginning, Braddock: Missing In Action III* and *Rambo: First Blood Part II*, for example, politicians are blamed for America's defeat in Vietnam. When John Rambo (Sylvester Stallone) is asked to return to Vietnam in search of American soldiers missing in action, he asks, with great bitterness: 'Do we get to win this time?'[49] In other words, will the politicians let them win? Second, it is a discourse about weak military leadership in the field. In *Platoon* and *Casualties of War*, for example, defeat, it is suggested, is the result of an incompetent military command. Third, it is also a discourse about civilian betrayal. Both *Cutter's Way* and *First Blood* suggest that the war effort was betrayed back home in America. Again, John Rambo's comments are symptomatic. When he is told by Colonel Trautman, 'It's over Johnny', he responds,

> Nothing is over. You don't just turn it off. It wasn't my war. You asked me, and I did what I had to do to win, but somebody wouldn't let us win. And I come back to the world and see these maggots protesting at the airport, calling me baby-killer. Who are they to protest me? I was there, they weren't!

Interestingly, all the films in this category are structured around loss. In *Uncommon Valor, Missing in Action I, II,* and *III, Rambo: First Blood Part II* and *POW: The Escape*, it is lost prisoners; in *Cutter's Way, First Blood* and *Born on the 4th of July*, it is lost pride; in *Platoon* and *Casualties of War*, it is lost innocence. It seems clear that the different versions of what is lost are symptomatic of a displacement of a greater loss: the displacement of that which can barely be named, America's defeat in Vietnam. The use of American POWs is undoubtedly the most ideologically charged of these displacement strategies. It seems to offer the possibility of three powerful 'truth effects'.[50]

First, to accept the myth that there are Americans still being held in Vietnam is to begin to retrospectively justify the original intervention. If the Vietnamese are so barbaric as to still hold prisoners decades after the conclusion of the conflict, then there is no need to feel guilty about the war, as they surely deserved the full force of American military intervention. Second, Jeffords identifies a process she calls the 'femininization of loss'.[51] That is, those blamed for America's defeat, whether they are unpatriotic protesters, an uncaring government, a weak and incompetent military command, or corrupt politicians, are always represented as stereotypically feminine: 'the stereotyped characteristics associated with the feminine in dominant U.S. culture – weakness, indecisiveness, dependence, emotion, nonviolence, negotiation, unpredictability, deception'.[52] Jeffords' argument is illustrated perfectly in the MIA cycle of films in which the 'feminine' negotiating stance of the politicians is played out against the 'masculine', no-nonsense approach of the returning veterans. The implication being that 'masculine' strength and single-mindedness would have won the war, whilst 'feminine' weakness and duplicity lost it. There can be little doubt that this aspect of Hollywood's discourse provides support for Bush's claims about the lessons to be learned from America's war in Vietnam. Third, perhaps most important of all is how these films turned what was thought to be lost into something which was only missing. Defeat is displaced by the 'victory' of finding and recovering American POWs. Puzzled by the unexpected success of *Uncommon Valor* in 1983, the *New York Times* sent a journalist to interview the film's 'audience'. One moviegoer was quite clear why the film was such a box-office success: 'We get to win the Vietnam War'.[53]

The second narrative paradigm is what I will call 'the inverted firepower syndrome'. This is a narrative device in which the US's massive techno-military advantage (as discussed earlier) is inverted. Instead of scenes of the massive destructive power of American military force, we are shown countless narratives of individual Americans fighting the numberless (and often invisible) forces of the North Vietnamese Army and/or the sinister and shadowy men and women of the National Liberation Front ('Viet Cong'). *Missing In Action I, II* and *III, Rambo: First Blood Part II* and *Platoon* all contain scenes of lone Americans struggling against overwhelming odds. John Rambo, armed only with a bow and arrow, is perhaps the most notorious example. *Platoon*, however, takes this narrative strategy onto another plane altogether. In a key scene, 'good' Sergeant Elias is pursued by countless North Vietnamese soldiers. He is shot continually until he falls to his knees, spreading his arms out in a Christ-like gesture of agony and betrayal. The camera pans slowly to emphasise the pathos of his death throes. In Britain the film was promoted with a poster showing Elias in the full pain of his 'crucifixion'.[54] Above the image is written the legend: 'The First Casualty of War is Innocence'. Loss of innocence is presented as both a realisation of the realities of modern warfare and as a result of America playing fair against a brutal and ruthless enemy. The ideological implication is clear: if America lost by playing the good guy, it is 'obvious' that it will be necessary in all future conflicts to play the tough guy in order to win. Such a narrative of course gives credence to Bush's Gulf War boast that this time America would not fight 'with one hand tied behind [its] back'.[55]

The third narrative paradigm is 'the Americanisation of the war'. What I want to indicate by this term is the way in which the meaning of the Vietnam War has become in Hollywood's Vietnam (and elsewhere in US cultural production) an absolutely American phenomenon. This is an example of what we might call 'imperial narcissism', in which the US is centred and Vietnam and the Vietnamese exist only to provide a context for an American tragedy, whose ultimate brutality is the loss of American innocence. And like any good tragedy, it was doomed from the beginning to follow the dictates of fate. It was something which just happened. Hollywood's Vietnam exhibits what Linda Dittmar and Gene Michaud call a 'mystique of unintelligibility'.[56] Perhaps the most compelling example of the mystique of unintelligibility is the opening sequence in the American video version of *Platoon*. It begins with a few words of endorsement from the then chairman of the Chrysler Corporation. We see him moving through a clearing in a wood towards a jeep. He stops at the jeep, and resting against it, addresses the camera,

> This jeep is a museum piece, a relic of war. Normandy, Anzio, Guadalcanal, Korea, Vietnam. I hope we will never have to build another jeep for war. This film *Platoon* is a memorial not to war but to all the men and women who fought in a time and in a place *nobody really understood*, who knew only one thing: they were called and they went. It was the same from the first musket fired at Concord to the rice paddies of the Mekong Delta: they were called and they went. That in the truest sense is the spirit of America. The more we understand it, the more we honor those who kept it alive.[57]

This is a discourse in which there is nothing to explain but American survival. Getting 'Back to the World' is everything it is about. It is an American tragedy and America and Americans are its *only* victims. The myth is expressed with numbing precision in Chris Taylor's (Charlie Sheen) narration at the end of *Platoon*. Taylor looks back from the deck of a rising helicopter on the dead and dying of the battlefield below. Samuel Barber's mournful and very beautiful Adagio for Strings seems to dictate the cadence and rhythm of his voice as he speaks these words of psycho-babble,

> I think now looking back, we did not fight the enemy, we fought ourselves. The enemy was in us. The war is over for me now, but it will always be there for the rest of my days. As I'm sure Elias will be, fighting with Barnes for what Rhah called "the possession of my soul".

Time magazine's review of the film echoes and elaborates this theme:

> Welcome back to the war that, just 20 years ago, turned America schizophrenic. Suddenly we were a nation split between left and right, black and white, hip and square, mothers and fathers, parents and children. For a nation whose war history had read like a John Wayne war movie – where good guys finished first by being tough and playing fair – the polarisation was soul-souring. Americans were fighting themselves, and both sides lost.[58]

Platoon's function in this scenario is to heal the schizophrenia of the American body politic. The film's rewriting of the war not only excludes the Vietnamese, it also rewrites the anti-war movement. Pro-war and anti-war politics are reenacted as different positions in a debate on how best to fight and win the war. One group, led by the 'good' Sergeant Elias (who listen to Jefferson Airplane's 'White Rabbit' and smoke marijuana), want to fight the war with honour and dignity, whilst the other, led by the 'bad' Sergeant Barnes (who listen to Merle Haggard's 'Okie from Muskogee' and drink beer), want to fight the war in any way which will win it. We are asked to believe that this was the essential conflict which tore America apart – the anti-war movement, dissolved into a conflict on how best to fight and win the war.[59] *Platoon* reduces the war to an American psychodrama. As Klein contends 'the war is decontextualized, mystified as a tragic mistake, an existential adventure, or a rite of passage through which the White American Hero discovers his identity'.[60]

Liberation from old ghosts and doubts

At one of the many homecoming celebrations for returning veterans of the Gulf War, Bush told his audience, 'You know, you all not only helped liberate Kuwait; you helped this country liberate itself from old ghosts and doubts . . . When you left, it was still fashionable to question America's decency, America's courage, America's resolve. No one, no one in the whole world doubts us anymore . . . Let this new spirit give proper recognition to the Vietnam veterans. Their time has come.'[61]

When, in the build up to the Gulf War, Bush had asked Americans to remember the Vietnam War, the memories recalled by many Americans would have been of a war they had lived cinematically; a war of bravery and betrayal. Hollywood's Vietnam had provided the materials to rehearse, elaborate, interpret and retell an increasingly dominant memory of America's war in Vietnam. Although academic and Vietnam veteran Michael Clark does not use the term, he is clearly referring to what I have called the 'memory industries' when he writes of how the ticker-tape welcome home parade for Vietnam veterans staged in New York in 1985, together with the media coverage of the parade and the Hollywood films which seemed to provide the context for the parade, had worked together to produce a particular memory of the war – a memory with potentially deadly effects. He writes of how

> they [the memory industries, especially film] had constituted our memory of the war all along . . . [They] healed over the wounds that had refused to close for ten years with a balm of nostalgia, and trans-formed guilt and doubt into duty and pride. And with a triumphant flourish [they] offered us the spectacle of [their] most successful cre-ation, the veterans who will fight the next war.[62]

Moreover, as Clark is at pains to stress, 'the memory of Vietnam has ceased to be a point of resistance to imperialist ambitions and is now invoked as a vivid warning to do it right next time'.[63]

At the end of the Gulf War, Bush boasted, as if the war had been fought for no other reason than to overcome a traumatic memory, 'By God, we've kicked the Vietnam Syndrome once and for all.'[64] Echoing Bush's comments, the *New York Times* featured an article with the title, 'Is the Vietnam Syndrome Dead? Happily, It's Buried in the Gulf'.[65] Vietnam, the sign of American loss and division had been buried in the sands of the Persian Gulf. Kick-ing the Vietnam Syndrome (with the help of Hollywood's Vietnam) had supposedly liberated a nation from old ghosts and doubts; had made America once again strong, whole and ready for the next war.[66]

Epilogue: a note of caution

I do not want to suggest that Hollywood's Vietnam was or is unproblematically consumed by its American audiences. My claim is only that Hollywood produced a particular regime of truth. Film (like any other cultural text or practice) has to be *made* to mean. To really discover the extent to which Hollywood's Vietnam has made its 'truth' tell requires a consideration of consumption. This will take us beyond a focus on the *meaning* of a text, to a focus on the meanings that can be made in the encounter between the discourses of the text and the discourses of the 'reader'. That is, it is not a question of verifying (with an 'audience') the *real meaning* of, say, *Platoon*. The focus on consumption (understood as 'production in use') is to explore the political effectivity (or otherwise) of, say, *Platoon*. If a cultural text is to become effective (politically or otherwise) it must be made to connect with people's lives – become part of 'lived cultures'. Formal analysis of Hollywood's Vietnam may point to how it has articulated the war as an American tragedy of bravery and betrayal; Bush's comments (and the comments of others) may provide us with clues to the circulation and effectivity of Hollywood's articulation of the war; but these factors, however compelling they may be in themselves, do not provide conclusive proof that Hollywood's account of the war has become hegemonic where it matters – in the lived practices of everyday life.[67]

Notes

1   I presented a version of this argument at the *Seventh International Seminar on Culture and Power*, University of Alcala, Madrid, October 2001. I would like to take this opportunity to thank the organisers of the conference for inviting me and the British Council for providing funding. I would also like to thank all those who made valuable comments on my paper.

2   See Michel Foucault, *Discipline and Punish* (Harmondsworth: Penguin, 1979); Michel Foucault, *History of Sexuality*, volume I (Harmondsworth: Penguin, 1981); 'Questions of Method: An Interview with Michel Foucault', in *Ideology & Consciousness*, 8 (1978), 3–14. I am aware that I make the American film industry sound too monolithic.

3   On articulation see Antonio Gramsci, *Selections From Prison Notebooks* (London: Lawrence & Wishart, 1971); Stuart Hall, 'The Rediscovery of Ideology: The Return of the Repressed in Media Studies', in

Veronica Beechey and James Donald (eds), *Subjectivity and Social Relations* (Milton Keynes: Open University Press, 1996), pp. 23–55; Stuart Hall, 'On Postmodernism and Articulation', in David Morley and Chen Kuan-Hsing (eds), *Stuart Hall: Critical Dialogues in Cultural Studies* (London: Routledge, 1996), pp. 131–50; Stuart Hall, 'Notes on deconstructing "The Popular"', in John Storey (ed.), *Cultural Theory and Popular Culture: A Reader*, 2nd edn (Hemel Hempstead: Prentice Hall/Harvester Wheatsheaf, 1997), pp. 442–53.

4 *Newsweek*, 10 December 1990.

5 Quoted in the *Daily Telegraph*, 17 January 1991. The fact that Vietnam became a key issue in the build up to the Gulf War can be demonstrated by 'A survey of 66,000 news stories that appeared in the US media between August 1990 and February 1991, found 7,000 references to Vietnam, almost three times more than the next most frequently cited phrase – "human shields"' (quoted in Jon Roper, 'Overcoming the Vietnam Syndrome: The Gulf War and Revisionism', in Jeffrey Walsh (ed.), *The Gulf War Did Not Happen* (Aldershot: Arena, 1995), p. 38).

6 Richard Nixon, *No More Vietnams* (London: W. H. Allen, 1986). Nixon did not coin the term, but he was a key player in giving it a particular political articulation. The Vietnam Syndrome began in the 1970s as a term to describe the psychological problems experienced by American Vietnam veterans (which also became known as 'Post-Traumatic Stress Syndrome'). In the 1980s the term was articulated in revisionist accounts of the war: no longer a psychological problem, it was now used to indicate a reluctance on the part of successive US administrations to pursue 'legitimate' political and military policies out of a fear that they would lead to another Vietnam (see Harry W. Haines, 'Putting Vietnam Behind Us: Hegemony and the Gulf War', *Studies in Communication*, 5 (1995), 35–67)). General William Westmoreland, commander of US forces in Vietnam, prefers the term Vietnam psychosis: 'Vietnam was a war that continues to have an impact on politics. I fear that one of the big losses, in fact, probably the most serious loss of the war, is what I refer to as the Vietnam psychosis. Any time anybody brings up the thought that military forces might be needed, you hear the old hue and cry "another Vietnam, another Vietnam". That can be a real liability to us as we look to the future' (cited in Roper, 'Overcoming the Vietnam Syndrome', p. 33). Noam Chomsky's gloss on the Vietnam syndrome is somewhat different: 'See, they make it sound like some kind of disease, a malady that has to be overcome. And the "malady" in this case is that the population is still unwilling to tolerate aggression and violence. And that's a change that took place as a result of the popular struggle against the war in Vietnam' (Noam Chomsky, 'The Lessons of the Vietnam War – An Interview with Noam Chomsky',

Vietnam Documents: American and Vietnamese Views of the War, ed. George Katsiaficas (New York: ME Sharpe Inc., 1992), pp. 230–1)).

7 Nixon, *No More Vietnams*, p. 13.

8 Nixon, *No More Vietnams*, p. 19.

9 Quoted in John Carlos Rowe and Rick Berg, 'The Vietnam War and American Memory', in John Carlos Rowe and Rick Berg (eds), *The Vietnam War and American Culture* (New York: Columbia University Press, 1991), p. 10.

10 Stephen Vlastos, 'America's "Enemy": The Absent Presence in Revisionist Vietnam War History', in John Carlos Rowe and Rick Berg (eds), *The Vietnam War and American Culture*, p. 69. Moreover, Reagan told Bobby Muller, a founder member of the Vietnam Veterans of America Foundation, 'Bob, the trouble with Vietnam was that we never let you guys fight the war you could have done, so we denied you the victory all the other veterans enjoyed. It won't happen like that again, Bob. . .' (quoted in Roper, 'Overcoming the Vietnam Syndrome', p. 30).

11 Quoted in Barbie Zelizer, 'Reading the Past Against the Grain: The Shape of Memory Studies', *Critical Studies in Mass Communication* (June 1995), 220.

12 Quoted in Rowe and Berg, 'The Vietnam war and American memory', p. 10.

13 Quoted in Andrew Martin, *Receptions of War: Vietnam in American Culture* (Norman: University of Oklahoma Press, 1993), p. 91.

14 Robert Burgoyne, *Film Nation: Hollywood Looks at US History* (Minneapolis: University of Minnesota Press, 1997), pp. 3–4.

15 Burgoyne, *Film Nation*, p. 122.

16 Robert Brent Toplin, *History by Hollywood: The Use and Abuse of the American Past* (Urbana: University of Illinois Press, 1996), p. vii. It is a commonplace of Vietnam literature that Hollywood's World War Two films helped recruit the veterans of the Vietnam War. For example, Michael Herr refers to the war movies that the US soldiers carried with them into the war: 'I keep thinking about all the kids who got wiped out by seventeen years of war movies before coming to Vietnam to get wiped out for good . . . [T]hey were actually making war movies in their heads, doing little guts-and-glory Leatherneck tap dances under fire; [driven by] movie-fed fantasies, [they were acting] the lowest John Wayne wet dream' (Michael Herr, *Dispatches* (London: Picador, 1978), pp. 169, 157, 24). Similarly, Vietnam veteran Thomas Bird recalls: 'It took me six months in Vietnam to wake up and turn all the World War II movies off in my mind' (quoted in Marita Sturken, *Tangled Memories: The Vietnam War, the AIDS Epidemic, and the Politics of Remembering* (Berkeley: University of California Press, 1997, p. 95)).

17 Michel Foucault, 'Film and Popular Memory', *Radical Philosophy* (1975), 28.
18 Maurice Halbwachs, *The Collective Memory* (Harper and Row: New York, 1980).
19 Sigmund Freud, *Introductory Lectures on Psychoanalysis* (Harmondsworth: Penguin, 1991); Sigmund Freud, *Interpretation of Dreams* (Harmondsworth: Penguin, 1991).
20 Halbwachs, *The Collective Memory*, pp. 22–3.
21 Halbwachs, *The Collective Memory*, pp. 50–1.
22 Halbwachs, *The Collective Memory*, p. 50.
23 Alison Landsberg, 'Prosthetic Memory: *Total Recall* and *Blade Runner*', *Body & Society* 1: 3/4 (1995), 176. French historian Pierre Nora makes a similar point: 'Modern memory is, above all, archival. It relies entirely on the materiality of the trace, the immediacy of the recording, the visibility of the image . . . The less memory is experienced from the inside the more exists only through its exterior scaffolding and outward signs . . . It adds to life . . . a secondary memory, a prosthesis-memory'. See Pierre Nora, 'Between History and Memory: les lieux de memoire', *Representations* 26 (1989), 13–14.
24 Landsberg, 'Prosthetic Memory', p. 179.
25 Elisabeth F. Loftus, *Eyewitness Testimony* (Cambridge, MA: Harvard university Press, 1996).
26 Gillian Cohen, *Memory in the Real World*, 2nd edn (Hove: Psychology Press, 1996).
27 Frederic Bartlett, *Remembering: A Study in Experimental and Social Psychology* (Cambridge: Cambridge University Press, 1967), p. 227.
28 Bartlett, *Remembering*, p. 212.
29 Halbwachs, *The Collective Memory*, p. 69.
30 Nora, 'Between History and memory', p. 7.
31 Sturken, *Tangled Memories*, p. 6.
32 Sturken, *Tangled Memories*, p. 20.
33 Quoted in Sturken, *Tangled Memories*, p. 86.
34 Michael Klein, 'Historical Memory, Film, and the Vietnam Era', in Linda Dittmar and Gene Michaud (eds), *From Hanoi To Hollywood: The Vietnam War in American Film* (New Brunswick and London: Rutgers University Press, 1990), p. 18.
35 Quoted in Klein, 'Historical Memory', p. 18.
36 H. Bruce Franklin, *M.I.A. or Mythmaking In America* (New Brunswick: Rutgers University Press, 1993).
37 Klein, 'Historical Memory', p. 17.
38 *Ibid*. Also see David Cortright, *Soldiers in Revolt* (New York: Doubleday, 1975); Rick Berg, 'Losing Vietnam', in John Carlos Rowe and Rick Berg (eds), *The Vietnam War and American Culture*; and the journal

Vietnam Generation (2: 1, 1990), which contains essays on the anti-war movement in the US armed forces.

39 Kathryn Marshall, *In the Combat Zone: An Oral History of American Women in Vietnam* (Boston: Little, Brown, 1987). According to Sturken the figure was 11,500 women (civilians and nurses) and 265,000 women in the military (Sturken, *Tangled Memories*, p. 67).

40 Wallace Terry, *Bloods: An Oral History of the Vietnam War by Black Veterans* (New York: Ballantine, 1984).

41 Susan Jeffords, *The Remasculinization of America: Gender and the Vietnam War* (Bloomington and Indianapolis: Indiana University Press, 1989), p. 190.

42 Franklin, *M.I.A. or Mythmaking In America*, p. 79.

43 John Pilger, 'Vietnam Movies', in *Weekend Guardian* (24–25 February 1990).

44 Quoted in Martin, *Receptions of War*, pp. 19–20.

45 Quoted in Martin, *Receptions of War*, p. 66.

46 Quoted in Franklin, *M.I.A. or Mythmaking In America*, p. 43.

47 See note 2 above.

48 Foucault, *Discipline and Punish*, p. 194.

49 Oliver North, often compared to Rambo, made a similar complaint when questioned by Congress (July 1987): 'We didn't lose the war in Vietnam, we lost the war right here' (quoted in Duncan Webster, *Looka Yonder! The Imaginary America of Populist Culture* (London: Routledge, 1988 p. 235)). If Rambo and North had bothered to read Nixon they would have known that America had not in fact lost the war in Vietnam. Chapter Four of Nixon's book is entitled, 'How We Won The War'. Nixon is astute enough to realise that this claim might require some defence: 'But win must be properly defined. We are a defensive power. We are not trying to conquer other countries. That is why we must have a policy in which we will fight limited wars if they are necessary to achieve limited goals. We win if we prevent the enemy from winning' (Nixon, *No More Vietnams*, p. 225).

50 Foucault, 'Questions of Method'. See Franklin, *M.I.A. or Mythmaking In America* and Elliott Gruner, *Prisoners of Culture: Representing the Vietnam POW* (New Brunswick: Rutgers University Press, 1993) for excellent discussions of what Franklin calls the 'near-religious fervor . . . [of] the POW/MIA fantasy' (xvi). Moreover, there can be little doubt, as Gruner observes, that the 'POW stories . . . delivered a victory in a lost war' (Gruner, *Prisoners of Culture*, p. 172).

51 Jeffords, *The Remasculinization of America*, p. 145.

52 Jeffords, *The Remasculinization of America*, p. 146. Hollywood's list of who was to blame for American defeat did not include those who are often blamed in the general discourse on the war – the US media. For

example, at the conclusion of the Gulf War, Ron Nessen, who had been White House Press Secretary during the Ford administration, claimed, 'The Pentagon has won the last battle of the Vietnam War. It was fought on the sands of Saudi Arabia, and the defeated enemy was the news media . . . Never again should the press [and other news media] be allowed open coverage of America at war' (quoted in Haines, 'Putting Vietnam Behind Us', p. 41).

53   Quoted in Franklin, *M.I.A. or Mythmaking In America*, p. 141.

54   The Christ-Like potential of the US soldier in Vietnam is also a feature of the Vietnam Women's Memorial, a statue depicting three uniformed women with a wounded male soldier, unveiled near the Vietnam Veterans Memorial in November 1993. The *Washington Post* described the memorial by saying: 'In spirit and pose the sculptor ambitiously invokes Michelangelo's "Pieta", the great Vatican marble of a grieving Mary holding the crucified body of Jesus' (quoted in Sturken, *Tangled Memories,* p. 69).

55   Quoted in the *Daily Telegraph*, 17 January 1991.

56   Linda Dittmar and Gene Michaud, 'America's Vietnam War Films: Marching Toward Denial', in Dittmar and Michaud (eds), *From Hanoi To Hollywood*, p. 13.

57   Harry W. Haines, '"They were called and they went": The political rehabilitation of the Vietnam Veteran', in Dittmar and Michaud (eds), *From Hanoi To Hollywood*, pp. 81–97. My italics.

58   *Time Magazine*, 26 January 1987.

59   The figure of John Rambo operates in much the same way. As Kellner points out, 'Rambo has long hair, a headband, eats only natural foods (whereas the bureaucrat Murdock swills Coke), is close to nature, and is hostile toward bureaucracy, the state, and technology – precisely the position of many 1960s counterculturalists'. See Douglas Kellner, *Media Culture* (New York: Routledge, 1995), p. 65.

60   Klein, 'Historical Memory', p. 10.

61   Quoted in Haines, 'Putting Vietnam Behind Us: Hegemony and the Gulf War', p. 48.

62   Michael Clark, 'Remembering Vietnam', in Rowe and Berg (eds), *The Vietnam War and American Culture*, p. 180.

63   Clark, 'Remembering Vietnam', p. 206.

64   Quoted in Franklin, *M.I.A. or Mythmaking In America*, p. 177.

65   *New York Times,* 2 December 1983.

66   William J. Bennett, writing in the *National Review*, claimed that the war in the Gulf had allowed the US to 'claim a victory on the magnitude of the Vietnam defeat' (quoted in Haines, 'Putting Vietnam behind Us', p. 52). Similarly, Paul Shinoff, writing in the *San Francisco Focus*, 'on February 27, the war ended. The Vietnam War, that is'

(quoted in Haines, 'Putting Vietnam Behind Us', p. 56). Against such triumphalism, Jon Roper claims that the Vietnam syndrome had not been overcome; it had informed Bush's decision not to pursue the war to its conclusion – defeat of Saddam Hussein. 'The "Vietnam syndrome" still existed as a constraint that counselled caution' (Roper, 'Overcoming the Vietnam Syndrome', p. 40).

67 See John Storey, *Cultural Consumption and Everyday Life* (London: Arnold, 1999).

6

The movie-made Movement: civil rites of passage

Sharon Monteith

> Memory believes before knowing remembers.
>
> (William Faulkner)
>
> Forgetting is just another kind of remembering.
>
> (Robert Penn Warren)

Film history cannibalises images, expropriates themes and techniques, and decants them into the contents of our collective memory. Movie memories are influenced by the (inter)textuality of media styles – Fredric Jameson has gone so far as to argue that such styles displace 'real' history. The Civil Rights Movement made real history but the Movement struggle was also a media event, played out as a teledrama in homes across the world in the 1950s and 1960s, and it is being replayed as a cinematic event. The interrelationship of popular memory and cinematic representations finds a telling case study in the civil rights era in the American South. This chapter assesses what films made after the civil rights era of the 1950s and 1960s express about the failure of the Movement to sustain and be sustained in its challenges to inequality and racist injustice. It argues that popular cultural currency relies on invoking images present in the sedimented layers of civil rights preoccupations but that in the 1980s and 1990s movies also tap into 'structures of feeling'. Historical verisimilitude is bent to include what Tom Hayden called in 1962 'a reassertion of the personal' as part of the political, but it is also bent to re-present the Movement as a communal struggle in which ordinary southern white people are much more significant actors in the personal and even the public space of civil rights politics than was actually the case. Historical facts as we retrieve and interpret them are only one facet of the movie-made Movement.

In a reception-driven analysis, film genres and sub-genres do not exist until they become necessary. It would be impossible to argue that something called 'civil rights cinema' existed before the end of the 1980s, by which time a provisional sub-genre of feature films had begun to develop around race and rights with reference out to the Movement. In the 1960s films that examined civil rights struggles in any guise at all were usually reviewed as 'small town movies' or 'southern melodrama' or 'social problem pictures'. Over the last two decades of the twentieth century, there has developed a critically self-conscious body of work on commemoration and retrieval and it is during this period that, as Richard Rorty has observed, 'the novel, the movie and the TV program . . . gradually but steadily replaced the sermon and the treatise as the principal vehicles of moral change and progress'.[1] Before this, movies with plots incorporating civil rights struggles could turn up in any popular genre from westerns to courtroom dramas, and even comedies.

Slowly a small but distinct body of films is developing in which Movement successes are celebrated and strategies and losses interrogated – *Freedom Song* (2000), *Boycott* (2001) and *The Rosa Parks Story* (2002), for example. But these films, like Spike Lee's *Malcolm X* (1992) and *A Huey P. Newton Story* (2001), fall outside of the broad (predominantly white) mainstream cinematic tradition. More usually, black activists (CORE and SNCC) and protagonists (Medgar Evers, Martin Luther King Jr.) have been caught in an epistemological drift, their stories dispersed and scattered through narratives in which white protagonists undergo a rites of passage or racial conversion. Most white directors and screenwriters espouse a liberal reformist vision in working out private salvations. But as Martin Luther King Jr. opined in *Where Do We Go From Here: Chaos or Community?* (1967), liberalism can be 'all too sentimental concerning human nature', leaning towards a 'false idealism'. Films made in our own historical moment tend to ensure that civil rights cinema becomes a cinema of integration and reconciliation. They function in a postmodern imaginary as socially symbolic texts in which racial tensions that remain unresolved in life find temporary resolution in narrative space. To do this, they focus on relationships between individuals, reducing larger historical events to personal histories, domesticating public memory of the Civil Rights Movement.

Memory and catechism

Shared cultural events are always 'historical', as George Lipsitz
has argued in *Time Passages* (1990), discussing the ways in which television in the 1950s naturalised the nuclear family as a touchstone
of modern American society. Collective memory functions to co-
ordinate and to fabricate national identity and unity. Movie memories
circulate among producers, directors, and audiences; an archival
memory-store of civil rights iconography, or an 'arcade' of motifs, to
borrow Walter Benjamin's terminology, finds space in the popular cultural imaginary that is contemporary cinema. Memories tied to place
as well as period can provide momentum in and of themselves. Car-
olyn Goodman, Andrew's mother, drove the road from Meridian in
1989, alone in the Mississippi night, still trying to come to terms with
what happened to her civil rights worker son, twenty-five years after
his brutal murder in 1964. In 1991 the gravestone of James Chaney,
the black activist murdered along with Goodman and Schwerner, was
defaced: a bullet fired into the photograph of the deceased. As I write,
the Mississippi Freedom Summer murder case may be reopened so
that those defendants acquitted by a hung (white) jury in 1967 may
be re-investigated. The history of the Civil Rights Movement is so
recent that dramatic personal re-enactments, historic cases of justice
deferred, and public commemorations proliferate.

In 2000, President Clinton, Martin Luther King Jr.'s widow,
Coretta Scott King, and civil rights leaders retraced the Selma to
Montgomery March that turned into 'Bloody Sunday' in 1965. They
marked the 35th anniversary on Edmund Pettus Bridge, itself a solid
signifier of the Movement past in popular memory. Commemorations reinforce the significance of the Movement as mythology and
as catechism, as well as history. Heritage tourism is the fastest growing feature of the leisure market according to Angela DaSilva, who
founded the National Black Tourism Network in 1996: 'Everyone
wants to march across the Edmund Pettus Bridge . . . And everyone
wants to do it singing "We Shall Overcome" at the top of their
lungs'.[2] In fact, a number of TV shows have picked up on this fascination from *Quantum Leap* to *I'll Fly Away*. Most recently in an
episode called 'Revisionism', *The Education of Max Bickford* (CBS
February 2002) included an African American professor who mis-
represented herself as a Freedom Rider. College principal (Regina
Taylor) admonishes her, 'People died. You can't take ownership of

that. It disrespects their memory', and in 1999 in an episode of *Touched By An Angel* (CBS April 1999) called 'Black Like Monica', Rosa Parks played herself as 'mother of the Civil Rights Movement' and honoured speaker when a small town in Illinois celebrates discovering a stop on the Underground Railroad. Popular memory fuses the pedagogical with the affective. It prefers to mythologise Rosa Parks as a tired seamstress rather than a trained activist and secretary of the Montgomery chapter of National Association of Colored People (NAACP). Those like Irene Morgan and Claudette Colvin, who took a stand on segregated public transportation and who refused to relinquish their seats to whites before Parks, have fallen out of history and are only just beginning to receive critical attention. The intervening years would seem to allow more creative space in which to interpret the past in order to deepen historical consciousness and yet movies often eschew hermeneutical struggles with form and changing definitions of heroism, tending to follow realistic conventions in 'authenticating' rather than re-visioning the Civil Rights Movement. Critical realism is not inevitably the most effective way of representing recent history in ways that continue to touch the popular imagination though, as television has shown. However, many working in history and cinema still betray in their work on film a reductive focus on fidelity – even historians David Herlihy and Natalie Zemon Davis, who have each acted as consultants for movies. Herlihy displays a keen awareness of the 'gaps, ambiguities and prejudices' in historical resources but he fails to see how films can 'carry' the same critical apparatus as historical texts – when they display the same *aporia*, they are dismissed as erroneous rather than historiography. Disciplinary essentialism of this kind fails to recognise movies as culturally conditioned productions embedded in the fabric of film history, or that the struggle with their accuracy can never be entirely separated from their 'ritual function'.[3] History has less epistemological hold on movies than memory.

Alice Walker's first published essay in the *American Scholar* in 1967 was an assessment of the Civil Rights Movement subtitled 'What Good Was It?', in which she described the Movement as 'a call to life' for people like herself who did not exist 'either in books or in films or in the government of their own lives'.[4] Much was invested in a defining social movement in the 1960s but just a generation later the Movement seems to find its continued meaning in images (Martin Luther King at the March on Washington; dogs and water cannons turned on black children in Birmingham; Autherine Lucy or Elizabeth Eckford braving rabid white racists alone to enrol in school; George Wallace standing in the schoolhouse door). Walter Benjamin has warned that ideas can evaporate in images because 'every image of the past that is not recognized by the present as one of its own concerns threatens to disappear irretrievably', and Fredric Jameson's critique of recycled clichés includes the recognition that time is fragmented into 'a series of perpetual presents'.[5]

An obvious problem for filmmakers is 'receding concreteness', to borrow Adorno's phrasing. In (re)connecting with a disappearing history, civil rights film narratives are typically recursive, but what they actually suffer from is 'presentism', whereby the pressures of the present distort our understanding of the past.[6] Character-led dramas (often based on autobiographical novels, and memoir – like *Crisis at Central High, Heart of Dixie,* and *Passion for Justice: The Hazel Brannon Smith Story*) promote a single monologic point of view to create what has ubiquitously come to be known as a 'useable past', in which resolution and reconciliation are valued over the propensity to grasp what might have been important to black and white southerners in the civil rights era. The priority becomes what is important to producers and audiences at the moment of the film's production; directors and screenwriters shape the tale into what James Snead calls 'replacement history'. For example, *Crisis at Central High* (1981) never mentions the role of Daisy Bates, head of the Arkansas chapter of the NAACP and the leading organiser during the Little Rock crisis of 1957–58. Rather, a 'Mrs Richardson' fulfils her role in two short scenes. Sensitive to public agendas that include the redemption of whiteness and white liberals, the movie is based on teacher Elizabeth P. Huckaby's journals in which a conservative moderate transforms into a spokeswoman for integration and takes a stand. This is an important story but since the Little Rock Nine are named and represented (though oddly Elizabeth Eckford is also renamed), one wonders what purpose there is in eliding the name of one of the most respected civil rights leaders in order to tell it. To foreground whiteness is often to withhold blackness; partial stories masquerade as objective understatement, or 'simply what happened' when framed by supposedly unemotional, fair-minded white professionals – like Huckaby, newspaper publisher Hazel Brannon Smith, and the student based on novelist Ann Rivers Siddons in *Heart of Dixie.*[7]

Synoptic cinema: the public/private distinction

Civil rights cinema does not sit comfortably within theories of genri-fication. For Rick Altman, genrification always operates dialectically, transforming an existing set of films until they are 'mashed, twisted and reshaped into unrecognizably new forms'.[8] Recent films share few semantic or syntactic elements with movies made in the 1960s. Nor are they 'new'. Instead they vault back, sidestepping brave little films like *The Intruder* (1961) and *Nothing But A Man* (1964), to reshape liberal social conscience movies like *Pinky* (1949), *Intruder in the Dust* (1949) and *Lost Boundaries* (1949), *Sergeant Rutledge* (1960) and *To Kill A Mockingbird* (1962), that are not 'about' the Movement at all. As Ralph Ellison opines, these films are 'not about Negroes at all; they are about what whites think and feel about Negroes'.[9] The tendency is to retell the movement as individual morality tales for a nation in which black and white individuals remain disconcertingly separate. While James Snead has argued that film 'translates the personal into the communal so quickly that eleva-tion of the dominant and the degradation of the subordinate are simultaneous and corporate', civil rights cinema operates conversely in translating the communal into the personal.[10] It is easy to deplore the retreat into the personal as a current 'fetish' of mass-market cul-ture. Adrienne Rich, for example, cites TV talk show culture from which the viewer 'might deduce that all human interactions are lim-ited to individual predicaments . . . personal confessions and revela-tions'.[11] Civil rights feature films of the 1980s and 1990s functioned as the kind of performed naivety Rich describes.

Of the many films one could use for exemplification – from *Crisis at Central High* to *Love Field* – *The Long Walk Home* (1994) is per-haps the clearest in that it domesticates a landmark civil rights strug-gle, the Montgomery Bus Boycott of 1955–56. It re-constructs the boycott along a trajectory of the lives of two women during the first weeks of the protest, a black domestic worker, Odessa Cotter (Whoopi Goldberg), and her white middle-class employer, Miriam Thompson (Sissy Spacek). The full significance of the boycott as a demonstration of collective black solidarity remains secondary to the primary focus on the women's relationship, and in particular on the white woman.[12] The development of Miriam's character from a smil-ing housewife and upholder of the racial status quo ('The rest of the world around you is living that way so you just don't question it') to

a tearful and determined participant in the movement for desegregation provides the narrative impetus of a film. Odessa is carved out
as the film's moral heroine but not its primary subject. If one takes
the subject as the character most affected by the ideological construction of the film text, Miriam clearly fulfills that role because the
film works as a 'racial conversion narrative' in Fred Hobson's analysis of the memoirs of white southerners who grow up racist but 'see
the light'. Novelist Reynolds Price, for example, allows 'Now when
I see films of the flocking brave faces, black and white, of the early
civil rights movement . . . I'm more than sorry that my face is missing'.[13] In the 1980s and 1990s Hollywood inserted the missing faces
into the civil rights story. White moderates, specifically those whose
silence had overwhelmed their hatred for cruelty (Price admits, 'All
these years later . . . my silence offends me') are delivered up in
movies that are really about a desire for forgiveness and regret for
the loss of hope in interracial coalitions.

In *The Long Walk Home*, hope for an enduring reconciliation
across racial, economic and class divisions is a considerable weight for
a single relationship to carry. Writer John Cork and director Richard
Pearce are not uncritical of the paradigmatic formulation of mistress
and maid; they deploy it to interrogate the fabric of segregation and
as a structural device to investigate the ways in which black women
were typically sutured into the lives of white women. However, in
foregrounding Miriam, the black struggle is superseded by a narrative
deemed to meet the affective needs of a white audience. Miriam's
position, morally satisfying as it is, remains tenuous and untypical.
Historically, there were many more women like those who play cards
at the bridge club and remain broadly antagonistic to reforms than
women like Montgomery's Virginia Durr, or Juliette Morgan, whose
letter to the *Advertiser* expressed support and deep respect for the
black protesters. Morgan was so hounded by angry whites that she
finally committed suicide. Cork and Pearce just manage to steer clear
of a utopian happy ending to a black and a white woman's precarious
alliance. But, the dominant story remains the white woman's racial
conversion in the face of her husband's disapproval.

To read the film historiographically is to recognise a series of
signifiers of the boycott. A white Montgomerian, Cork painstak-
ingly, if somewhat lyrically, re-presents the atmosphere of a city
engaged in a 'war of wills in the cradle of the Confederacy', as he
casts the conflict between the protesters and their opponents. As

factory employees, including Odessa's husband, gather to read the
flyer urging them to boycott the buses on 5 December 1955, the
incident of Claudette Colvin refusing to relinquish her seat to a
white person is referred to as 'the Colberg case', repeating the mistake in the original boycott notices and exemplifying the film's bid
for authenticity at the level of detail. The mayor, W. A. Gayle, and
Grover Hall, editor of the *Advertiser*, are referred to directly and
Miriam is seen reading the *Advertiser* on the first morning of the
protest with its headline 'Extra Police Set For Patrol Work in Trolley
Boycott'. Mass meetings at Holt Street Baptist Church are recreated
and although Reverend Martin Luther King Jr. is typically concealed
in a series of cutaway shots, the first speech he delivered as head of
the Montgomery Improvement Association rings out for the con-
gregation ('If we are wrong . . . then the Supreme Court is wrong . . .
And we are determined here in Montgomery to work and fight until
justice runs down like water, and righteousness like a mighty
stream'). Police Commissioner Clyde Sellers is represented, as is his
attendance at the White Citizens Council rally of early January 1956
at which he expressed his support for the Council in general and for
its battle against the desegregation of public transport in particular.
The reaction of black Montgomerians to the bombing of King's
home is portrayed, as are Commissioner Sellers' comments at the
time. The city of Montgomery itself is textualized in director
Richard Pearce's patterning of empty yellow City Lines buses
threading their way to Washington Park and Capitol Heights. The
inclement weather of December/January 1955–56 is specifically represented, as Odessa braves the wind and rain to make her way across
town to work.

Pearce worked for many years as a documentary cameraman
(*Woodstock* and *Hearts and Minds*) and at the formal level, *The Long
Walk Home* is naturalistic, the camerawork intended to reveal the
historical Montgomery of the 1950s as the small southern town
impacts our popular memory. The credits move into a monochrome
establishing shot of the town that slips into colour as dawn breaks
on another Montgomery morning. The camera sweeps the skyline
before swooping down to reveal black domestic workers paying
their fare at the front of a bus before dismounting to re-enter at the
back, as required under Jim Crow. This archetypal sequence, shots
of black people walking to and from work at dawn and dusk, and
lining the pavement outside the King house after it is bombed, act as

'image facts', units of impression assembled to coalesce in the drive for historical verisimilitude.[14] And, I would add, as talismanic motifs of what the Movement struggled to change framed as images in our popular memory.

Clayborne Carson has described the iconography of the Civil Rights Movement as confrontations of good versus evil, and Pearce assembles scenes to locate this feature of the Montgomery struggle; white intransigence, often very vocal and translated into brute force, is opposed by black moral certainty and courageous calm. A pragmatic desire to maintain the domestic status quo that enables her own lifestyle, combined with something close to an altruistic concern for the difficulties her employee encounters in getting across town, propels Miriam to support her domestic of ten years standing when she upholds the boycott. Many white women ignored Mayor Gayle's demand that they desist from driving their domestics to work. They famously retorted that since he was unprepared to undertake domestic work in their homes himself, they would continue to support those who were. Self-interest and southern tradition were powerful forces which led to white women incidentally and inadvertently aiding the boycott. It is from this position that Miriam shows her support of Odessa. But, a change ensues that spurs Miriam into supporting the boycott itself, beyond the efficacies of her own self-interestedness. This change derives as much, if not more, from her shock and shame at her husband's reactionary behaviour in aligning himself with his bigoted brother and the White Citizens' Council, than it does from her developing appreciation of Odessa.

No matter how carefully the boycott has been visually established, it is finally Norman Thompson (Dwight Schultz) who pushes his wife from private sympathy to a public display of support. He is 'a good husband and a good provider' turned bad in the classic iconography of civil rights movies. On Christmas Eve he is held in the frame, hugging his two daughters, as they are backlit in such a way that a halo of light arcs around the trio as Miriam looks on with a smile. But he is caught up in the recalcitrance of his peers; his manhood challenged by his younger brother. Besieged, Norman follows the morally reprehensible path in a film that is carefully coded around ethical decision-making; unlike Odessa's daughter, who rides the bus because she places her own desires before the needs of the community for a brief aberrant moment, he does not learn from his mistakes. The final shots of Norman are of his helplessness in the face of white violence against his wife. He gazes hopelessly at Miriam as she and their young daughter join the boycotters, and in so doing step outside his jurisdiction.

Despite the sentimental claims of the reviewer for *Jet* who believes that 'Suddenly a bond is created and the women finally begin to learn about each other, finding out about each other's strength and inner beauty', Odessa continues to refer to her employer as 'Miss Thompson' throughout the film.[15] Odessa's character does not change over the course of the narrative. She is self-possessed throughout; progressively more tired but never defeated. She is a paradigm of the ennobled, resolute black citizen who has the decorum and poise that Jo Ann Robinson attributed to Rosa Parks, as signalled in the title of Parks' memoir, *Quiet Strength* (1994). In the opening sequence she stands on the bus on her way to work. Her face composed. She is alone. The final freeze-frame is of her face in close-up as she holds her place in the line of passive resistance the black women have formed against the white men who seek to destroy the carpool and humiliate the women who use it. The camera moves laterally as she and Miriam exchange tearful, apprehensive smiles but it is on Odessa's face – a picture of dignity – that it rests. Her face is the closing image of the film. Odessa is Cork's tribute to those June Jordan has described as the 'invisible women' of the civil rights epoch. The narrator makes this clear: '50,000 boycotted the buses in Montgomery. I knew one. Her name was Odessa Cotter'.[16]

The emphasis shifts towards the white family as soon as it is swiftly understood that the black family will endure. The vicissitudes within the white household become the main subject matter of a white family melodrama located within the context of the boycott. When Miriam first expresses her intention to drive for the carpool, Odessa reminds her of the consequences she will inevitably face: 'Once you step over there, I don't know if you can ever step back.' My reading, therefore, militates against the promotional publicity for the movie that declares, 'Their forbidden friendship changed a nation'. Despite around ten years of daily contact, there is no evidence in the film of any intimate exchange between the women before the boycott triggers communication. As a direct result of the boycott, however, Norman Thompson's racist fears of change in the South are made manifest and his college-educated wife is forced either to align herself with his bigotry, ignore it (and Virginia Durr amongst others have repeatedly argued that the Southern lady was often expected to meet a situation by simply acting as if it hadn't happened),[17] or oppose it. That she chooses the latter course is, of course, the salient focus of the film. Miriam is one of Betty Friedan's suburban housewives for whom 'the problem with no name' begins to come into focus as a need to be useful in a community in which her symbolic status as a southern lady can operate to deny her autonomy. The film is actually Miriam's story about wresting back her autonomy; civil rights history is reshaped into a (white) feminist coming-of-age story.

Mississippi burning and squirming

The recycling and consumption of the past as nostalgia fortifies popular cultural representations of the civil rights era as an integrationist success story in which the racist past is 'overcome' with the help of well-meaning whites. But the effect of such films can be much more complicated and far-reaching than first appears. Alan Parker purposefully rewrites history when he decides that the FBI bribing a Klansman to give up details of the Chaney, Goodman and Schwerner murders (Delmar Dennis was paid $30,000) does not fit the ideological project that is *Mississippi Burning* (1988). He tells a different story in which the FBI roots out the corrupt police and Ku Klux Klan members who conspired to kill the civil rights workers. They succeed with a little help from locals with a conscience, a hint of romantic love, a lot of trickery, and some swaggering aggression. When the film is raked over by former activists, historians, journalists, a newly-revived Klan, and the Sheriff in the 1964 murder case, it becomes the stuff of public debate and Parker's rescripting of events enters popular memory.

In Parker's version of events, FBI agents Ward, a northerner, Harvard-graduate and serious stickler for playing by the rules (Willem Dafoe), and Anderson, a former Sheriff and volatile, if reconstructed, southern redneck willing to break the rules (Gene Hackman), arrive in fictional Jessup County, Mississippi to investigate the disappearance of three civil rights workers, two white and one black. Basing the story on history, they discover their bodies in an earthen dam forty-four days after they were reported missing. In the interim, violence ensues at every turn as the FBI cuts through the

customs of a small town's strained race relations; the two main
protagonists learn to respect each other; and Anderson's chivalry
towards a law officer's wife leads to information as to where the
dead are buried.

Mississippi Burning was the first Hollywood blockbuster to focus
on the Movement. What actually happened in 1964 (and at the
'Mississippi Burning Trial' in 1967 when seven men were convicted
of civil rights violations rather than murder) may be mutated into a
clearer moral geography but it is also recast in a buddy buddy
action-movie format. While this formula secures audiences, Parker
became the scourge of the 'historian cops', to borrow Robert Sklar's
term, for representing FBI heroics over historical fact. Hollywood's
redescription of events fired up former activists like Executive
Director of the NAACP, Benjamin Hooks, and Coretta Scott King
who decried the film's distortion of history, while film critics Vincent
Canby and Robert Ebert declared *Mississippi Burning* the best movie
of the year. That Parker represented whites over blacks is not in
doubt. In fact, Parker outlines in the Production Notes that 'the
formal energy of our narrative was firmly placed on their [Hackman
and Dafoe's] shoulders'. He realises that the murder of Chaney,
Schwerner and Goodman is the catalyst for his movie and that
'hopefully, one day someone will also make a film about the importance of these young men's lives'.[18] In the 'Notes on the Making of
the Film' that few critics or reviewers cite, Parker allows:

> Our film cannot be the definitive film of the black Civil Rights strug-
> gle. Our heroes are still white. And in truth, the film would probably
> never have been made if they weren't. This is a reflection of our soci-
> ety not the Film Industry. But with all of its possible flaws and short-
> comings I hope our film can help to provoke thought and allow other
> films to be made because the struggle still continues.[19]

The construction of Parker as a *bête noir* was exacerbated by
reviewers who took little account themselves of the civil rights history they accused Parker of ignoring. Parker fails to put James
Chaney in the driving seat in the opening sequence in which the
activists' car is pulled over by their murderers, but Sean French is
one of a number of reviewers who fails even to recognise Chaney's
activism when he describes the murder of 'two white civil rights
workers and a local black man'.[20] FBI champions of civil rights *are*
set against largely silent and passive black victims of segregation,

when J. Edgar Hoover's baiting of King and his dismissal of civil rights struggles is almost as well documented as the examples of black courage and non-violent resistance that eventually wore down a government reluctant to intervene. What jars most forcibly is that the film condones, even celebrates, the Agency's use of its own brand of vigilante violence against the Klan because it gets results, echoing the promotion for box office hits like *Dirty Harry* (1971) and the kind of cop who 'doesn't break murder cases, he smashes them', and reminding us of other hard-hitting mavericks like Charles Bronson in *Death Wish* (1974). Pauline Kael most deplored this feature of the film, describing it as 'morally repugnant'.[21] But critics writing in *Time* better capture the way in which the movie extrapolates from a historical event while projecting that event back into popular consciousness when they compare *Mississippi Burning* to Warner Brothers' exposés of racist violence, like *Black Legion* and *They Won't Forget*, both released in 1937.[22]

It may be all too easy to over-egg the melodramatic pudding but the 1964 murder case was in and of itself one of the most sensational events of the civil rights era. *Mississippi Burning* may owe more to film history than social history but FBI agents who discovered the men's bodies did pose as Klansmen to draw out suspects. Some of the film's dialogue is excerpted directly from the 1967 trial and, most importantly, the power of the big screen is such that the men acquitted in 1967 were brought back into the social spotlight by the film, even twenty years later. The clearest example is that of Lawrence Rainey who decided to sue Orion Pictures for $8 million when he saw himself portrayed as the paradigmatic Sheriff ('The character in the movie was a big man like me and he chewed tobacco like I chewed tobacco all the time').[23] The interpenetration of repressed history and the potent images of *Mississippi Burning* impacted on the southern state that Martin Luther King famously described as 'sweltering in the heat of injustice' in ways that echoed the turmoil of the 1960s. On the one hand, civil rights campaigners were prompted into setting up a new voting registration promotion and, on the other, the local Klan instigated a recruitment drive.[24] The Klan recruiters were wrong: ten robed men found themselves out-numbered by press. But Philadelphia, Mississippi will always be remembered for the events that happened there in 1964, no matter how much it may try to move on; in 1989 there was a furore over whether to screen *Mississippi Burning* in the town. While Parker's film underlines the rage and resentment that can be touched off by intervening in collective memory, it is the crime that remains rooted in place, no matter how it may be rewritten, and the iconography of good and evil that transcends period, as discussion of *A Time to Kill* (1996) will show.

Real to reel: Canton, Mississippi

'Welcome to the Home of *A Time To Kill*, Historic Canton, Mississippi'. This proud statement aligns film and history and blurs distinctions between them. One extra on the movie summarised, 'For a lot of people here, this is not history, it's memory.' When a town becomes a movie set, the movie mythos becomes rooted in place and community. This fusion took place in Canton, twenty-five miles north of Jackson in Mississippi. The town now has a Film Office and its own version of Hollywood's Walk of Fame. It continues to offer tours of the Hollywood sound stage Joel Schumacher and his crew left behind and tells tourists, 'Tour the office of the young lawyer, Jake, and experience the *actual* feeling of being part of Hollywood' (my italics). When Larry Fulton, production designer for *A Time To Kill*, first came across Canton in a photo book, he says, 'It looked perfect'. Director Joel Schumacher had emphasised the importance of moving the production to a small southern town: 'The people that lived in the town needed to be a part of the fabric of the movie. It would feel and smell and look real, and it would add to the integrity of the piece.'[25] Tonea Stewart (Gwen Hailey in the film) echoes Richard Rorty when she says 'There's almost a ministry in what we're doing . . . presenting it [the South] as it is'.[26] Around six hundred locals took part as extras. John Grisham's imaginary Clanton in the 1989 novel became Canton, with the blessing of the locals. Readers of *The Summons* (2002) in which Grisham returns to Clanton find Hollywood's Canton colonising their mental pictures of the southern town.

In the movie, Carl Lee Hailey (Samuel L. Jackson), enraged by the rape and attempted murder of his ten-year-old daughter by two redneck racists on a drunken spree, guns them down inside the seat of southern justice, the courthouse on the square ('I hope they burn in Hell!'). Carl Lee is freed when his lawyer, Jake Brigance, convinces the jury to 'see the light': had a white girl been the victim of black rapists, a white father's crime of murderous revenge would have been commuted, even validated. Carl Lee's crime galvanises the small southern town and its factions – black and white. His trial is the movie's centrepiece and its scenes, including ubiquitous shots on the courthouse steps with the American flag flying proudly, are key to the film's affective patterning. The courtroom drama is an all-encompassing public ritual of self and national disclosure in which the legacy of legal segregation collapses in ruins: Jake's final words to Carl Lee are 'I just thought our children could play together'. Jake feels noble; his position made racially permeable because of the changes wrought by Carl Lee's acquittal on a town polarised by race. As Allison Graham has pointed out, the function of white criminal lawyers in southern cinema is to act as 'cinematic historians, researching the past, explaining it, and bringing it to a close'.[27]

A Time To Kill may initially seem a strange choice as a Movement movie but it borrows heavily from the store of rhetorical and dra-maturgical images of racial struggle that coalesce in earlier films. Richard Schickel felt sure that the film would 'induce a certain sense of déjà vu among veteran viewers. Yes we have intruded in this dust, killed this mockingbird before . . . before we became a full-time cul-ture of irony'.[28] It harks back to movies of the 1980s like The Long Walk Home because it involves a racial conversion story but it also relies as much on the tabloid sensationalism and buddy-buddy dynamic of Mississippi Burning as the quieter southern tropes and the courtroom drama of Intruder in the Dust and To Kill A Mock-ingbird. A Time to Kill is a racially-charged blockbuster, just like Mis-sissippi Burning. Variety correctly judged it could 'translate into sizeable crossover business' and Rolling Stone called it a movie 'in the old potboiler tradition'. Set in the 1990s, it harks back to the 1960s by positing an axiomatic question, 'Is it possible for a black man to get a fair trial in the South?' and audience members admit to not realising at first that the events on screen actually take place 'now' because they feel tugged back into 'then'.[29] Grisham is clearly aware of the tenacity of images of the unreconstructed South. In the novel when the newly-revived Klan burn a cross in Jake's yard, he feels as if 'I'm looking at an old issue of Time magazine', or 'a chap-ter from an old Mississippi history textbook'.[30] Or a scene from Parker's Mississippi Burning.

A Time to Kill's reception is bound up with a tussle over popular memory of what the Movement sought to change and a pervasive feeling of late twentieth-century declension. In Hollywood's wake the media came to town. 'Lights, Camera, Canton!' (1996) is a *48 Hours* special in which CBS anchor and newsman Dan Rather and colleagues visit Canton during the making of the film. They demystify the movie-making process (special effects and casting choices) but perpetuate movie mystique by profiling actors and the director with 'Canton the movie town' as backdrop. A year later, Christie Herring and Andre Robinson made *Waking in Mississippi* (1997), an hour-long documentary, to ask a much more pertinent question about popular memory: 'Is Hollywood waking Mississippi from its hateful slumber?' Although CBS spent two segments of their programme on the core scene of *A Time To Kill*'s race riot, they omitted to pay more than lip service to local views. *Waking in Mississippi* centres on the local and national media struggle over the town's representation in local memory. In 1994 National Guardsmen had been alerted to the possibilities of racial strife and rioting in the town square when the town voted to elect its first black mayor, Alice Scott, and found itself forced by a tie to vote a second time. Within the year Schumacher is choreographing the race riot that never happened in that same square for *A Time To Kill*.

Like Philadelphia, Canton was the site of a voter registration drive in the early 1960s and it has a bloody civil rights history. Dave Dennis and George Raymond, trying to organise voter registration in Canton, lived in danger on a daily basis. Ann Moody left the South for eleven years after seeing a man 'get his brains spattered all over the church grounds' in Canton; 'That was just too much'. The Freedom House was bombed and on one occasion in 1964 someone called to enquire 'How many did we get?' In 1967 Mississippi newsman Ira B. Harkey was calling Canton 'one of the hottest spots in the Negro revolution'. Where Grisham's imaginary Clanton is located in a county that is 74 per cent white, Canton's population of 10,000 is around 72 per cent black and has been since the 1960s. Most pertinent in the context of *Waking in Mississippi*, in January 1964 when blacks boycotted white stores, white businessmen were threatened if they didn't join the town's Citizens' Council. One white businessman, Phil Mullen, refused and his newspaper collapsed as a result. He left the state.[31] Thirty years later, in 1994, Christie Herring began to receive messages at Duke where she was studying film. She was informed politely but firmly that it was known that she had not cast her absentee ballot. As a white Canton resident she should cast her vote in the second election to ensure the town re-elected the white mayoral candidate. Herring had decided to vote for Scott but felt her privacy threatened: 'I was reading *Coming of Age in Mississippi* at the time and saw 60s elements in everything that was happening; which is to say that I saw discrimination, racism, deliberate intimidation of those who challenged the system, whether that was simply because they were black or because they were white and not staying in line. It was horrific to me at the time.'[32] Herring's experience reminds us that Annie Devine, the Canton activist celebrated in Ann Moody's *Coming of Age in Mississippi* (1968), told Tom Dent in 1991 that just maybe the Civil Rights Movement in Canton had simply 'opened up the Pandora's Box of race', and a local attorney described the town as 'a generation behind every other place in Mississippi'.[33] Herring and co-director Robinson begin to get to grips with the racism that continued to permeate Canton politics and Herring discovered that 'my struggle with my "role" in the community was not an isolated struggle'. What Herring found most striking was that:

> No one seemed to be making connections between the election and *A Time To Kill* and that really surprised me . . . There were vague references to the 60s by the local and national media but, given what had happened and so recently, I felt that someone must tell that story. I felt a responsibility to do so. I didn't plan on a two-year project though, until after Andre and I went there the first time, experienced what it was like for us to simply be there as a black man and a white woman, and experienced the carnival that was the *A Time To Kill* set.[34]

Waking in Missisippi forms an important intertext with *A Time To Kill* in that it combines a keen sense of contemporaneity with an unsettled racial past and makes us aware of the shadow relationship between past and present.

By extension, when people play themselves in movies about the civil rights era (Medgar Evers' children and detective 'Benny Bennett' in *Ghosts of Mississippi*) or when they have a vested interest (the children of organisers Chuck McDew and Dave Dennis were extras in *Freedom Song*), the distinction between movie-made memories and historical past becomes blurred, especially for the figures who experience both. In *A Time to Kill*, Dr William Truly, a member of the NAACP plays a member of the NAACP and actress Elizabeth Omilami hits an Imperial Wizard in the face during the scene of confrontation between black supporters of Carl Lee Hailey and the Klan in the town square. She reports that she felt as though she were acting out the release of deep-seated anger. As a child she had marched with her father, Reverend Hosea Williams, a veteran of the Selma to Montgomery march of 1965, who was jailed a total of 135 times for his civil rights activism. As recently as 1987 in predominantly white Forsythe County, marchers led by Reverend Williams were attacked by members of the Klan hurling bricks and bottles. Like Christie Herring, in creative ways Omilami brought personal memories of public history to bear, this time by harnessing the anger she needed to fulfil her role on screen. Similarly, actress Sandra Bullock (Jake's assistant Ellen Roark in the film) remembers that during the shooting of such scenes for *A Time To Kill* she felt afraid that when the director shouted 'Cut' the riot might not stop. Extras remembering the experience when interviewed by Herring and Robinson and by journalists describe it as 'Almost too real' and declare, 'Some of this has happened'.[35]

When Hollywood comes to town, the very tropes that act as catalysts for bad memories are packaged as collective fantasies. *A Time To Kill* is both a movie and a collective memory for the residents of Canton. Where *The Long Walk Home* has been adopted in schools, largely because it extols a strong (white) female role model, and *Mississippi Burning* remains most renowned for the furore of its reception, *A Time to Kill*, despite Grisham's conservative but fair-minded legal eagle saving the day, successfully plays out movie-made southern stereotypes while pandering to the kind of heritage tourism that supports the 'New South' of racial reconciliation.

Towards a movie-made movement

Barbara Melosh complained in 1988 that a 'sanitized version' of the Civil Rights Movement had entered 'the canon of consensus history' and Fred Hobson, with his usual unruffled good sense, allows that 'the Bad Old Days' before 'the South Triumphant' are far more intriguing than the 'New South'.[36] Whichever way film directors turned their cameras in the 1980s and 1990s, they failed to reshape our visions of the Movement, instead reflecting 'our' timidity and sentimentality in white redemption stories set in the 'bad old days', or our primal thrill at seeing morally-charged action heroes succeed against evil racists by deploying the requisite quotient of violence. Herring and Robinson's low-budget creative intervention in the wake of *A Time To Kill* shows that bitter memories of the 1960s continue to simmer just below the racially-charged politics of the 1990s. *A Time To Kill* illustrates that while films that *recreate* civil rights struggles are rarely box-office smashes, those that revisit their interpretive grid to imagine a dialectical relationship between race and rights with affective *echoes* of civil rights scenes successfully harness the imagistic power of film memory.

Few feature films capture what Todd Gitlin has called the movement's 'divine delirium'. Rarely do directors stretch to present a character like Vernon Johns whose bleak, stirring sermons at Dexter Avenue Baptist church ('it's safe to murder Negroes') animate what is an excellent – though one fears little known – TV movie, *The Road to Freedom: The Vernon Johns Story* (1994). Only as recently as 2001 has the brilliant civil rights strategist Bayard Rustin, black, communist, and queer, been allotted screen space, in *Boycott*. Someone is yet to make the movie that juxtaposes the legacy of the first black graduate of Central High, Ernest Green, with that of Governor Orval Faubus who tried to block his progress: by the mid-1970s Green was Assistant Labor Secretary to President Carter and Faubus was a bank teller. Safe, sensible and sensitive evocations carry the day but too often fail to convey the excitement, fear and urgency one feels reading novels like Alice Walker's *Meridian* (1976) or Charles Johnson's *Dreamer* (1998). Few films capture what Cornel West has described as the 'boiling sense of rage and a passionate pessimism regarding America's will to justice' that characterised the civil rights years for many black people in the South.[37] Yet *A Time To Kill* does tap in to that sense of disquiet, its racial enclaves congealed into custom until shaken by the angry black father breaking open a legacy of race hatred that whites found morally reprehensible but many tacitly sanctioned for so long. Carl Lee as reconceived in Akiva Goldsman's screenplay, is a reminder of Clyde Franklin's assertion in 1994 that 'in America adult black males have only been "men" for about twenty years' and that they are still seldom recognised as 'societally approved men'. Goldsman and Schmacher make Carl Lee an African American populist hero.[38]

When considering the movie-made Movement, one begins to detect a new battle over audience that divides along racial lines, with directors fighting over custody of the past in order to protect the 1960s and its icons. Spike Lee campaigned against a white director, Norman Jewison, directing a film based on *The Autobiography of Malcolm X* (despite the older director's success with films like *In The*

Heat Of The Night and *A Soldier's Story*). In a similar way, if, as
Maurice Halbwachs maintains, we need historical witnesses to confirm our recognition of the past in collective memory, the casting of
Medgar Evers and Martin Luther King Jr.'s children in *Ghosts of
Mississippi* and *Boycott* garners a sense of authenticity for black
audiences and exhibits a kind of moral deference to African American shared memories.

Richard Rorty claims that post-war it has become difficult to tell
a 'convincing story of social hope' and Manning Marable and Leith
Mullings have stated that it is 'exceedingly difficult to advocate radical ideas for democratic social transformation when there are few,
if any, actual models which express one's hopes and aspirations'.[39]
The Civil Rights Movement remains perhaps the only model to
which contemporary writers and filmmakers can turn with some
certainty. But palliative rites of passage stories – works of contrition
frozen in the past – have been a soft and spongy fulcrum for movies
of this sub-genre for too long. When they mutate into a political
battleground like *Mississippi Burning*, they reflect an equally viti-
ated sense of Hollywood's scope for representing the Movement
and remind us that film reflects but also limps behind reality. There
is room for more of the kind of creative-critical archaeology that
Waking in Mississippi begins to undertake with regard to *A Time To
Kill*. Even white psychodramas can have important and unexpected
effects. In *Long Night's Journey Into Day* (2000), a documentary
about South Africa's post-apartheid Truth and Reconciliation Commission, one of the white subjects interviewed said he decided to
seek amnesty for his part in the murder of black South Africans
after watching *Mississippi Burning*. Eric Taylor had the opposite
response to Lawrence Rainey when he realised he had indeed
become like those Sheriffs he saw on screen whose primary task was
to break rather than uphold the law. Similarly, *A Time To Kill* has
been cited by an American Senator when speaking out against racist
bigotry; he forgoes any problematic discussion of vigilante justice
to dwell on 'A Time to Heal', the words that follow 'A Time to Kill'
in the Book of Ecclesiastes. And local newspapers like the *Jackson
Clarion Ledger* and *Madison County Journal* continue to credit *A
Time To Kill* with 'bringing [Canton's] residents closer together . . .
across racial boundaries [more] than any other experience in the
city's history'.[40] Filmmakers and audiences are only just beginning
to excavate the layers of film and history – our reel and real

memories of the courageous successes and gridlocked failures of the Movement.

Notes

I am grateful to Richard H. King for his comments on an earlier draft of this essay and to Christie Herring for her thoughtful reconsideration of the events that surrounded the making of *Waking in Mississippi*.

1 Richard Rorty, *Contingency, Irony, and Solidarity* (Cambridge: Cambridge University Press, 1989), p. xvi. See also John Bodnar, *Remaking America: Public Memory, Commemoration, and Patriotism in the Twentieth Century* (Princeton, NJ: Princeton University Press, 1992); Marita Sturken, *Tangled Memories: The Vietnam War, the AIDS Epidemic, and the Politics of Remembering* (Berkeley: University of California Press, 1997).

2 Quoted in Tim Funk, 'Black History Comes Alive in Southern Cities', *The Daily Helmsman* (5 February 2002), 11.

3 David Herlily, 'Am I A Camera? Other Reflections on Films and History', *American Historical Review* 93: 5 (December 1988), 1191; Natalie Zemon-Davis, *Slaves on Screen: Film and Historical Vision* (Cambridge, MA: Harvard University Press, 2000).

4 Alice Walker, 'The Civil Rights Movement: What Good Was It?', in *In Search of Our Mothers' Gardens* (London: The Women's Press, 1984), p. 122.

5 Benjamin, *Illuminations* trans. Harry Zohn (London: Fontana, 1973), p. 247; Fredric Jameson, 'Postmodernism and Consumer Society', in John Belton (ed.) *Movies and Mass Culture* (New Jersey: Rutgers University Press, 1996), p. 202.

6 Theodor Adorno, *Minima Moralia: Reflections From Damaged Life*, trans. E. F. N. Jephcott (London: Verso, 1974), p. 235. For a more positive view of 'presentism' and its effects, see Maurice Halbwachs, *On Collective Memory*, ed. and trans. Lewis A. Coser (Chicago: University of Chicago Press, 1992).

7 For example, Martha Douglas uses just these terms when praising *Crisis at Central High*, 'Crisis at Central High: Grim, Tense, Scary, Real', *Arkansas Gazette* (2 February, 1981), B1.

8 Rick Altman, *Film/Genre* (London: BFI, 1999), p. 195.

9 Ralph Ellison, 'The Shadow and the Act', in Ralph Ellison, *The Shadow and the Act* (New York: Vintage, 1994), p. 277. Ellison is reviewing a clutch of films released in 1949.

10 James Snead, *White Screens, Black Images: Hollywood From the Dark Side* (New York: Routledge, 1994), p. 4.

11 AdrienneRich, 'Arts of the Possible', *The Massachussetts Review* 38: 3 (Autumn 1997), 326.
12 This exemplifies what Benjamin De Mott has called 'friendship orthodoxy' in *The Trouble With Friendship: Why Americans Can't Think Straight About Race* (New Haven: Yale, 1998) and is a component of the framework through which I read a variety of relationships between black and white southern women in *Advancing Sisterhood? Interracial Friendships in Contemporary Southern Fiction* (Athens: University of Georgia Press, 2000).
13 Fred Hobson, *But Now I See: The White Southern Racial Conversion Narrative* (Baton Rouge: Louisiana University Press, 1999), p. 129.
14 The term 'image facts' is André Bazin's and is part of the 'aesthetic of reality' he argues for Rossellini's neo-realist *Paisa*. See *What Is Cinema? Volume II* (Berkeley: University of California Press, 1972), p. 37.
15 Unnamed reviewer, *Jet* (25 March 1991), 58.
16 June Jordan, 'The Mountain and the Man Who Was Not God: An Essay on the Life and Ideas of Dr. Martin Luther King, Jr., in *Moving Towards Home: Political Essays* (London: Virago Press, 1989), pp. 200–1. Jordan refers by name to Jo Ann Robinson, Rosa Parks and Ella Baker, women directly involved in the boycott or the organisations that it spawned, but there were many others, unnamed and unacknowledged, whose imaginary representative Odessa Cotter becomes. The narrator echoes Lenwood G. Davis's words: 'The Montgomery story is one with 50,000 actors and each playing a different role. It is impossible to name and to give equal space to all of the personalities', *The Life and Times of Martin L. King, Jr.* (Connecticut: Negro Universities Press, 1969), p. 43.
17 Virginia Durr, *Outside the Magic Circle: The Autobiography of Virginia Foster Durr*, ed. Hollinger F. Bernard (Tuscaloosa: The University of Alabama Press, 1985), p. 267.
18 Alan Parker, 'Notes on the Making of the Film', in *Mississippi Burning* Production Notes, p. 16.
19 Parker, 'Notes', p. 27.
20 Sean French, review of *Mississippi Burning*, *Sight and Sound* 58: 2 (Spring 1989), 132.
21 Pauline Kael, *The New Yorker*, 64: 45 (26 December 1988), 73.
22 Elizabeth L. Bland, Jack White and Richard Corliss, 'The Fire This Time', *Time* (9 January 1989), 56.
23 Lawrence Rainey quoted by Ron Harris, 'Ex-Sheriff is Seeking Filmmaker Retraction', *The Commercial Appeal*, 1 February, 1989, B8. Lawless southern sheriffs in the movies are usually re-presentations of people like Mississippi's Harold Strider ('I just want to tell all of those people who've been sending me those threatening letters that if they ever come down here, the same thing's gonna happen to them that happened to

Emmett Till'), or Safety Commissioner Bull Connor, who turned water cannons and dogs on black children in Birmingham in 1963.

24 Mark Perrusquia, 'Klan Recruiters Use Movie', *The Commercial Appeal* (2 March 1989), B2.

25 Press kit for *A Time To Kill*, p. 8.

26 *Entertainment Weekly* 337 (26 July 1996), 21.

27 Allison Graham, *Framing the South: Hollywood, Television, and Race During the Civil Rights Struggle* (Baltimore: Johns Hopkins University Press, 2001), p. 189.

28 Richard Schickel, *Time* (29 July 1996), 76.

29 Audience members sampled by the author at the University of Memphis, Tennessee, January 2002; *Rolling Stone* 740, p. 68. In the early 1960s Silvan Tomkins pioneered a psychological approach to memory that he called script theory. Although his work offers a methodology for the study of personality, when applied to the structuring of film narrative, his unit of the 'scene' helps to map those cinematic sequences that act as 'core', magnified by memory either in positive terms (variant magnification) or negatively (analog magnification). Core scenes in my extrapolation are cinematically tried and audience tested; they anchor the narrative and read alongside Tomkins' theory of affect have increasing relevance. This affective pattern accounts for linked signature scenes that transcend historical context – and even period in the case of *A Time to Kill* – and reinforce both film history and popular memory. See, for example, Tomkins, *Affect, Imagery, Consciousness: Cognition: Duplication and Transformation of Information* (New York; Springer, 1992).

30 John Grisham, *A Time to Kill* (London: Arrow, 1992), p. 184.

31 Ann Moody in a lecture at Millsaps College, 26 February 1985, as quoted by Gayle Graham Yates in *Mississippi Mind: A Personal Cultural History of an American State* (Knoxville: University of Tennessee Press, 1990), p. 80; 'Riders Throw Bomb at Freedom house', *The Student Voice* 5: 14, 9 June 1964; Ira B. Harkey, *The Smell of Burning Crosses: An Autobiography of a Mississippi Newspaperman* (Jacksonville, Illinois: Horns Wolfe and Co., 1967), pp. 90–1.

32 Christie Herring, correspondence with the author, March 2002.

33 Tom Dent, *Southern Journey: A Return to the Civil Rights Movement* (New York: William Morrow & Co, 1997), p. 349.

34 Christie Herring, correspondence with the author, March 2002.

35 Marc C. Malkin, 'In the Works: *A Time To Kill*', *Premiere* (March 1996), 35; Press kit for *A Time To Kill*, p. 11.

36 Barbara Melosh, '"History" and Memory in Fiction: The Civil Rights Movement in Three Novels', *Radical History Review* (Winter 1988), 64; Hobson, *But Now I See*, p. 122.

37 Cornel West, *Race Matters* (Boston: Beacon, 1993), p. 18.
38 Grisham has generally admitted that Goldsman develops Carl Lee beyond his depiction in the novel. Goldsman captures something of the mood epitomised by the founding of the National Council of African American men in 1990 and the Million Man March in 1995. Clyde Franklin, 'Ain't I A Man? The Efficacy of Black Masculinities for Men's Studies', in Richard Majors and Jacob Gordon (eds), *The American Black Male: His Present Status and His Future* (Chicago: Nelson-Hall, 1994), p. 242. Nick Cassavetes' recent film starring Denzel Washington, *John Q* (2002), also represents the passionate black father willing to commit a crime for the sake of his child.
39 Manning Marable and Leith Mullings, 'The Divided Mind of Black America: Race, Ideology and Politics in the Post Civil Rights Era', *Race and Class* 36: 1 (1994), 70.
40 Senator O'Donnell in the Nevada Legislature, February 10, 1997; Duane Gordon, 'TV Star to play Skip in Movie', *Madison County Journal* (7 May 1998, n.p.).

7

Prosthetic memory: the ethics and politics of memory in an age of mass culture

Alison Landsberg

Memory is not commonly imagined as a site of possibility for progressive politics. More often, memory, particularly in the form of nostalgia, is condemned for its solipsistic nature, for its tendency to draw people into the past instead of the present. This is the case, for example, in Kathryn Bigelow's 1995 film *Strange Days*, in which the use of memory – usually another person's memory – is figured as a form of addiction. The film is set in Los Angeles, on New Year's Eve 1999. The Los Angeles of the film is a chaotic, multicultural world of violence, epitomised by the assassination of Jeriko One, an important African-American rapper and a vocal opponent of white oppression. Rather than confront this bleak reality, people buy 'wire trips', which are memories that can be played back again and again. A wire trip, as the 'dealer' Lenny Nero (Ralph Fiennes) explains to a potential buyer, 'is life. It is a piece of someone's life'. On a wire trip, 'You are there – doing it, seeing it, hearing it, feeling it'. A wire trip is analogised to a drug trip, and as with drugs, these 'playbacks' of memories are addictive, a form of escape from the present. Available on the black market, these memories circulate as commodities; consuming them threatens to prevent individuals from acting in the present, from being productive, politically engaged members of society. Indulging in memory 'playback' has the anti-social, apolitical effect of atomising people. This retreat from the 'real world' – especially in the face of urban crisis – makes impossible any form of politics, any strategy for bringing about social change. To be a socially responsible person, Nero must 'kick the habit', turn away from the private prison world of memory in order to live productively in the public world.

This negative depiction of memory is more than just the conceit of a science fiction film. The image of memory as an obstacle to, rather than a catalyst for, progressive politics and collective action is shared by many scholars as well. Historians Roy Rosenzweig and David Thelen, in their important recent book, *The Presence of the Past*, reject the frequently heard criticism that Americans are ignorant about history. Through an ambitious survey project aimed at examining qualitatively and quantitatively how contemporary Americans feel about history, they demonstrate that most are, in fact, fascinated with the past.[1] Yet despite the multiple forms of 'popular history-making' their survey uncovers, Rosenzweig, in particular, remains concerned that the way many Americans remember the past has the effect of atomising them, rather than building collective solidarities. Because many of the Americans surveyed emphasise first-hand experience and the familial, they tend to construct a more privatised version of the past, which might as a negative consequence 'reinforce rather than break down barriers between people, resist rather than promote change'.[2] The concern here is that these more personal memories are less useful in the task of forging political alliances between different groups of people. In other words, Rosenzweig echoes the critique implied in *Strange Days* that private memory is an obstacle to collective politics. The commodification of memory, as depicted in *Strange Days*, only exacerbates this problem. By purchasing the memories they want, the film's addicts retreat into their own private fantasies rather than participate in the public sphere of social responsibility. Similarly, the commodification of memories through history films, television, museums and the Internet threatens to construct pasts that are privately satisfying rather than publicly useful.

This critique is legitimate, but not necessarily insurmountable. It might be possible to imagine a relationship to memory that facilitates, rather than prevents, the formation of progressive political alliances and solidarities. In fact, the conditions of possibility for such a relationship emerged at the turn of the last century when two developments radically changed the conditions and contours of memory in American culture. Modernisation and industrialisation sparked an unprecedented movement of peoples across the globe, while the birth of the cinema and other technological innovations led to the emergence of a truly mass culture. In the context of mass migrations, memory would be required to play a crucial new role. The US experienced its largest waves of immigration from Europe in the first decades of this century, even as it witnessed the mass migrations of African Americans to the industrial centres of the North. With these movements of peoples came the rupture of generational ties, rendering the traditional modes for the transmission of cultural, ethnic, and racial memory – both memories passed from parent to child and those disseminated through community life – increasingly inadequate. At the same moment, the cinema and the technologised mass culture that it helped inaugurate transformed memory by making possible an unprecedented circulation of images and narratives about the past. Thanks to these new technologies of memory on the one hand and commodification on the other, the kinds of memories that one has 'intimate', even experiential, access to would no longer be limited to the memories of events through which one actually lived. This essay will argue that the effects of capitalist commodification and mass culture are not exclusively privatising and therefore conservative; these forces have also opened up the potential for a progressive, even radical politics of memory: such a politics instrumentalises what I have called 'prosthetic memory'.[3]

In 1913, Max Scheler published *The Nature of Sympathy*, in which he attempts to explore the contours of sympathy, empathy and what he regards most highly of all, 'fellow-feeling'.[4] Fellow-feeling, a sense of collective responsibility, is to Scheler a position of high moral value, which he defines in opposition to 'emotional infection' and 'emotional reproduction': if, for example, when confronted with a drowning man one is stricken with fear for oneself, if one feels a twinge of pain, this is emotional infection and has a lower moral value than the 'purer and truer' fellow-feeling.[5] Scheler rejects the mere reproduction of feelings on the grounds that 'it entails that our fellow-feeling must necessarily be confined to processes and incidents in other people's experience such *as we have already met with ourselves*'.[6] Scheler posits instead that one can easily participate in someone else's joy or sorrow without having lived through, or 'sampled that particular quality of experience before'.[7] Fellow-feeling is possible, according to Scheler, because man has an '*innate* capacity for comprehending the feelings of others, even though he may never on any occasion have encountered such feelings (or their ingredients) in himself'.[8]

What Scheler is describing as fellow-feeling, then, is really what is now defined as empathy. And what Scheler actually articulates here is the distinction between 'empathy' and 'sympathy'.[9] Sympathy, a feeling that arises out of simple identification, often takes the form of wallowing in someone else's pain. In it, there is a presumption of sameness between the sympathiser and her object. Whether or not there is actually a 'sameness' between them, an actual shared experience, matters little, for in the act of sympathising, one projects one's own feelings onto the other. This act can be imperialising and colonising, taking over, rather than making space for, the other's feelings.[10] In the act of sympathising, not only is the victimhood of the other reinforced, but hierarchies are established; sympathy implies condescension, for the sympathiser looks down on his/her object, and in the process reaffirms his/her superiority. The experience of empathy, by contrast, is not purely emotional, but has a crucial cognitive component. It therefore takes work and thought to achieve. The connection one feels when one empathises with another is not simply a feeling of emotional connection, but a feeling of cognitive, intellectual connection – an intellectual coming-to-terms with the other's circumstances. As the philosopher Emmanuel Levinas argues, any ethical relationship to the other requires empathy: a recognition of the profound difference and unknowability of the other, and a simultaneous sense of commitment and responsibility toward him/her even in the face of such differences.[11]

If Scheler's essentialist and universalising argument – that man has an '*innate* capacity for comprehending the feelings of others' – seems antiquated today, his sense that one can commiserate with another without having shared that person's particular experience opens up the possibility of bridging perceived differences in order to form political alliances. And yet in positing an instinctual basis for fellow-feeling, Scheler neglected to consider the cultural effects of the new forms of mass culture emerging at the time he wrote – in particular the cinema. It is not simply, as he suggests, that humans are intrinsically able to 'comprehend the feelings of others', but rather that technologies of memory have exponentially increased the opportunities for such empathetic understandings.[12] It may very well be the case that humans are unique in their *capacity* for empathy. But empathy is not instinct; it is a faculty whose exercise is more or less likely depending on social and cultural context. The emerging technologies of mass culture had the potential to create the understanding necessary for the formation of political alliances across chasms of difference. In this connection, empathy's emergence into the language in 1904 is suggestive:[13] like Scheler's discussion of fellow-feeling, the concept of empathy seems to have become imaginable – distinguishable from sympathy – against the backdrop of a burgeoning mass culture.

Of course, others have reflected on the political potential of technologies of mass culture, notably Siegfried Kracauer and Walter Benjamin. Writing in the 1930s, Kracauer and Benjamin began to theorise both the experiential nature of the cinema, the power of film to speak to, and move, the human body as well as its ability to influence the way one sees the world. For Kracauer, film actually addresses its viewer as a 'corporeal-material being'; 'it seizes the "human being with skin and hair"' as 'The material elements that present themselves in film directly stimulate the *material layers* of the human being: his nerves, his senses, his entire *physiological substance*'.[14] The cinematic experience has an individual, bodily component even while its mode of reception is collective. For Kracauer, film quite literally has the capacity to move the spectator. Benjamin, too, argues for the radical political potential of technologies of reproduction. He famously describes the way the camera enables one both to see objects outside of one's immediate experience and more importantly to recognise new dimensions of commonplace objects: 'Our taverns and our metropolitan streets, our offices and furnished rooms, our railroad stations and our factories appeared to have us locked up hopelessly. Then came film and burst this prison-world asunder by the dynamite of the tenth of a second.'[15] For Benjamin the camera has the capacity to make visible that which, through repression and reification, remained inaccessible to the naked eye. But what I hope to underscore here is the unique capacity of film and other technologies of reproduction to generate empathy. By revealing perspectives otherwise inaccessible, and by addressing the individual body in the intimate ways that they do, these technologies of reproduction serve as particularly powerful conduits for the generation of empathy.

One of the most dramatic instances of how the mass media generate empathy is through the production and dissemination of memory. Such memories bridge the temporal chasms that separate individuals from the meaningful and potentially interpellative events of the past. It has become possible to have an intimate relationship to memories of events through which one did not live: these are the memories I call prosthetic. 'Prosthetic memories' are indeed 'personal' memories, as they derive from engaged and experientially-oriented encounters with the mass media's various technologies of memory. But because prosthetic memories are not natural, not the possession of a single individual, let alone a particular family or ethnic group, they conjure up a more public past, a past that is not at all privatised. The pasts that prosthetic memory open up are available to individuals across racial and ethnic lines. This form of memory is historically specific and quite distinct from the various forms of collective memory, which are usually circumscribed by a particular community or group. In contrast to collective memories, which tend to be geographically specific and which serve to reinforce and naturalise a group's identity, prosthetic memories are not the property of a single group. Rather, they open up the possibility for collective horizons of experience and pave the way for unexpected political alliances.

I call these memories 'prosthetic memories' for four reasons. First, they are not 'authentic' or natural, but rather are derived from engagement with mediated representations (seeing a film, visiting a museum, watching a television show, using a CD-ROM). Second, like an artificial limb, these memories are actually worn on the body; these are sensuous memories produced by an *experience* of mass mediated representations. And like an artificial limb, these memories often mark a trauma. Third, calling them 'prosthetic' signals their interchangeability and exchangeability and underscores their commodified form. In this sense, I agree with those who have rejected the 'culture industry' model in which mass culture is seen solely as a site of domination and deception. I argue that commodification, which is at the heart of mass cultural representations, is precisely what makes images and narratives widely available, available to people who live in different places, come from different backgrounds, from different races and from different classes. Furthermore, reception is more complicated than such critics allow, as spectators have greater intelligence and agency than the 'brainwashing' model permits; commodities, and commodified images, are not capsules of meaning that spectators swallow whole, but rather the grounds upon which social meanings are negotiated, contested, and sometimes constructed. Finally, I call these memories prosthetic to underscore their usefulness; because they feel real they help to condition how an individual thinks about the world, and might be instrumental in generating empathy and articulating an ethical relation to the other. A sensuous engagement with the past, which prosthetic memory enables, is the foundation for more than simply individual subjectivity; it becomes the basis for mediated collective identification and for the production of potentially counterhegemonic public spheres.

In beginning to theorise their political potential, two elements of prosthetic memory are particularly relevant: their indebtedness to commodification and mass culture on the one hand, and on the other, their unique ability to generate empathy, a crucial step in the formation of political alliances and solidarities. Perhaps in a perfect world there would be some alternative to commodity culture, but for those living in the early hours of the new millennium, a commodity-saturated capitalism prevails. And yet it is the very pervasiveness of commodification – reaching as it does into the realm of mass cultural representation – that makes images and narratives about the past available on an unprecedented scale. Prosthetic memory, as I have been arguing, is quite literally made possible by the advanced state of capitalism and its ensuing commodity culture. It is through buying a movie ticket, paying the entrance fee to a museum, or acquiring access to the Internet, that one gains access to these images and narratives about the past. So instead of simply condemning commodity culture, as many cultural critics have done, I will argue that the only way to bring about social transformation is by working within the capitalist system.[16] There is not, I am afraid, some pristine world of politics apart from the world of consumption. In what follows, I will highlight particular instances where commodified prosthetic memories work towards politically progressive ends.

Scholars in a variety of fields have long challenged the notion of the passive consumer. According to Daniel Miller, the reception or use of a commodity 'is the start of a long and complex process, by which the consumer works upon the object purchased and recontextualizes it, until it is often no longer recognizable as having any relation to the world of the abstract and becomes its very negation, something which could be neither bought nor given'.[17] While the kinds of commodities disseminated by the mass media are different in form from more traditional commodities, they require a similar kind of analysis. Stuart Hall, John Fiske and others have emphasised the point that meaning-making occurs at two moments in the mass communication process – both at production and reception, at moments of 'encoding' and 'decoding'.[18] Hall, in particular, emphasises that there are always several possible readings of a given cultural text; some reinforce the existing power structures and status quo while other, more oppositional ones, challenge it.[19] Even in the complicated case of mass cultural commodities, reception is conditioned by and mediated through the cultural, political and social worlds of the consumers.

It is important here to underscore the fact that there is indeed a limit to the number of possible readings of any mass cultural commodity. While these commodities might be multivocal, they are not infinitely so; the commodity itself imposes certain constraints on its interpretation as does the social world, or system of signs, in which it gets decoded. The mass cultural texts in which I am most interested are those that attempt to make possible progressive, or counterhegemonic readings; but because of the multivocality of commodities, even those cannot predetermine the meanings ultimately negotiated by individuals.

Nevertheless, because these mass cultural commodities, these images and narratives about the past, are mediated through the cultural, political and social worlds of individuals, they have the capacity to affect profoundly an individual's subjectivity. The radical potential of prosthetic memory derives from the fact that the subjectivities they produce are not 'natural', not premised on some count of authenticity. Furthermore, prosthetic memories cannot be owned exclusively. Despite the fact that these memories are made possible by a commodity culture, and circulate like commodities, they can never be owned as private property, and as a result they occupy a unique position within and yet implicitly opposed to capitalism. In fact, one might even say that they function as what Etienne Balibar has called 'universal property'. In reflecting on property, Balibar wonders 'whether the principle of total possession brings with it intrinsic limits, that is, whether there are "objects" that, by nature, cannot be appropriated, or more precisely that can be appropriated but not totally possessed'.[20] I would argue that mass cultural commodities, and in particular the prosthetic memories that I am describing, pose a powerful challenge to the concept of private property; at the dawn of the twenty-first century, this challenge is lodged even more strongly by the Internet, with its capacity to disseminate freely texts, information, music and so forth. As memories that no individual can own, that individuals can only *share* with others, and whose meanings can never be completely stabilised, prosthetic memories themselves become a challenge to the 'total possession' of private property.

Perhaps more than in any other realm, the political potential of prosthetic memory has been explored in science fiction film. In Paul Verhoeven's *Total Recall*, a film with a much more sanguine attitude towards memory than *Strange Days*, Quade (Arnold Schwarzeneggar), the protagonist, has a life-long dream of visiting Mars. The world he inhabits is both technologically advanced and commodity-saturated, and he is therefore able to buy memories of just such a trip. The political conditions on Mars are dire, for there is a class of people, the Mutants, whose fate lies in the hands of the evil capitalist Cohagen: he alone controls their access to oxygen through an elaborate venting mechanism. Quade later learns that even before he had opted to purchase his 'memory trip', he had already received implanted memories and that Quade, the identity constructed on the basis of those memories, is actually 'inauthentic'. Quade, then, has to choose which identity to inhabit: the identity of Quade, or the identity of 'Hauser', whom he is told was his authentic identity. Capitalism has thus given Quade some choices about who to be. However, the mere fact that both options are in some ways made possible by capitalism does not mean that they are both equally reactionary or equally progressive. One of the identities, that of Quade, is motivated by a social conscience, a desire to save the oppressed underclass on Mars. In other words, the prosthetic memories he has taken on enable him to think ethically; on the basis of those memories – and in particular, the memories of the oppression and ghettoisation of the Mutants – he experiences empathy. Quade acts in a socially responsible way by turning on the oxygen mines and freeing the Mutants from the tyrannical grip of Cohagen. *Total Recall* illustrates Hall's point that capitalist commodities offer choices – not unlimited choices, but choices nevertheless – some of which have the potential to challenge the status quo and subvert social norms and hierarchies. Commodified memories might be used in unexpected ways, in ways that actively challenge the exploitative drive of capitalism.

To underscore this point, I would like to turn to a mass cultural text that aims to produce prosthetic memories: John Singleton's 1996 film *Rosewood*. *Rosewood* raises the question of whether white children – and by extension, a white audience – can take on memories of racial oppression and in the process develop empathy for African Americans. Singleton's film documents the events that transpire over the course of five days in a small Florida town called Rosewood. Because the film is first and foremost an attempt to put into history that which has been left out, Singleton situates his story *in* history: the narrative begins on Thursday, 31 December 1922. This film dramatises a moment in the history of two neighboring Florida towns, Rosewood and Sumner – the former is primarily black, the latter primarily white. Despite the presence of much racism, the two towns manage to coexist until a white woman in Sumner, after receiving a beating at the hands of her white lover, cries rape and blames it on an unknown black man. Her allegation ignites the town of Sumner and violent lynch mobs decimate Rosewood. By 'remembering' cinematically the lynch mobs that lived on long after the abolition of institutional slavery, Singleton makes visible a history of racial oppression that has been radically underrepresented.

But Singleton is doing more than making oppression visible. He reconstructs a radiant image of Rosewood and its citizens. In an inversion of stereotypes, Rosewood, not Sumner, is the thriving town. In Rosewood, black families own the land and all but one of the businesses. Tranquil scenes of family and community life in Rosewood are juxtaposed against scenes of the coarser, more chaotic and unkempt life in Sumner. The hard-working African Americans he depicts in Rosewood are living the American dream. Significantly, in this film, African American characters are privileged with point-of-view shots. To watch *Rosewood* the spectator must, in effect, look at the world through black eyes. Singleton is thus directing cinematic technology toward the task of producing empathy in his spectators.

Children play a crucial role in the film's vision. Not only is the narrative driven by the harrowing escape of the black children of Rosewood, but the importance of saving the children is underscored at the end by a textual epilogue which informs the viewers that the film was made possible by the sworn testimony of the children of Rosewood. It was their words which make visible this under-represented history.

But this film also foregrounds a white child. In one of its first scenes, a white man in Sumner – one who subsequently is revealed as the most virulently and violently racist of the bunch – teaches his son Emmett to hunt. This scene initiates what becomes a veritable obsession of the film: the teaching of children. When Emmett and Arnett, the African American boy from Rosewood, are playing together at the beginning of the film, Emmett's father warns, 'I don't want you around that nigger boy – You'll be a man soon. I'll getya there'. Racial prejudice, the film suggests, is not natural but learned.

Emmett is brought along with the lynch mob and experiences a series of pedagogical events; in one instance his father teaches him to make a noose. Later his father forces him to look into a mass grave. Emmett shakes his head and walks away with tears in his eyes. When his father asks him why he is crying he says, 'There's babies in there.' 'Nigger is nigger, boy', his father responds. The lesson here, the fundamental premise of racial prejudice, is that blacks are black before they are human.

At the end of the film, many of the children of Rosewood do successfully escape, but at great cost: the once thriving town is smoldering ash, destroyed by racial hatred. But the film does not end there. It ends in the white town of Sumner. In the final scene Emmett is standing outside his father's cabin with all of his worldly possessions tied to a stick. 'Where you going boy?' his father asks. 'I hate you', Emmett responds, 'You ain't no man.' And then he walks away. The film's vision here is intimately tied to children's 'vision': that of both the children of Rosewood who have testified to this past and Emmett, the white child, who has the capacity to see differently. By looking as if through black eyes he is able to see through the reified, naturalised structures of societal and institutional racism. The price of this vision, though, is high for it requires him to disinherit himself. In some ways, then, Emmett becomes the model for the white spectator. It is the white spectator, like Emmett, who needs to learn to see as if through black eyes, and this is achieved cinematically. This kind of vision, Singleton suggests, generates empathy, and it is the only way to prevent the structures of oppression from reproducing themselves. Through the character of Emmett, Singleton's film stages a process whereby white viewers can come to recognise and reject racism. Seeing through black eyes in *Rosewood* means seeing 'through' the reified ideologies of white supremacy.

Singleton uses cinematic identification to create the conditions under which audience members can take on prosthetic memories. The film deploys specific cinematic techniques intended to elicit identification both with the African American characters, but also, at the end, with the little white boy, Emmett. This kind of cinematic identification has pedagogical value because it forces identification across racial lines; it positions white people to look at the world through black eyes. Similarly, cinematic identification can enable viewers to acquire prosthetic memories. Emmett's ability to turn away from his father and to reject his father's white supremacist beliefs is enabled by his memories: his memory of his father calling his friend Arnett a nigger, his memory of being forced to make a noose, his memory of the mass grave filled with black bodies – and babies. And in identifying with Emmett, we too take on those memories. They are not memories of events we lived through, as they are for Emmett, yet through an act of prosthesis enabled by cinematic identification, they become part of our archive of memory. The point here is not that we forget who we are as we watch the film, but rather that we are enabled, for a short period of time, to see through different eyes, and think beyond our own social position. Prosthetic memories enable us to 'remember' the specific event, the Rosewood massacre, but also the broader historical terrain – the vitality of organised racism that persisted well into the twentieth century. In other words, the past that the film makes visible is one that has social relevance in the present and might be instrumental in enabling a white individual to experience empathy for African Americans, as Emmett does for the residents of Rosewood.

To help white audiences see through black eyes, and to force white viewers to interrogate the prejudices which are the legacy of whiteness, is certainly the intention of this film. And yet, as post-structuralism has taught us, texts are polysemic. There is no way to assure a particular reading of a text, no way to completely stabilise meaning. For some viewers, the vulgarity of the white characters will be read as an exaggeration, making it easier to dismiss the film as anti-white propaganda. For others, the circumstances and specificities of their own lives might radically alter what they take from the film. Non-African American viewers might well see *Rosewood* as a reflection of their own experience; in other words, instead of working to generate empathy for African Americans, the film might actually reproduce an individual's sense of his or her own victimisation, foreclosing the possibility of learning about difference. There is ultimately no guarantee of how any text will be read.

But if the active engagement of individuals with mass cultural texts means that the meanings of prosthetic memories cannot be predetermined, this engagement is also precisely what gives prosthetic memories their special power. As memories taken on and experienced sensuously, even viscerally, they become powerful tools in shaping one's subjectivity. At the same time, though, these memories are not essential, not simply an individual's birthright – one can imagine, for example, a white person 'remembering' racism and racial persecution in this country. Because prosthetic memories enable individuals to have a personal connection to an event they did not live through, to see through another's eyes, they have the capacity to make possible alliances across racial, class and other chasms of difference. As *Total Recall* demonstrates, the political potential of prosthetic memory lies in its capacity to enable ethical thinking. Technologies such as the camera and the cinema enable people to take on memories of difficult pasts and thereby facilitate the experience of empathy. In so doing, they open up new doors for consciousness raising and progressive political alliance formation.

The idea that mass cultural technologies are inherently atomising and apolitical has re-emerged in the debates surrounding the latest such technology: the Internet. Like both the cinema and television before it, the Internet has generated a great deal of discussion, both among academics and in the popular press, about its potential and its dangers. In addition to celebrating its ability to grant easy access to vast amounts of information, champions of the Internet, such as Howard Rheingold, have tended to celebrate its capacity to generate 'virtual communities', which he defines as 'social aggregations that emerge from the Net when enough people carry on public discussions long enough, with sufficient human feeling, to form webs of personal relationships in cyberspace'.[21] Critical of precisely those claims, its detractors have challenged the idea that a virtual community looks anything like a 'real' community.[22] Kevin Robins, for one, has argued that cyberspace is often imagined as a utopia divorced from the social, material and political landscapes of the 'real world'.[23] For Robins, communities in cyberspace are fundamentally anti-political.[24] And he is by no means alone in this position. Cyberspace, Michele Willson argues, sanctions 'a withdrawal from the active political sphere of real space'.[25] But she is equally concerned with the ethical ramifications of 'virtual communities', claiming that such disembodied interactions, the immaterial and transient connections people share in virtual communities, render an ethical or political concern for the Other 'impotent and unrealizable'.[26]

These critiques, it seems, bring us back to the world of *Strange Days*, to anxieties about the ways in which new technologies might atomise, rather than politicise individuals. Like the memory playbacks to which Lenny Nero is addicted, cyberchats seem to limit an individual's ability to engage in meaningful politics. But while it might be the case that virtual communities differ in quality and depth from the real thing, we should hesitate before embracing an unqualified celebration of real communities. At least in the US, patterns of racial and economic segregation have meant that most communities that exist in real space are distressingly homogeneous and exclusive. The Internet, like the cinema, has the capacity to speak to a wide range of people who hail from radically different backgrounds, and to foster the formation not necessarily of communities, but of political alliances across those differences. Cyberspace offers an arena in which large-scale, strategic alliances can be mobilised quickly and efficiently to enable political activism. For example, the Internet was crucial in coordinating the public demonstrations that interrupted the IMF and World Bank meetings in Seattle in December of 1999. In that case, too, a diverse public came together not to form a permanent community, but to combine forces on the basis of shared political interests. By enabling farmers, union workers, college students and environmentalists, among others, to recognise, in previously unimaginable ways, a shared set of political concerns, the Internet enabled these disparate groups to take collective action. By focusing on communities as the grounds for politics in cyberspace, the critics might have overlooked other kinds of associations and networks in cyberspace where individuals actively engage real world politics.

My aim here is not to be an apologist for the Internet, particularly given its marriage to unbridled capitalism. But as with capitalism itself, the Internet has made available texts and archives that were accessible only to the privileged few. Many critics, for example, overlook the great strides that have been taken to make the Internet a legitimate tool in both the dissemination and archiving of history: the work of some historians has shown the capacity of the Internet to be educational, not just commercial.[27] Furthermore, as an increasingly experiential medium, the Internet has the potential to generate prosthetic memories. Because of its fundamental interactivity, it engages the individual body. As its mode of address becomes more complex both visually and aurally, the Internet might be another mass cultural mechanism capable of generating empathy and ethical politics. While I share Willson's concern about the ethical ramifications of virtual communities, I am more sanguine about the possibilities the Internet opens up for disseminating prosthetic memories that might enable grassroots political activism and consciousness-raising.

I do not mean for even a moment to suggest that there is anything *inherently* positive or progressive about this new form of memory.

What I mean instead to underscore is the unique power of prosthetic memory to affect people in profound ways – both intellectually and emotionally – in ways that might ultimately change the way they think, and how they act, in the world. My call, therefore, is to take seriously both the desire individuals feel to be part of history and the potential of prosthetic memory to bring about social justice. The mass cultural technologies that enable the production and dissemination of prosthetic memories are incredibly powerful; rather than disdain and turn our backs on these technologies, we must instead recognise their power and political potential. As surfing the Internet reveals, hate groups and Holocaust deniers have embraced these powerful technologies; and so must progressively-minded individuals. The taking on of memories, particularly traumatic memories, and the disenfranchisement and loss of privilege that the experience often necessitates, can have a profound effect on one's politics and one's understanding of who one's allies might be.

What I am describing here is a utopian dream, a dream where ethics and politics converge. My dream is the antithesis of the nightmare in *Strange Days*. And it is a dream that has not yet materialised. As we embark on this next century, where inevitably we will find that capitalism continues to permeate all aspects of life and culture, we must resist the temptation to throw up our arms in resignation. Commodification does not necessarily mean atomisation. Paradoxically, it can help overcome the atomising effect of private memory that Rosenzweig identifies by making memory more radically public. There will be new technologies and the further development of old ones – museums, the cinema, the Internet – and they will continue to disseminate stories and images about the past. The utopian dream that I have named prosthetic memory is a call to take seriously these technologies, these sites for the production of prosthetic memories, as they might well serve as the ground on which to construct new political alliances, based not on blood, or family or kinship, but on collective social responsibility.

Notes

1 Using standard survey practice, and random-digit dialing, they completed 808 national interviews; as a pool, the interviewees reflected the varied demographics of America. Because they were also interested in the way that minority groups articulate their relationship to the past

and to American history, they also developed three minority samples: African American, Mexican American and American Indian. For a detailed discussion of how the survey was conducted see 'Appendix 1'. Roy Rosenzweig and David Thelen, *The Presence of the Past: Popular Uses of History in American Life* (New York: Columbia University Pess, 1998), pp. 209–31.

2   Rosenzweig and Thelen, *The Presence of the* Past, p. 186. The kind of memories of the past most people favour are private ones, memories that have some personal component to them: a 71–year-old woman reflecting on World War Two does not focus on the 'patriotic narrative of the nation-state', but instead remembers that 'she learned self reliance from the war: "My husband was in that. It was a lot of heartache with both of us being young and him being away in his early twenties. I learned how to be independent and how to take care of myself."' (p. 115).

3   For more on 'prosthetic memory', see Alison Landsberg, 'Prosthetic Memory: Blade Runner and Total Recall', *Body and Society* 1: 3–4 (November 1995). Also collected in Mike Featherstone and Roger Burrows (eds), *Cyberspace/Cyberbodies/Cyberpunk: Cultures of Technological Embodiment* (London: Sage Publications, 1995), pp. 175–89, and most recently in David Bell and Barbara M. Kennedy (eds), *The Cybercultures Reader* (New York: Routledge, 2000), pp. 190–201; Alison Landsberg, 'America, the Holocaust and the Mass Culture of Memory: Towards a Radical Politics of Empathy', *New German Critique* 71 (Spring–Summer 1997), 63–86; Alison Landsberg, 'Prosthetic Memory: The Logics and Politics of Memory in Modern American Culture' (PhD dissertation, University of Chicago, 1996).

4   Max Scheler, *The Nature of Sympathy*, trans. Peter Heath, ed. W. Stark (Connecticut: Archon Books, 1970) [published 1913 (1923 was the second edn)].

5   Scheler, *The Nature of Sympathy*, p. 47.

6   *Ibid.*

7   *Ibid.*

8   Scheler, *The Nature of Sympathy*, p. 48.

9   According to the *Oxford English Dictionary*, the word sympathy first appeared in 1567 and was understood to mean 'agreement in qualities, likeness, conformity, correspondence'. In 1596, its usage reflected a new shade of meaning, not just a conformity, but a 'conformity of feelings, inclinations, or temperament, which makes persons agreeable to each other'. This sense of conformity, of adapting oneself to be like the other, or more commonly reimagining the other to conform to oneself, has for centuries been central to the meaning of sympathy.

10 The ideological problem of 'speaking for' the other has been widely

theorised in the field of subaltern studies. See, for example, Gayatri
Spivak, *In Other Worlds* (New York: Routledge, 1988).
11 Emmanuel Levinas, *Time and the Other*, trans. Richard A. Cohen
    (Pittsburgh: Duquesne University Press, 1987). This text, originally
    delivered as four lectures in 1946/47, was first published in 1948.
12 It should be noted that Scheler rejects empathy, but the 'empathy' he
    rejects sounds more like what the *Oxford English Dictionary* defines as
    sympathy. He writes, 'When all is said, the theory of empathy offers no
    grounds for assuming the existence of other selves, let alone other indi-
    viduals. For it can only serve to confirm the belief that it is *my* self
    which is present 'all over again', and never that this self is other and dif-
    ferent from my own' (p. 242). My working definition of empathy
    seems moreakin to what he calls 'fellow-feeling'.
13 'Empathy', *Oxford English Dictionary*, 2nd edn.
14 Miriam Hansen, '"With Skin and Hair": Kracauer's Theory of Film,
    Marseilles 1940', *Critical Inquiry* 19.3 (Spring 1993), 458.
15 Walter Benjamin, 'The Work of Art in the Age of Mechanical Repro-
    duction', in Benjamin, *Illuminations* (New York: Schocken, 1968),
    pp. 236–7.
16 In her powerful critique of the ideological grip of the 'heterosexual
    matrix' Judith Butler famously argues that there is no outside to the
    symbolic economy. In order to bring about change, one must work not
    outside of, but within, the existing sign system. Change is possible by
    changing how certain things signify, through what she calls redeploy-
    ment – attaching new meanings to existing concepts. See Judith Butler,
    Gender Trouble (New York: Routledge, 1990). I am indebted also to
    Daniel Miller's claim that the possibilities for social change are 'clearly
    immanent within the consumption activities of mass populations
    today'. See Daniel Miller, *Material Culture and Mass Consumption*
    (Oxford and Cambridge: Blackwell Publishers, Ltd., 1987), p. 6.
17 Miller, *Material Culture*, p. 190.
18 Stuart Hall, 'Encoding, Decoding', in Simon During (ed.), *The Cultural
    Studies Reader* (New York: Routledge, 1993), pp. 90–103.
19 Importantly, for Hall, there are three identifiable decoding positions:
    the 'dominant hegemonic position' which takes the meaning at face
    value and operates hegemonically within the dominant code, the 'nego-
    tiated code or position' which draws on both hegemonic and opposi-
    tional elements and tends to focus on situational or local meanings, and
    the 'oppositional code' in which the viewer decodes the message in
    an oppositional or 'globally contrary' way, rejecting the cultural/
    political framework in which the message was encoded, in favor of an
    'alternative framework of reference'. See Hall, 'Encoding, Decoding',
    pp. 90–103.

20 Etienne Balibar, 'What Is a Politics of the Rights of Man?', in *Masses, Classes, Ideas*, trans. James Swenson (New York: Routledge, 1996), pp. 205–20.

21 Howard Rheingold, *The Virtual Community: Finding Connection in a Computerised World* (London: Secker & Warburg, 1994), p. 5.

22 See, for example, Kevin Robins, 'Cyberspace and the World We Live In', in David Bell and Barbara M. Kennedy (eds), *The Cybercultures Reader* (New York: Rotledge, 2000), pp. 77–95; Michele Willson, 'Community in the Abstract: A Political and Ethical Dilemma?', in Bell and Kennedy (eds), *The Cybercultures Reader*, pp. 644–57; and Ziauddin Sardar, 'ALT.CIVILIZATIONS.FAQ: Cyberspace as the Darker Side of the West', in Bell and Kennedy (eds), *The Cybercultures Reader*, pp. 732–52.

23 Robins, 'Cyberspace and the World We Live In', p. 86.

24 Robins, 'Cyberspace and the World We Live In', p. 90.

25 Willson, 'Community in the Abstract', p. 655.

26 Willson, 'Community in the Abstract', p. 645. Similarly, Ziauddin Sardar condemns the Internet as yet another Western apparatus involved in the project of colonising 'Others'; cyberspace, a space charted and created firmly in the West, is inevitably inflected by the 'subconscious perceptions and prejudices, conscious fantasies and fears' (Sardar 750) of its architects.

27 The Center for History and New Media, at George Mason University, for example, is dedicated to the furthering of historical knowledge online. See http://chnm.gmu.edu.

8

'Forget the Alamo': history, legend and memory in John Sayles' *Lone Star*

Neil Campbell

> History is inseparable from the earth [*terre*], struggle is underground
> [*sous terre*], and, if we want to grasp an event, we must not show it, we
> must not pass along the event, but plunge into it, go through all the
> geological layers that are its internal history . . . to connect it to the
> silent layers of earth which make up its true continuity . . . It is there-
> fore now the visual image, the stratigraphic landscape, which in turn
> resists the speech-act and opposes it with a piling-up.
>
> (Gilles Deleuze)[1]

John Sayles' *Lone Star* examines 'life beneath the ashes or behind the
mirrors' by excavating the 'geological layers' of what is remembered, who remembers and how these memories are constructed and
recycled to form a particular history within the border community
of Frontera ('frontier'), Texas, 'a pretty lively mix' of ethnic histories.[2] The US/Mexico borderlands are a 'kind of dysfunctional family
. . . [with] all these secrets that go way, way back' and yet, as in the
US itself, a dominant history has emerged by 'generalized assent . . .
to regulate the present . . . [until] for better or for worse, history
increasingly became the discipline of memory' and the burier of
secrets.[3] *Lone Star* begins in the earth, its pre-title sequence shows
two soldiers collecting spent shells at a disused firing range stum-
bling across a skeleton, a Mason's ring and a sheriff's badge buried
in the desert. Their conversation jokily mentions the 'Coronado
Expedition', locating the significance of colonial history to this film
and suggesting its continued relevance to the present day lives of this
border community; 'This country's seen a good few disagreements
over the years', we are told. Digging for relics of the past, to transform into art-objects of the future (the bullets will make sculptures),
one comments, 'You live in a place, you should learn something
about it'. In their archaeological resurrection of the 'buried' and

'forgotten' they set the tone for the film's interest in sites of memory and their relationships to official history, as well as to its critique and expansion via 'learning' about place through its stories and uncovered memories. Similar 'collectors' throughout the film, like Otis Payne, Wesley Songbird, Bunny and Sam Deeds himself contribute to this 'piling-up' of alternative, buried voices and versions of the past, providing a framework for Sayles' reconsideration of relations of memory and history. As the skeleton of ex-sheriff Charlie Wade is exhumed from the desert, Sayles enacts a process of revision, layer by layer through the community's 'stratigraphic landscape', that 'conceives historical understanding as an after-life of that which is understood, whose pulse can still be felt in the present'.[4]

Through these acts of retrieval, Sayles' film can be seen as in dialogue with the 'culture wars' debates of the 1980s–90s in which issues of identity politics, multiculturalism and the representation of US history came to the fore, often embedded in the looser exchanges and controversies over so-called political correctness. George Lipsitz cites Lynne Cheney, E. D. Hirsch, Allan Bloom and others, who began to attack new forms of history teaching for betraying particular established knowledges about America and its past. As Cheney wrote in 1988, history textbooks needed to be like those of the 'early decades of the century . . . filled with stories – the magic of myths, fables, and tales of heroes', providing 'symbols to share . . . help[ing] us all, no matter how diverse our backgrounds, feel part of a common undertaking'.[5] Cheney's belief that national identity was best served by the articulation of history as 'heroic' and unidirectional was at odds with the growing emphasis upon multicultural representations insisting upon 'the complex realities of American history itself'.[6] A similar debate emerged specifically around the way American Western history was represented in 1991 at the art exhibit in Washington, D.C., 'The West As America: Reinterpreting Images of the Frontier', in which the very 'heroic', 'shared' and 'common undertaking' that Cheney appreciated in the traditional version of westward expansion as the producer of national identity, was re-cast as a quasi-imperial project whose artifacts were in need of a revisionist interrogation. As William Truettner, the curator of the exhibition, put it, 'myth functions to control history, to shape it in text or image as an ordained sequence of events. The world is rendered pure in the process; complexity and contradictions give way to order, clarity, and direction', and, therefore, it is vital to examine these mythic formations and the ideological assumptions they maintain.[7] Sayles' film responds to these tensions within American cultural life re-situating the debates over identity, memory and myth on the frontier itself where a multiplicity of histories collide and struggle for prominence in a society traditionally dominated by the very ideological vision of the West that the exhibition sought to critique. It was for these reasons that *Lone Star* was referred to as a 'prophetic allegory' by Mary Helen Washington in her Presidential Address to the American Studies Association in 1997, offering a new approach to studying America in which the 'differences of language, politics, historical vision' were not allowed 'to dissolve in a soothing movement toward consensus', but instead 'presents the multicultural moment as one of tension, struggle, discomfort and disagreement'.[8] The following year Janice Radway re-iterated the significance of *Lone Star* by using it too as a locus for her questioning of the meaning of 'American' within American Studies and the possibility of an interdisciplinary practice of 'intricate interdependencies' reflected in the 'cultural menudo' of Sayles' frontier community.[9] All these examples testify to the centrality of *Lone Star* as a document engaging in a popular dramatisation and exploration of major cultural themes of history, legend and memory and how they might relate closely to wider redefinitions of power relations and personal/national identity within the shifting cultural landscapes of the USA.

Lone Star is a story of multiple borders, from the ever-present geopolitical southwest border, to those drawn through the diverse lives that intersect within the community of Frontera. As Sayles said, '[i]n a personal sense, a border is where you draw a line and say, "This is where I end and somebody else begins". In a metaphorical sense, it can be any of the symbols that we erect between one another – sex, class, race, age'.[10] The film interrogates these spatial and communal tensions as complex contact zones, 'space[s] of colonial encounter' where 'disparate cultures meet, clash and grapple with each other' and 'subjects are constituted in and by their relations to each other . . . in terms of co-presence, interaction, interlocking understandings and practices'.[11] Indeed, the film ultimately questions the rigidity of these borders and frontiers by demonstrating that their apparent authority can be challenged by individual choices and collective, communal change. Annette Kolodny, in the spirit of revisionist history, argued that 'both geography and chronology must be viewed as fluid and ongoing, or as a continuously unfolding palimpsest' in which 'hybridised forms and tropes constitute the focus of textual analysis'.[12] For her, the revised 'frontier' breaks down 'our grand obsessions' about territorial identities, separated lives and unrelated histories and re-thinks border space as 'that liminal landscape of changing meanings on which distinct human cultures first encounter one another's "otherness" and appropriate, accommodate, or domesticate it through language . . . [in an] inherently unstable locus of . . . environmental transitions and cultural interpenetrations'.[13] Sayles' characters are perpetually engaged with the consequences of living amid centuries of 'intercultural crossing and mixing', through which particular stories and memories become 'official' whilst others become marginalised.[14]

Central to this '*transfrontera* contact zone' is the mixing of history and memory and the 'borders' that run between them.[15] The notion that history is fixed and final, 'out there' and official, written down in textbooks and taught from one generation to the next, is questioned through the intersecting and contradictory memories of Frontera's multicultural citizens whose different 'versions' structure the complex layering of the film. Memory, according to Sturken, is always 'entangled' with history; 'Indeed, there is so much traffic across the borders of cultural memory and history that in many cases it may be futile to maintain a distinction between them'.[16] Sayles' film articulates this 'border traffic' showing how official history is dialogised by alternative versions and counter-memories that emerge in the unravelling of a murder mystery in which the subject under enquiry is much more than the dead sheriff, Charlie Wade. The film's sheriff-detective-historian, Sam Deeds, delves into the past, as history and memory, to discover that there are many 'boundary crossings' between the two making 'true distinctions' impossible.[17] Hence, he discovers that memory, as Raphael Samuel argues, 'far from being merely a passive receptacle or storage system, an image bank of the past, is rather an active, shaping force . . . dynamic' and 'what it contrives symptomatically to forget is as important as what it remembers . . . [for] it is dialectically related to historical thought, rather than being some kind of negative other to it'.[18] In making these discoveries, Sam's own memory-journey directs the audience into a wider reconsideration of borders and of the nature of history itself.

De Certeau claims 'the historian is no longer a person who shapes an empire . . . [but] comes to circulate *around* acquired rationalizations

. . . works in the margins . . . becomes a prowler. In a society gifted
at generalization, endowed with powerful centralizing strategies, the
historian moves in the direction of frontiers of great regions already
exploited . . .'.[19] He theorises the 'historian' as 'playing on the borderlines', discovering 'lapses in the syntax constructed by the law of a
place',[20] just like the hesitant and confused figure of Sam Deeds often
filmed 'on the edge of things, looking on, observing . . . unsure of
himself, so often off-center' and pushed to the margins of the actual
frame to underline his position.[21] Sam is a man haunted by his dead
father, literally and metaphorically the 'law', the ex-sheriff Buddy
Deeds, who in the official, dominant, white history of Frontera is a
'legend', 'a unique individual' with a reputation born from a benign
dictatorship in which a kind of equality was maintained within very
strict rules about race and power. As his ex-deputy Hollis tells
Sam, 'Mexicans that know, that *remember*, understand what Buddy
was to their people'. Sam's efforts to explore the 'lapses' and gaps in
this 'official' story involve him in the uncovering of multiple and contested memories that relate to the whole community and its complex,
layered history.

Sayles visualises this entangled, layered 'after-life' of history,
legend and memory through techniques such as intertextuality,
superimposition, montage, seamless transitional editing, a
hybridised soundtrack commenting on the film's narrative, reitera-
tive, liminal spaces within the film (drive-in, café, school, river,
roadside stall, borderlands), as well as the complex web of characters and relationships that enhance the central themes of the film –
secret histories, new identities and hybrid communal relations. For
example, in demonstrating the relationships of the past 'whose pulse
can still be felt in the present', Sayles edits without 'a cut or a dissolve' because they 'say this is a border, and the things on opposite
sides of the border are meant to be different in some way, and I
wanted to erase that border and show that these people are still
reacting to things in the past'.[22] Thus, as Hollis tells Sam in the present his version of Buddy's 'stand-off' with Wade, the camera
focuses on a bowl of tortillas on the table becoming a bowl in the
past as the camera re-focuses upon Buddy. The sequence ends with
Buddy asking for a 'cerveza', and as the camera moves back into the
present, Hollis uses the very same words. In 'erasing' the border
between past and present cinematically, Sayles shows that history
and memory are alive in the present, informing and shaping the

choices people make, so that it feels 'almost not like a memory – you don't hear the harp playing. It's *here*'.[23] 'It was [said Sayles] a way of suggesting that kind of shared past that's still in the town, even though it's not written history.'[24] Thus every relationship in the film is steeped in the entanglements of history and memory with much of the drama based on how these diverse people deal with its 'weight' – 'do I want to carry this? Is [the history] good, or is it possible to say "I'm going to start from scratch? Do I still live my life in reaction to – for or against – my father?"'[25]

Similarly, *Lone Star* deliberately echoes other texts and genres, from classic westerns, border movies, film noir, murder mysteries, to Mexican-American writing, such as Americo Paredes' *With His Pistol in His Hand*.[26] Sayles has said that the film 'is more film noir than a Western, where the story turns back on the detective . . . But I hope it's more like Raymond Chandler, where the trip is the point, and not "Who Shot the Sheriff?"'[27] The film investigates and unravels a 'legend', Buddy Deeds, a reference to John Ford's reflective *The Man Who Shot Liberty Valance*, and yet pays homage to Orson Welles' *Touch of Evil* with the border as a space of complex exchange and porosity, where corruption and the law are entwined like the very histories of the people who live there. *Lone Star* also refers ironically to the events of the Alamo as a mythic historic marker of border relations, especially John Wayne's *The Alamo*, with its insistent myth of white sacrificial victory over the duplicitous and cowardly Mexicans, encouraging its audience to both 'remember' and 'forget' its importance. In contrast, *With His Pistol in His Hand* examined the 'corrido' of Gregorio Cortez, a Mexican border hero, to reveal 'his story, the fact and the legend of it', demonstrating how myths emerged on both sides of the borderline, 'partaking of influences from both cultures' and with 'cultural conflict [seen as] many-layered'.[28] The multi-layered border culture is reflected in and illuminated by the depth of reference that Sayles builds into the genre memory that its audience draw upon to comprehend its rich, complex and unfinished history. Like the action that opens the film, once we begin to dig into the past of the border country or the text itself, what is unearthed is layered and interconnected rather than an epic, grand narrative about heroic events and last stands.

Such layerings create a 'complex movie where the effect is more cumulative than linear', since Sayles is not providing a direct route through to a single conclusion, but offering instead his Chandler-like 'trip' in which the audience engages with a host of interconnected, complementary and simultaneous elements.[29] There is no simple borderline to divide past and present, truth or legend, history or memory since these ambiguous elements are woven together; 'You know', says Sayles, 'history has the word *story* in it.'[30] In uncovering and gathering these stories throughout the film, the audience is displaced beyond the borders of conventional historical frameworks with preferred and approved versions, encouraging choice and the possibility of alternative notions of what constitutes history and identity. This unsettling of history is represented in the film by Sayles' disorientating visual techniques, like the seamless editing already discussed, and in his use of acute camera angles, low shots, expressionist close-ups, superimposition and dissolves that draw us critically into the many layers of Frontera's stories.

In a key scene Sam is represented undergoing a layered memory-journey, a microcosm of the broader 'trip' represented in the film, as he sifts through the records, notes and dates of his father's 'history', as if the detective is becoming the historian delving into the interconnected archives of the border, emphasised by the lines that he draws between different elements of the past. The layered, superimposed dissolves swirl around from all angles integrating Sam's face with the maps, written, official records and his own scribbled jottings, binding his 'personal', inner memory with that of the border itself as the blues soundtrack links it all still further to both Wade and to Otis (connected through 'R and B' in the film). As the sequence returns to Sam's actual office, the words of the Mexican janitor echo across all we have just seen, 'Time marches on', reminding us that too much dwelling in the past can only stifle the future.

The weight of this past is, however, guarded by the older, white, male generation, of Hollis the Mayor and Fenton, a local businessman, who resent change and display a racist dislike of the erosion of their dominance on the border: 'They call everything else in the country after Martin Luther King and we can't have one measly courthouse [named after Buddy] . . . it's bad enough that all the street names are in Spanish.' When Sam reminds them that 'they were here first', he replies, 'Well then let's call it after Big Chief Shit-in-the-Bucket . . . He had the Mexes beat by centuries.' This exchange reveals the complex history of the cultural landscape that Sayles is keen to explore in the film:

A lot of what this movie is about is history and what we do with it. Do we use it to hit each other? Is it something that drags us down? Is it something that makes us feel good? You can have six different people look at the Alamo and they have six different stories about what actually happened and what its significance was. The same goes for your personal history. At what point do you say about your parents that was them, this is me and I take responsibility for myself from this day on. That's also what this movie is about.[31]

For *Lone Star* is about 'the burden of history' shown through the interrelated narratives of Sam, Pilar and Delmore, 'and about whether you can make the choice to not carry it, and whether that's a good thing or not'.[32] This is dramatised when a school meeting discusses how history should be taught, bringing into sharp focus issues of memory and cultural tension. 'You're tearing down the heritage, tearing down the memory of those people who fought and died for this country', one Anglo parent says, whilst a Mexican replies, 'We fought and died for this land too. We fought the US army, the Texas Rangers.' 'Yeah, and you lost buddy . . . Winners get the bragging rights, that's how it goes.' Pilar, the history teacher, is accused of breaking away from the official 'textbook'; 'the way she's teaching it she's got everything switched around . . . her version is not . . . what we set as the standard'. As Mexican voices call for 'historical perspective', someone shouts 'you call it history, I call it propaganda and they might have their own story of the Alamo on the other side but we're not on the other side'.

Pilar's defence of her teaching is central to the position of the film itself and recalls a particular response to the 'culture wars' of the 1990s: 'I've only been trying to get across part of the complexity of our situation down here, cultures coming together in both negative and positive ways.' This, however, can only be accepted in a limited manner by the meeting: 'If you're talking of food and music . . . I have no problem with that, but when you start changing who did what to who . . .'. For this is a community where such 'complexity' is seen by many as a rejection of an essential identity based upon rooted, fundamental, national myths about Manifest Destiny and, therefore, about the loss of local power and status. Pilar's revisionism of public and personal 'his-story' highlights how gender 'borders' are also critiqued in this film and indicative of the wider social changes taking place throughout these communities as old, established, patriarchal regimes begin to fragment. Pilar is a 'pillar' of the community like her mother, Mercedes, a successful, independent business woman despite having entered the US illegally, later seen aiding border-crossers to make a new start in America. And yet for much of the film Mercedes denies her past, as she has severed her connections to Mexican history and blocked out all her memories of the crossing and of the loss of her young husband Eladio at the hands of Wade. But as ever in the film, memory returns, provoked by contact with the actual present, for as Mercedes chooses whether or not to help a new generation of wetbacks, it triggers her memory of crossing and draws her to a point of reconciliation with that past. Although she has no desire to go 'home' to Mexico with her daughter and grandson, who has a 'Tejano roots thing', Mercedes will ultimately choose to help Enrique and his fiancée cross to the US, showing the 'mercy' her name suggests.

Similarly, Sam investigates the history of his father, a local hero whose life has taken on an almost religious, mythic significance, underlined by Hollis's comments that 'Your father was my salvation' and Fenton's line 'Your mother was a saint'. Elsewhere, Sam is told 'Sheriff Deeds is dead, you're just sheriff junior', to which he replies, 'That's the story of my life'. It is against this powerful hagiography that Sam's interrogation of the past revises both his father's and his own life-story whilst revealing the community's underlying relationships. Self-consciously echoing *The Man Who Shot Liberty Valance*, we are told how Buddy was a 'goddamned legend' with 'the finest sense of justice of any man I ever knew', but rather than 'print' that legend, *Lone Star* investigates it, unravelling the relations that constitute the secret history of the Deeds family and the border family/community. The surname suggests 'an act, something done, an exploit' and the 'written evidence of a legal transaction', whilst echoing the proverb 'the deeds of the father are visited on the son'.[33] Sam's investigation into the 'deeds' of his family history begins with Hollis's memory developing into a deeper examination of interviews, written documents, archives, family records and forensic evidence, as he pieces together his alternative history. In this, Sayles dramatises a version of what Lipsitz calls 'counter-memory':

> [A] way of remembering and forgetting that starts with the local, the immediate, and the personal. Unlike historical narratives that begin with the totality . . . counter-memory starts with the particular and the specific and then builds outward . . . [it] looks to the past for the hidden histories excluded from dominant narratives. But unlike myths that

seek to detach events and actions from the fabric of any larger history, counter-memory forces revision of existing histories by supplying new perspectives about the past . . .[It] embodies aspects of myth and aspects of history, but it retains an enduring suspicion of both categories.[34]

In 'countering' the history and memory of his father, Sam acts against the monolithic 'totality' of his legend, uncovering the 'the local, the immediate and the personal' and all the 'hidden histories' clinging to that reputation and replayed throughout the film by the likes of Hollis, Fenton and Otis. Sam's paternal investigation reveals the connections across the community just as Sayles' film interweaves the various stories that echo and relate to each other both directly and indirectly. He has said, 'the best metaphor for history is fathers and sons. Inheriting your cultural history, your hatreds and alliances . . . is what you're supposed to get from your father in a patriarchal society.'[35] Of course, in *Lone Star* many parent/child relationships reassess 'history', but the film is drawn to fathers as the source of patriarchal authority and control, symbolic of the genealogical order of the border country and embodied in the 'dead fathers' of Buddy Deeds and Charlie Wade. In a flashback establishing Wade's brutality over the young Otis, he says: 'You learn to know your place *son*, this isn't Houston', reminds him that he 'sent his father to the Farm once' and finally, when pointing his gun at Otis says, 'Come to Papa'. Power, authority, the control of history itself, lay in the hands of real and symbolic fathers, as this scene reminds us, drawing obvious parallels with the master/slave relations invoked by Wade over Otis. Later in the film Sam's ex-wife, Bunny, is represented as a sedated, neurotic woman still ruled by the 'master/father' and unable to break free of his patriarchal control. 'I've only got my little girl now, she's my life-line', she mutters, voicing her father's words, adding, while supposedly commenting on a weight-lifter on the television, '[i]magine all that weight pressing down, it'd be hard to breathe, hard to swallow'. The weight of the past, the dead weight of the father in the lives of Sam and Bunny, the film suggests, may or may not be overcome to allow change to take place.

Otis Payne, the African-American bar-owner, brutalised by the 'master/father' Wade, in turn rejects his own young son Delmore, who returns as the new colonel at the local Army base. Delmore's life is conditioned by his surrogate Army 'family' with clear rules and lines to follow, revealed after a shooting at 'Big O's', when he

makes an 'official visit' to question his father. In contrast to Delmore's 'spit and polish' officialdom, Otis interjects memories that
present an alternative history of Frontera's blacks, since 'over the
years this is the one place that's always been there . . . There's Holi-
ness Church or Big O's'. To which Delmore replies, 'And people
make a choice?' and Otis answers, 'Most of them choose *both*. You
see it's not like there's a borderline between the good people and the
bad people – you're not on either one side or the other.' This pragmatic version of social practice shows how people attempt to live
with contingency and the 'fuzzy logic' of border cultures, 'choosing
both' as a way of living with the multiple and hybrid whilst refusing
the arbitrary historical lines of 'demarcation' that divide people and
keep them apart. Memories and unrecorded histories cut through
and coexist with the official lines and disciplined authority of history
represented by Delmore's military bearing, and as with Sam's delving into Buddy's life, a 'counter-memory' is formed that 'embodies
aspects of myth and aspects of history' whilst retaining 'an enduring
suspicion of both categories'.[36] Delmore leaves, saying 'You'll get
official notification when I make my decision', asserting his power
over his father and simultaneously authorising a particularly regi-
mented and systematised view of history 'by the book', and yet the
scene has also presented something countering this, offering the
audience a more complex rendition of cultural relations.

Delmore's son, Chet, inherits these tensions, caught between a
disciplinarian father and a 'legendary' grandfather whose image he
knows only from the label for his barbeque sauce. Disinterested by
Pilar's history lesson, as it seems removed from and irrelevant to his
own experience, Chet like Sam, must uncover the history of and
division within his own family and see its complex relationships to
everyday life. When Chet visits Otis's Black Seminole Indian
museum, a hybrid mix of escaped slaves and Native Americans
whose 'border' identities reveal notions of origin or essence inadequate, he asks about one John Horse/Juan Caballo, 'is he a black
man or an Indian?' 'He's *both*', answers Otis, echoing the earlier
scene with Delmore, since, 'Blood only means what you let it'. In his
own way, Otis asserts choice, self-determination and rejects the mas-
tery of history to define our lives as he had earlier resisted Wade's
assumed power and authority. If the obsession with 'blood', origins
and 'history' is so reductionist it cripples the ability to live together
and build decent communities, then what has been lost is a balance

that acknowledges, values and uses the past without being imprisoned and conditioned by it at the expense of new relationships and alliances. Chet comments, 'My Father says that from the day you're born, you start from scratch, no breaks and no excuses', which is another extreme position that the film argues against, for it suggests that the past has no significance and has to be screened out. The film's view is rather that the past has to be known, lived and worked through – like the legend of Buddy Deeds – before people can choose to move on.

However, there are borders everywhere that divide people arbitrarily and deny them the opportunities to develop identities and relations, epitomised by men like Wade and Buddy, agents of official history, who in different ways kept the lines clearly drawn. From a Mexican perspective, when Sam crosses the border, he's told, 'a bird flying South, you think he sees this line? You think half way across that line they're thinking different? Why should a man?' Whereas an Anglo bar tender longs for the clarity of segregation:

> we are in a state of crisis, the lines of demarcation are getting fuzzier and to run a successful civilization, you have got to have your lines of demarcation between right and wrong, between this-un and that-un, your Daddy understood that . . . people don't want their salt and sugar in the same jar . . . you're the last white sheriff this town's gonna see . . . this is it right here Sam, this bar is the last stand.

In the bar our attention is drawn to the Army couple, one black, one white, as an example of the changing racial borders of the town and the nation, not in the terms outlined by the bar tender, but rather as a sign of possibility. Ironically, Buddy helped to make the lines of demarcation fuzzier because of his relationship with Mercedes and the birth of Pilar, even though he claimed otherwise in his public life. His hypocrisy reveals the countering layers that the film uncovers and which De Certeau, echoing Deleuze, defined as the nature of history and place:

> The kind of difference that defines every place is not on the order of a juxtaposition but rather takes the form of imbricated strata . . . The revolutions of history, economic mutations, demographic mixtures lie in layers within it, and remain there, hidden in customs, rites, and spatial practices . . . This place, on its surface, seems to be a collage. In reality, in its depth it is ubiquitous. A piling up of heterogeneous places.[37]

Sam's subsequent relationship with Pilar means that the fuzzy lines of the border run right through their lives to the point that their incest becomes a metaphor for the hybrid mixing taking place throughout the region. Just as the multi-layered soundtrack shifts seamlessly between Tejano music, to mariachi, rock and roll, R and B, country and western and back again as a measure of the cultural mix of the border, so the film explores the implications of a world with no boundaries in which there is an 'imbricated' 'piling up' into a sophisticated cultural 'collage'. In the scene that reconciles Sam and Pilar at her mother's empty café, they dance to Freddy Fender's 'Desde que conosco', the English version of which, 'Since I met you baby', was playing when Delmore met his father earlier in the film, triggering the shift towards reconciliation in the film's central relationships. In a conversation after they have made love in Sam's apartment, Pilar comments that 'There's nothing on the walls. No pictures', to which he replies, 'There's nothing I want to look back on.' It is as if the past has had no dynamic relationship with the present; 'Like your story's over', says Pilar, borrowing words from her son Amado earlier about her own life. At this shared recognition of emptiness and reconciled to their new love, Pilar adds 'It [his story] isn't [over] . . . not by a long shot', for as the film asserts, one cannot be imprisoned by the past, but instead one must comprehend and use it in order to move on – to continue the 'story' of your life.

Following this scene of reconciliation between the past, present and future, Sayles instigates other related compacts; between Otis and Delmore, when the latter sees the 'shrine' to him at Big O's home; between Mercedes and her past when she helps Enrique's fiancée to safety in the US; and between Chet and Delmore when the latter softens to both his son and his father, accepting that the 'Army isn't for everyone' and they might have a barbecue to reconcile the family. The central reconciliation is, of course, Sam and Buddy's as he goes to Hollis and gives his 'version', concluding with 'Buddy Deeds was a murderer', and then hears the truth from Otis. The creation of the 'legend' is explained, and as Otis says, 'As time went on, people liked the story we told better than anything the truth might have been.' It is now up to Sam to act, to make a choice as to whether or not Wade's murder by Hollis should be revealed, but he opts for silence, to bury the truth and allow the legend to remain: 'It's just one of your unsolved mysteries', he says. The knowledge of the past and the delving into communal and personal memory has brought Sam and others to these moments of reconciliation not as an act of closure, but as the possibility of beginning, for new relationships commencing out of this joining of past and present.

Sam and Pilar's reconciled love provides a productive revision of the oldest taboo of miscegenation across races and suggests a new hybrid American identity, a mixing of bloods, not in war, violence and 'disagreement', but in hope and renewed possibility as an ironic, revisionist, Edenic couple heading a symbolic new 'family'. The final scene of the film is played out in an abandoned drive-in cinema, with Pilar and Sam looking up at the blank screen as she asks 'when does the movie begin?' It is a key site of memory in the film, being their place of love and denial – it is here that Buddy found them and broke up their relationship – and also a reminder of communal collective experience of the movies where different peoples came together to enjoy film. Earlier in a flashback sequence, the drive-in, ironically called 'Vaquero', reminding us of the Mexican roots of the 'American' cowboy, is playing *Black Mama, White Mama*, a film about a black and a white prisoner hand-cuffed and escaping from jail, chosen by Sayles because 'it's about people of different races being chained together whether they want it or not'.[38] Here, Buddy, denying such hybrid relations, splits up Pilar and Sam, reinforcing the cultural and racial borders that both the place and the movie being watched challenge to some extent. Of course, Sayles' 'movie' itself is a complex revision of the old myths projected endlessly onto this screen in the past, and Pilar, who finds out about their incest in this scene, calls for a clean break, a new beginning: 'We'll start from scratch' [linking her back to Chet earlier] . . . All that other stuff, all that history, to Hell with it right? Forget the Alamo'. Looking up at the blank screen ravaged by time passing, Sayles creates 'the sense that they are going to go forward, something could be projected on that thing. But they're not the fourteen-year-old kids that they were. They've had some damage. Things have fallen away. They're different people'.[39] This 'difference' comes with the knowledge that will let them escape Frontera in the same way that a movie traditionally offers its audience an 'escape' from the everyday through the imaginative 'free space' of the cinema encouraging 'ways of asking and answering questions' that 'reposition us for the future by reshaping our memories of the past'.[40] Pilar and Sam look up to the screen ready to 'project' their new vision upon it, ready to take over the role of the movie as the 'escape' from the everyday borders and restrictions of their lives and in the creative imagining of alternative identities. As the film *Lone Star* ends, Sayles suggests that the latent possibility inherent in the experience of movies can be carried forward into life itself – that is, into the imaginative reconstruction of identity, community and nation.

As Sayles has said, 'American culture is not monolingual or monoracial. It's always been a mix', and in this moment of decision Sam and Pilar 'choose to cross that border of moral opinion' and assert this new 'family'.[41] Their incipient migratory movement and willingness to break the 'rule' and social taboo are signs of a wider recognition of the necessity for that very dialogical, hybrid mix that Sayles sees as fundamentally American. As if to directly respond to the kind of one-dimensional notions of identity and nation associated with conservative historians and theorists, Sayles allows Sam and Pilar a 'second life' as an anti-essentialist identity forged from movements and migrations rather than formed by a single and rooted attachment to one place.[42] The territorialism and essentialism that the film works against is further challenged as their 'new beginning' begins with a 'line of flight', a Deleuzian 'deterritorialisation' in which their identities are re-formed as acts of hybrid 'becoming'.[43]

In Sayles' new history, knowing about the past is vital as a way forward rather than as something to dwell upon or be imprisoned by, existing as part of a multifaceted spatial appreciation of living in the West with its many stories and many peoples. The film challenges a world of borderlines and the oppressive weight of 'dead' fathers, and proposes a more productive, imbricated way of living where the past and present interconnect within hybrid communities and 'enables other positions to emerge . . .displaces the histories that constitute it, and sets up new structures of authority . . .[that give rise to] to something different, something new and unrecognisable, a new area of negotiation of meaning and representation'.[44] In these postcolonial borderlands, Sayles creates a sense of optimistic newness, of Sam and Pilar as hybrids on 'the cutting edge of translation and negotiation, the *in-between space*', about to begin a life somewhere in the New West by displacing the old histories and prejudices and commencing 'something different, something new'.[45]

Stephen Cook writes that 'Frontera is not unlike a forest whose roots have overlapped and grafted. One may not tear out any tree without damaging the others', and indeed one might go further to argue that Sayles' layered histories suggest that 'roots' in the final analysis are unsubtle tools to define the complex subtleties of border identities seeing in the 'overlapped and grafted' rather more of the 'rhizomatic' as defined by Deleuze and Guattari as 'a set of relations not separable from each other'.[46] Indeed, Chicana Gloria Anzaldua's optimism for the future is based on a similar belief that 'There will be a hybridity of equal parts instead of a graft and a major tree'.[47] For her, identity

> is an arrangement or series of clusters, a kind of stacking or layering of selves, horizontal and vertical layers, the geography of selves made up of different communities you inhabit . . . Where these spaces overlap is nepantla, the Borderlands. Identity is process-in-the-making . . . you shift, cross the border from one to the other.[48]

Anzaldua's 'nepantla' is an 'in-between' space that facilitates transformation since within it, as in *Lone Star*, traditionally assumed and fixed borders break down, compelling us to find new ways of defining ourselves and our communities. The forbidden or taboo (like the incest motif and the hidden histories in the film) ruptures the smooth surfaces of the everyday, forming an 'interface' so 'in the cracks between worlds and realities . . . changes in consciousness can occur. In this shifting space of transitions, we morph, adapt to new cultural realities'.[49] Through the retrieval of memory and the reconstruction of Frontera's multiple histories, Sayles' film reaches points of knowledge and reconciliation from which choices can be made about living with the past rather than in its shadow and about identity as a process rather than a fixed and rooted essence, for ultimately '[w]e can and must visit the past, but we do not have to live there, no, not anymore'.[50]

Notes

1 Gilles Deleuze, *Cinema 2* (London: The Athlone Press, 1994), p. 25.
2 Deleuze, *Cinema 2*, pp. 256–7.
3 Diane Carson (ed.), *John Sayles Interviews* (Jackson: University of Mississippi, 1999), p. 203; and Richard Terdiman, *Present Past: Modernity and Memory Crisis* (Ithaca and London: Cornell University Press, 1993), p. 31.
4 Walter Benjamin, *One-Way Street* (London: Verso, 1997), p. 352.
5 George Lipsitz, *Time Passages: Collective Memory and American Popular Culture*. (Minneapolis: University of Minnesota Press, 1990), pp. 24–5.
6 Lipsitz, *Time Passages*, p. 27.

7   William Truettner (ed.), *The West America: Reinterpreting Images of the Frontier*. (Washington, DC: Smithsonian, 1991), p. 40.

8   Mary Helen Washington, '"Disturbing the Peace: What Happens to American Studies If You Put African American Studies at the Center?": Presidential Address to the American Studies Association, 29 October 1997', *American Quarterly*, 50: 1, (March 1998), p. 16.

9   Janice Radway, '"What's in a Name?" Presidential Address to the American Studies Association, 20 November 1998', *American Quarterly*, 51: 1 (1999), 6.

10   Carson (ed.), *John Sayles Interviews*, p. 210.

11   Mary Louise Pratt, *Imperial Eyes: Travel Writing and Transculturation* (London: Routledge, 1995), pp. 6–7.

12   Annette Kolodny, 'Letting Go Our Grand Obsessions: Notes Towards a New History of the American Frontiers', *American Literature*, 64: 1, March 1992, 9.

13   Kolodny, 'Letting Go', pp. 9–10.

14   J. D. Saldivar, *Border Matters: Remapping American Cultural Studies* (Berkeley: University of California, 1997), p. 11.

15   Saldivar, *Border Matters*, p. 13.

16   Marita Sturken, *Tangled Memories: The Vietnam War, The AIDS Epidemic, and the Politics of Remembering* (Berkeley: University of California Press, 1997), p. 5.

17   Sturken, *Tangled Memories*, p. 6.

18   Raphael Samuel, *Theatres of Memory* (London: Verso, 1994), p. x.

19   Michel De Certeau, *The Writing of History* (New York: Columbia University Press, 1988), p. 79.

20   De Certeau, *Writing of History*, pp. 85, 4.

21   Tod Lippy, 'Writing and Directing *Lone Star*', www.scenariomag.com/interviews/sayles.html

22   Carson (ed.), *John Sayles Interviews,* p. 204.

23   *Ibid.*

24   Lippy, 'Writing and Directing *Lone Star*', p. 4.

25   Carson (ed.), *John Sayles Interviews,* p. 204.

26   Americo Paredes, *With His Pistol in his Hand: A Border Ballad and Its Hero* (Austin: University of Texas Press, 1986).

27   R. Pride, 'John Sayles', in *Hollywood Scriptwriter*, www.hollywoodscriptwriter.com/saylesuncut.html, p. 3.

28   Paredes, *With His Pistol in His Hand*, p. 247, and quoted in Saldivar, *Border Matters*, p. 41.

29   Lippy, p. 13.

30   Gavin Smith (ed.), *Sayles On Sayles* (London: Faber and Faber, 1998), p. 217.

31   Johns Sayles, 'Interview at Cannes', www.filmscouts.com/films/lon-sta.asp

32 Lippy, 'Writing and Directing *Lone Star*', p. 3.
33 Smith (ed.), *Sayles On Sayles*, p. 226.
34 Lipsitz, *Time Passages*, p. 213.
35 Carson (ed.), *John Sayles Interviews*, p. 214.
36 Lipsitz, *Time Passages*, p. 213.
37 Michel De Certeau, *The Practice of Everyday Life* (Berkeley: University of California Press, 1988), p. 201.
38 Smith (ed.), *Sayles on Sayles*, p. 228.
39 *Ibid.*
40 Lipsitz, *Time Passages*, pp. 164–5.
41 Carson (ed.), *Interviews*, p. 213, p. 216.
42 Smith (ed.), *Sayles on Sayles*, p. 225.
43 See G. Deleuze and F. Guattari, *A Thousand Plateaus* (London: The Athlone Press, 1992).
44 Homi Bhabha, 'The Third Space', in J. Rutherford (ed.), *Identity, Community, Culture, Difference* (London: Lawrence and Wishart, 1990), p. 211.
45 Homi Bhabha, *The Location of Culture* (London: Routledge, 1994), p. 39.
46 Stephen Cook, 'The New West in John Sayles' *Lone Star*: Texas as a Mirror of California', Unpublished Paper at Western American Literature Association Conference, Sacramento, 1999, 1–17, p. 16. G. Deleuze and C. Parnet, *Dialogues* (London: The Athlone Press, 1987), p. vii. See also Deleuze and Guattari, *A Thousand Plateaus*.
47 Gloria Anzaldua, *Interviews/Entrevistas* (London: Routledge, 2000), p. 278.
48 Anzaldua, *Interviews/Entrevistas*, pp. 238–9.
49 Anzaldua, *Interviews/Entrevistas*, p. 280.
50 Cook, 'The New West', p. 17.

III

Mediating memory

9

'Mortgaged to music': new retro movies in 1990s Hollywood cinema

Philip Drake

> The most powerful cultural force operating in the seventies was definitely nostalgia . . . it will be impossible, twenty years hence, to revive the seventies; they have no style of their own.
>
> (James Monaco)[1]

> History is the subject of a structure whose site is not homogenous, empty time, but time filled by the presence of the now.
>
> (Walter Benjamin)[2]

As every decade passes, so claims about how it will be recalled and re-remembered emerge. Looking back to the past solidifies years into publicly memorialised decades, reconstructing the past as an episodic narrative. This narrative dramatises the relationship between past and present, constructing a memory of the past through the recycling of particular iconography that metonymically comes to represent it. Particular fashions, music and visual images are memorialised, and become subject to reinterpretation in the present. Memories of the 1970s in the 1980s, for example, are quite different from those of the 1990s, as James Monaco's remark above illustrates. Thus, whilst the 1970s has proved a rich source of nostalgia for popular culture in the 1990s, commentators in the 1980s saw the 1970s as a decade obsessively concerned with recycling the past and hence lacking its own historicity. In this chapter I shall argue that the selectiveness and historical contingency of this remembered, memorialised past is increasingly dependent upon, and recycled within, audiovisual representations such as those found in popular film. My aim is to consider how 1990s Hollywood cinema has activated a selective, revised sense of the past, and how memory approaches to film history are able to analyse this. In particular, I will stress how popular cultural memory is drawn upon as an aesthetic and commercial strategy of Hollywood; that is, how the styles of the past provide a powerful means through which a film can be branded and marketed to audiences. Often ignored in this process is the deployment of film music, and hence this chapter will focus in particular on the use of music as a significant means through which memories of the past may be evoked in the present.

Mediated memory

As many of the chapters in this book make clear, a distinguishing feature of memory approaches to history is their concern with the *process* of memory on historical knowledge, in particular the contingency of the historically remembered past. Thus what we call the past is accessible only through private and publicly articulated memories, narrated through the perspective of the present. David Lowenthal has termed this *memorial knowledge*, knowledge of the past based upon selective and strategic remembering in the present, and suggests that this is made up of a mixture of personal memory and public memories that over time become fused and indistinguishable.[3] Not only does it become impossible to discern primary from secondary memories ('remembering things from remembering remembering them' as Lowenthal puts it),[4] but also that the memories of others are necessary in order to affirm the validity of our own. Strategic remembering, then, transforms the terrain of the past, often eliminating (or in psychoanalytic accounts, repressing) contradictory or unwanted memories and prioritising those more favourable or immediately useful.[5]

In an article identifying what he calls 'new memory', Andrew Hoskins argues that mediated forms of memory increasingly serve to confirm history and structure the memorialising of knowledge. Through mediated memory historical events become memorialised through their media representation – remembered by their mediation and remediation – and this iterative process helps to construct a sense of the past as episodic. The recognisable narrative of the past as a succession of definable decades (such as 'the sixties' and 'seventies') is therefore largely a product of its media articulation. Hoskins' account of new memory describes the influence of such forms of memory thus:

> Fundamental to the process of both individual and collective memories
> is that they are increasingly mediated. In this way our understanding

of the past is 'manufactured' rather than remembered. At the same time, our sense of collective memory or history is also much more of an electronically mediated one, or, rather reconstructed, from the ever more manipulable global image banks of television and film.[6]

Not only, then, have memories become increasingly mediated with the rise of mass media, but they are also more often the memory of a mediated experience in the first place. Hence it is almost impossible to untangle, for instance, memories of seeing a film for the first time from seeing it subsequently. The impact of visual media is often argued to have intensified the process of memory recall through this iterative process. Through repetition the initial experience is continually re-remembered and remade. The recent work on mediated memory therefore offers a useful starting point to examine the memoralisation and recycling of the past in popular cinema. The concept of 'flashbulb memory', originally developed in psychology by Roger Brown and James Kulik, offers an interesting parallel to this argument.[7] Using the metaphor of the camera, it suggests that flash-bulb memories are those particularly vivid, intensively experienced, memories that are tied to a strong affective and emotional response. Memories of the footage of the assassination of President Kennedy, the death of Princess Diana, or the resignation of Margaret Thatcher are examples of this; through their media circulation and repetition their resonance increases. Disentangling the event from its performance in the media becomes impossible, and its circulation adds to its memorialisation. Thus 'flash-bulb' memories may be strongly related to media memories, or mediated forms of memory.

However, the concept of flash-bulb memory also illustrates the prioritisation of the visual field in writing on memory recall. With a few exceptions film theorists examining the relationship between history, memory and film have focused upon visual images. I want to suggest that the photographic metaphor used by 'flash-bulb' memory theorists is problematic in that it presumes the transparency and fixity of the original memory as an *image*, and downplays other strong sensory triggers such as sound or music. Furthermore whilst the concept of flashbulb memory can help to explain the strong response to specific public events or personal experiences, it is less helpful in understanding memory of the past 'in general' (that is, a sense of *duration* that describes the connections between the memorialised past and the present). In this chapter I shall therefore focus in particular on the function of film music, as musical memory seems to be less specifically tied to space and place than visual images, and more intertwined with issues of affect and audience response. Music is able to index popular memory and nostalgia in ways that are specific to the medium, and quite unlike visual forms. I shall argue that this offers some advantages for Hollywood cinema, which has been concerned with mobilising the commercial potential of memory. In significant cases, this has been achieved through the alternative narration provided by film music, allowing a film to be set visually in the present yet evoke a sense of pastness through its soundtrack. Hollywood cinema has made substantial use of the pop soundtrack to evoke a sense of time past and this is especially the case in the retro film, a cinematic mode that wears stylistic referencing, and pastiche, overtly on its sleeve.

In an article exploring the notion of pastiche, Richard Dyer argues that the very point of pastiche in art is its unapologetic imitation of something else, and that this often involves an affective complicity with its audience.[8] The pleasure of pastiche is therefore partly in its very ostensiveness. Film music provides an interesting example of this. Dyer examines the film music of Nino Rota (most famously known for the theme of *The Godfather*), suggesting that Rota's use of pastiche sets up a register whereby 'we are allowed to feel the emotional appeal of the music and yet also able to recognise its historical and constructed character'.[9] Pastiche, then, is based on the memorised knowledge of that which is imitated rather than aiming for any specific historical accuracy. As Dyer comments, 'pastiche imitates wide-spread perceptions of the art to which it refers rather than being an archaeologically precise reproduction of it'.[10] The same might be said of retro art, which selectively draws upon widely received perceptions of the past in the present. By addressing the affective dimensions of the past in the present, embodied by music in the retro film, I want to examine how musical memory can function performatively, transforming the meaning of visual narration. This chapter suggests that Hollywood cinema in the 1990s evoked the past in the present in a number of identifiably different ways. It is first necessary to clarify some terms, however. As such, I present a typology identifying three categories of popular film that activate memorialised knowledge. Focusing on the third of these – what I call the 'retro film' – I shall suggest that Hollywood's fascination with retro perspectives derives from a commercial opportunism based upon nostalgia for selected and revised pasts and their connection to the present.

History/period/retro

Much film criticism makes the assumption that the representation of pastness is measurable against a retrievable original past to which it is to be compared. Thus many Hollywood films are judged to have been unfaithful to this 'actual' past (*Forrest Gump* (1994), *Titanic* (1997), *Pearl Harbor* (2000)) by introducing new themes, conflating historical characters, or presenting historically inaccurate events.[11] Both Lowenthal and Hoskins, however, argue that this 'retrieval' model of memory recall is inaccurate, relying as it does upon a notion of an original experience to which it may be compared. Hoskins suggests that there is no 'fixed' moment to recall, only 'a (re)construction of an event, person or place which is ultimately contingent on (or rather, in) the present'.[12] Whilst emphasising the importance of 'process' to memory recall, this does present difficulties in dealing with qualitatively different kinds of memories – those ostensibly of a specific past event and those of a sense of the past (or of duration) in general.

In order to clarify terms and avoid this problem, I wish to make a distinction here between three impulses in contemporary Hollywood cinema's activation of the past: the 'history film', the 'period film' and the 'retro film'. The history film is perhaps the most familiar, often dealing with historical trauma or a famous character, as for instance in a biopic such as *Nixon* (1995) or a film centred on a known event such as that in *Titanic* or *Saving Private Ryan* (1998). As these examples can be taken to suggest, the history film is indexical to a *referential* past, measurable against the memorialised knowledge of a particular event or person and audiovisual recordings and accounts of them. The reconstruction of details of the actual Titanic, or the resemblance of Anthony Hopkins' performance to televised footage of Richard Nixon, are key aspects of this impulse.

My second category – the 'period film' – describes a film that is indexical to a *historical* past. Unlike the history film it does not deal with a publicly memorialised event or figure, but instead with the past in general. As such the period film often tends to be typified by reconstruction aesthetics – for instance the lavish reconstruction of New York in *The Age of Innocence* (1993) or Rome in *Gladiator* (2000). Although the historical film will usually also be concerned with the reconstruction of period detail, the referentiality of the period film is the memorialised knowledge of a period rather than a specific historical event or person. The characters in *Gladiator*, for instance, are recognisable historical types, but the specific events depicted are not indexical to a referential past but to a past 'in general'. Again this is measurable although not to the same specificity – for instance in the authentic detail of the mise-en-scène rather than the events depicted.

The third category to be defined is what I call the 'retro film'. The 'retro film' mobilises particular codes that have come to connote a past sensibility as it is selectively re-remembered in the present (i.e. 'the seventies' or 'the sixties') as a structure of feeling, and these codes function *metonymically*, standing in for the entire decade. As such, the retro film is less concerned with historical accuracy than with a playful deployment of codes that connote pastness. Such a formulation of the 'retro film' shares similarities with Fredric Jameson's formulation of the 'nostalgia film' in that it refers to those films that evoke the past through previously mediated representations and stereotypes of the past. However, I use the term 'nostalgia' to describe the mode of engagement between film performance and audience rather than as a descriptive category for the film texts themselves. The past in the retro film has less to do with the reconstruction of the past (as in the period film) or a historical event (as in the history film) than with its memorialisation and re-imagining in the present. I should make clear that these categories are not mutually exclusive. Films can often occupy more than one category and I use these categories primarily for their heuristic usefulness. For instance both *Titanic* and *Saving Private Ryan* also focus on individual fictionalised stories as well as publicly known events, thus moving between the first two categories. Indeed, entwining the collective and the individual is often a strategy for making history 'accessible' to contemporary audiences, usually through the narration of events that appear to unfold on screen as if in the present.

The past as a style

In his book, *The Seventies Now*, Stephen Paul Miller remarks that upon watching the film *Pulp Fiction* (1994) he wondered whether it was set in the 1970s. Noting that virtually all the music, cars and cultural references were from the 1970s or before, he relates that his awareness of the presentness of the film's setting was only provoked by flashbacks to the 1970s as part of the film's diegesis. This time-lessness – a fusion of past and present – is the essence of the retro film. Thus, in Miller's words, 'the present seemed like the Seventies, and the film conveyed an impression of a past and a present entangled in that decade'.[13] Retro cultural objects deploy codes that operate as catalysts for recollection, and stand in for a historical 'feeling'. Thus the exact ways in which this film, or the retro films that I shall go on to discuss, evoke the past are difficult to pin down precisely. Retro films play on a fascination with fusing past and present, and retro styles are only retrospective because they involve looking back knowingly from the present time. Retro, then, is both a playful and knowing deployment of the past in the present, and frequently involves irony. For instance, writing on retro fashion in the *New York Times* in 1975, Kennedy Fraser suggests that, 'retro represents the desire to find style, *but obliquely*, and splendour, *but tackily*, and so to put an ironic distance between the wearers and the fashionableness of their clothes'.[14] Finding political potential in retro fashion, Kaja Silverman argues that it 'avoids the pitfalls of a naïve referentiality, by putting quotation marks around the garments it revitalizes'.[15] This suggests that the knowing use of selective signifiers from the past (fashion, music, intertextual references) in the retro film ostends its signification, creating a shared discourse with the audience through their awareness of the film's avoidance of direct referentiality.

However, as Stuart Tannock has noted, the politics of nostalgia has sharply divided critics. Jameson, for instance, largely takes a negative view, arguing that nostalgia and the popularity of retro is symptomatic of the problem of defining the current historical period and its distinctness.[16] His well-known argument is that the current period is experiencing a crisis in its sense of the present and therefore its relation to the historical past – a result of what he calls a 'waning of historicity'.[17] Instead he argues that nostalgia substitutes a memory of history with a memory of the *idea* of history. The nostalgia film operates as a 'bad object' for Jameson, as Richard Dyer points out, functioning as a way of regulating and commodifying the past.[18] It is not concerned with representing/critiquing history but with evoking the past through selective stylistic iconography such as fashion and music, in ways in which I have described. Thus, argues Jameson, it empties history of politics, reducing it to a recombination of stereotypes of the past.

There is insufficient space here to fully discuss the debate that Jameson's work has provoked. Linda Hutcheon, in particular, questions Jameson's negative theorisation of nostalgia by pointing out the possibilities of revising history through irony and play, rather as Silverman has argued that retro clothing recuperates the past in a political form.[19] Nostalgia, then, may be used to characterise a number of quite different and even contradictory impulses. It can be conceptualised as conveying a knowing and reflexive relationship with the past, as a yearning for a better but irretrievable past, or, in more sceptical accounts, as emblematic of an engrossing but ultimately fabricated approximation of the past. As such, the term needs to be deployed with care. In his article examining nostalgia as a cultural style, Paul Grainge suggests that it is useful to map a distinction between articulations of nostalgia as a 'mood' and as a 'mode'.[20] He argues that discussions of nostalgia as a mood orientate themselves around affective and experiential discourses of nostalgia as a form of yearning. However, Grainge questions the reduction of nostalgia critiques to this single formulation, suggesting as it does the loss of a past authenticity. Instead he suggests that nostalgia also operates quite removed from this concept of loss, as evidenced by the popularity of retro objects that are less about articulating a connectedness to a lost 'authentic' past than with consuming objects whose signification has become loaded with connotative markers of taste in the present. The fashionability of retro objects as markers of style in the present complicates any totalising theorisation of nostalgia as embodying a sense of loss. Articulations of nostalgia as a 'mode', on the other hand, Grainge argues, may overemphasise nostalgia as an 'empty' style at the expense of understanding the complex configurations of consumption through which retro objects gain their signification. As this argument suggests, there is a need to conceptualise nostalgia as encompassing affective, stylistic and historical dimensions, and for the cultural and discursive specificity of nostalgia to be fully historicised.

My own position on nostalgia is informed by a notion of collective play rather than yearning or historical blockage; I am inclined to look positively at nostalgia as a mode that can actively renegotiate and reconfigure the past in the present. Whilst I accept some of Jameson's central observations on nostalgia, I inflect them somewhat differently, less concerned with a theorisation of waning historicity than with offering attention to the stylisation of the past in retro-cinema. In considering this point, Jameson's argument remains significant. Indeed, an important aspect of his formulation of the nostalgia film is its strategy of selective re-remembering; evoking the past through the deployment of a limited iconography that erases contradictions in the past in favour of a coherency of style. Jameson argues that films evoke particular historical periods through their repeated citation of generic conventions, cultural stereotypes, and symbolic objects of the period, especially style/fashion objects. His analysis of *American Graffiti* (1973) suggests that its evocation of the early 1960s (through diners, rock 'n' roll, Elvis, short hair, domestication but also teenage rebellion) is one rooted in a 1970s selective revisioning of the late 1950s and early 1960s. Rather than accept his final conclusions about pastiche as 'blank parody', however, I am persuaded by Dyer's argument that the importance of pastiche might be in its obviousness, rearticulating the signifiers of the past in an ostensive rather than blank or necessarily self-reflexive way.

Jameson's provocative comments, along with the more recent insights offered by writers on memory and culture, provide a useful basis for analysing the popularity of retro-cinema in the 1990s. Hollywood uses retro perspectives for aesthetic and commercial purposes, as both a stylistic and marketing strategy. The aspects identifiable in 1990s Hollywood retro-cinema are: a) the selective mobilisation of iconography of the past becoming fused with the present, b) the accentuation of pastness as a stylistic feature, and c) the commodification of pastness and its market exploitation. In order to give my argument some specificity I now wish to focus on two 1990s Hollywood films that I shall argue exemplify the 'new retro' movie in 1990s Hollywood: *Sleepless in Seattle* (1993) and *Jackie Brown* (1997). Both these films are set contemporarily in the 1990s yet, I argue, evoke an earlier period – in *Jackie Brown* a 1970s blaxploitation aesthetic and in *Sleepless in Seattle* the classical Hollywood romantic comedy of the 1930s to 1950s.

Mortgaged to music: retro perspectives in *Jackie Brown* and *Sleepless in Seattle*

Jackie Brown was the long-awaited follow-up to director Quentin Tarantino's *Pulp Fiction*. The film stars blaxploitation movie icon Pam Grier and 1970s television and movie star, Robert Forster, as

well as Samuel L. Jackson. Most of the critical reviews of the film
pointed out the obvious positioning of Grier in *Jackie Brown* as a
product of Tarantino's enduring fandom of 1970s blaxploitation
movies, in particular her key roles in *Foxy Brown* and *Coffy* in the
early 1970s. The marketing of the film emphasised Tarantino's rein-
statement of Pam Grier as an icon, and his efforts to produce a
homage to her earlier films, as well as his boldness in casting a forty-
something black woman and fifty-something white man as the love
story in the film.

What is particularly interesting about *Jackie Brown*, like *Pulp Fiction* before it, is that it feels like a 1970s film despite being set in
1995. Sharon Willis, writing on the relationship between Tarantino
as an auteur and the cult status of his work, argues that his films
'embody a nostalgia for 70s that is continually circulating in television, video, and radio'.[21] Highlighting the mediated recycling of
retro culture, she suggests that 'later appropriations of the products
of the 70s recycle them as a kind of nostalgia to the second degree –
nostalgia for nostalgia'.[22] According to the typology I outlined earlier, *Jackie Brown* is neither a historical film (based on historical
event) nor a period film (recreating a historical moment). It is, I suggest, a good example of the retro film, evoking a nostalgic and
metonymic historicity through its steady deployment of 1970s
iconography. The film may be set in the 1990s, with predominantly
1990s mise-en-scène, but it insistently invokes the 1970s. It simultaneously has both a 'presentness' and 'pastness', set in the present
but evoking a 1970s 'structure of feeling'. Raymond Williams
coined this phrase to describe the affective sense that the past continues to hold over the present, what he called 'social experiences in
solution', whereby the constituent parts become inseparable, the
past and present dissolved together.[23] A number of elements therefore combine to contribute to the retro feel of *Jackie Brown*. Most
obviously there is the casting of two 1970s stars – Pam Grier as
Jackie Brown and Robert Forster as Max Cherry. The narrative centres on their growing relationship which itself functions as a mediation on time and memory (both in terms of their star images and the
characters that they play). The mise-en-scène too harks back to this
period, with the bail-bond office and Jackie's flat, in particular,
exuding signifiers of seventies-ness, evident in the brown décor, the
prominence of her vinyl record collection full of 1970s music, as
well as the clothing of the principal characters.

The opening of the film immediately signals its retro intentions. The first scene introduces us to Jackie, whilst the soundtrack plays Bobby Womack's 1970s soul classic 'Across 110th Street', a key song that both starts and ends the film. This establishes a retro frame of reference, as Womack's song is the eponymous title music for a 1972 film, *Across 110th Street*. Referring to the opening of the film, where Grier as Jackie strides through an airport, Tarantino described one of his aims as to achieve the best Pam Grier walk ever put on celluloid, clearly harking back to her earlier blaxploitation roles.[24] In the opening shot, Jackie stands immobile on a moving walkway at the right of the frame. The colour and style of her uniform evokes a seventies-ness, complimented by the colours of the mosaic tiles behind her. Even the film titles deliberately evoke the 1970s through their typeface: the unfurling of the bubble-like characters and two tone colour look out of place in the contemporary era of digital imaging and matting. The credits, and the retro font of the film title, work to frame the film by selectively drawing upon 1970s iconography, signalling its retro mode.[25]

My main point of interest however is the use of music in the film. Little work on memory has been concerned with music, although Lowenthal does note that music is often a means of activating memory, and Jameson tantalisingly comments that the nostalgia film is 'mortgaged to music'.[26] Most discussions of memory and film tend to prioritise visual memory over musical memory, thus downplaying the significance of music and the soundtrack.[27] However, it is the work of the soundtrack and the memorialised knowledge it conveys that particularly helps to establish the retro feel to the film, and the deliberate deployment of musical memory is therefore an important aspect of the aesthetic and commercial strategy of 1990s Hollywood retro-cinema. In particular, the use of period songs re-key narrative events, evoking an associational structure of feeling of the period, even where the narrative events are taking place contemporarily. Thus in the opening scene of *Jackie Brown* the credits and movement of the film title are all timed to appear in pace with the structure of the song. As the scene progresses, Jackie/Grier starts to walks through the airport, the low camera angle emphasises the timing of her gait with the rhythm of the song, as if her movement is motivated by the music.

In his book on the soundtrack, Jeff Smith has suggested that the pop score operates what he calls a 'juke-box narrative'.[28] He argues

that whilst the pop song may be used in a conventional way to reinforce or comment upon a character or their emotions, it always
retains an autonomous identity and resists full integration into narrative. This means that recognition of songs by audiences will influence interpretation of narrative events, most obviously where lyrics
are used to comment on the action or music is used as an ironic coun-
terpoint to action onscreen. The pop music soundtrack creates a relationship between sound and image that is layered, where music plays
an active role in the construction of narrative through its partial
autonomy. In *Jackie Brown*, songs are often deployed as a narrational
device, most notably in the function of The Delfonics' 'Didn't I (Blow
Your Mind This Time)', a 1970s song that narrates the emotions of
the characters through the film. This takes on a symbolic function in
establishing the relationships between characters and their nostalgia
for the past. When Jackie plays the song to Max it is supposed to indicate her investment in the past (and in vinyl). His subsequent purchase of a Delfonics tape endows the song with a specific narrative
function, conveying a sense of emotional connectedness between
characters never made explicit in their conversation. The music is
used internally and self-consciously – the characters comment upon
the music, and it is passed between them symbolically.

One reviewer of the film – Erik Bauer, writing in *Sight and Sound*
– found this use of music objectionable, suggesting that 'the emotion
of the songs is often used as a lazy prod towards what the inscrutable
Jackie might be feeling at any moment'.[29] His pejorative tone is interesting – of course the same accusation could be levelled at the use of
the visual close-up as a signifier of character interiority, or such other
cinematic conventions as elliptical editing, point-of-view shots and
more. However, here music is foregrounded; it articulates a complex language for emotion that lacks visual cognisance and enunci-
ates a nostalgic feeling of duration rather than presentness. The use
of music from the 1970s and earlier (including Bobby Womack, The
Delfonics, Brothers Johnson, Randy Crawford and Bill Withers)
evokes a historicity in the film that is located less in the reconstruction of a historical period than in a 1970s structure of feeling.

Sharon Willis also objects to the ostensive signalling of the retro
film, suggesting that 'the same cinematic moves that figure history as
cultural waste, as trash to be collected and recombined, allow for the
production of false social anchors in, say, images drawn from blaxploitation films'.[30] However the ahistoricism of retro-cinema seems

to me to be precisely the point, and its stylistic appropriation of the past marks out something that is also dynamic about cultural recycling. Retro films such as *Jackie Brown* are not reducible to questions about falsifying the historical past, as I have outlined above, but need to be placed within patterns of consumption and cultural taste. The ways in which history is reconfigured in the retro film, and retexualised through music, are complex, involving an affective address that marks out the pastness in the retro film as stylish or 'cool', hence the particular appeal of retro objects to youth or style-driven markets. Thus the ways in which retro-cinema functions as a commercial strategy need to be explored if we are to make sense of popular commercial cinema. The accentuation of pastness in the retro film operates simultaneously as a stylistic feature and a means of marketing the film and its ancillary products. Thus the soundtrack to *Jackie Brown*, available on release of the film, not only included songs from the film but also quotable dialogue, creating a hybrid product where film and soundtrack are mutually reinforcing, appealing to those who may invest in and recycle styles of the past as markers of taste in the present.

I now want to consider a very different 1990s retro film, the romantic comedy *Sleepless in Seattle*. This attracted a largely female audience compared with the significant male audience for *Jackie Brown*. *Sleepless in Seattle* was released in 1993 and although it is not as easily classifiable as retro as *Jackie Brown*, was nonetheless perceived as following in the retro-romantic comedy tradition of *When Harry Met Sally* (1989), *Pretty Woman* (1990) and *Ghost* (1990). These films were substantial box-office hits and were seen as reinvigorating the romantic comedy genre, mobilising, as Peter Krämer has noted, an audience traditionally neglected by Hollywood: the female audience aged over twenty-five.[31] The average age of cinema-goers in the US domestic market rose in the 1990s, and older audiences began to displace the industry's prime focus on the youth market. By the start of the 1990s, according to Krämer, the 25–49 year old age group made up 46 per cent of all admissions, whereas the 12–24 year-old age group – Hollywood's traditional audience – had declined to 44 per cent. According to MPAA figures, the overall composition of cinema-goers changed in the 1990s, with those in the 40+ age group accounting for 40 per cent of total cinema-goers in 2000, compared to only 32 per cent in 1990.[32] A more substantial, and significantly older, female audience was a facet of this shift, beginning to form a growing percentage of Hollywood's potential market in the 1990s. This fact accounts in part for increased attention to genres traditionally deemed 'female-oriented'. 'Sleeper' hits such as *Sleepless in Seattle* and *Pretty Woman* represented lower risks than blockbuster productions due to their relatively low production costs. The films also created a cluster of stars (Meg Ryan, Sandra Bullock, Tom Hanks, amongst others) whose images differed from dominant gender representations of the previous decade, and gradually permeated across other Hollywood genres through the 1990s. No doubt this renewed interest was driven by Hollywood's commercial imperatives. As a number of high-budget action films failed to recoup their massive investments, the studios took notice of sleeper hits. Costing only $21m, *Sleepless in Seattle* was a huge box-office hit, grossing $228m in worldwide theatrical receipts alone, and proving extremely successful as a video and soundtrack album.

On its release, many of the reviewers noted *Sleepless in Seattle*'s emphasis on 'retro-romance', seeing it as a nostalgic revisiting of the classical Hollywood romantic comedy.[33] The trajectory of the film works gradually towards bringing the two protagonists, Sam (Tom Hanks) and Annie (Meg Ryan), together as a 'magical' encounter. This involves them negotiating obstacles encountered in the present day. For instance, Sam has to rediscover the rules of dating after fifteen years and manage single parenthood, and Annie has to cast off an existing partner in favour of Sam. The film does indeed evoke the classical romantic comedy both explicitly, through its showcasing of period 'standards' on the soundtrack, and implicitly, through its non-cynical investment in a narrative centred around romantic love, observing such time-honoured conventions as keeping the two lovers apart until the finale of the film, making all other partners absurdly unsuitable and invoking the classical 'magic' of romantic love. The inclusion of intertexts within the film, particularly *An Affair to Remember* (1957) and *Casablanca* (1943), have the effect of emphasising a nostalgic yearning for a past innocence, particularly in the re-visiting of the former film's key symbolic site (the observation deck of the Empire State Building) and the inclusion of the song 'As Time Goes By', made famous in the latter. This intertextual referencing plays on the impossibility of a golden past – as represented by the classical Hollywood romance – even as characters yearn for its simplicity. Indeed, much of the comedy in the film focuses on the difficulty of conducting romance in the present, or the need to adopt romantic clichés whilst at the same time distancing oneself from them by deploying them knowingly. Thus the scene where the female characters sob at *An Affair to Remember* (reprised when the male characters discuss *The Dirty Dozen* (1967)) is comic because it pokes oblique fun at their sense of nostalgia for how things used to be in the movies, rather than in life.

Perhaps even more than with *Jackie Brown*, music plays a key role in establishing the retro perspective of the film. In addition to 'As Time Goes By', the film showcases a number of 'standards' including 'Somewhere Over the Rainbow', 'Stand by Your Man', 'Making Whoopee', 'In the Wee Small Hours' and 'Stardust', all of which musically locate the film in the past. However, the nostalgic evocation of romance associated with these standards is qualified through the deployment of the songs in uncommon versions. For instance the version of 'As Time Goes By', sung by Jimmy Durante, is comic, with his voice straining to reach the high notes. Likewise, the version of 'Making Whoopee', sung by a rasping Dr John rather than a crooning Frank Sinatra, qualifies the romantic sentiment with 'knowing' humour.

Such knowingness is common in retro-cinema. In his article examining the relationship between the pop 'standard' and the narrative in *Sleepless in Seattle*, Ian Garwood points out that this musical strategy, rather than acting as a traditional underscore, puts some distance between song and narrative, suggesting that the estrangement between the two allows the music to commentate as an alternative narrational form to the visual action.[34] The point, then, is that retro-romance (and retro-cinema generally) is knowing, often overdeterminedly so, and its evocation of the past is often qualified by its ostensiveness. *Sleepless in Seattle*'s showcasing of recognisable hits not only offers a commentary on the drama at any given point, but also points us determinedly towards the soundtrack section of our nearest music-store, a neat alignment of Hollywood's commercial and aesthetic interests.

The past in these two films, and the retro film more generally, is not about historical truth but rather about mobilising a popular memorialised sense of pastness. Retro aesthetics are a way of commercialising popular memory; their recognition allows them to connect into a public nostalgia for a past derived from earlier representations, such as those shown in the retro-romance of *Sleepless in Seattle* or in the stylised seventies-ness of *Jackie Brown*. The success of retro films, and period compilation soundtracks in 1990s Hollywood cinema – ably demonstrated by the *Pulp Fiction* soundtrack which sold over four million copies – is significant to the establishment of brand awareness, important in the package-unit mode of production in contemporary Hollywood. By fusing a sense of pastness with the present, the 'retro' film (and soundtrack album) commodifies this pastness as a commercial style amenable to product differentiation by the post-Fordist audio-visual industries. The niche marketing of recent 'retro' films, particularly those associated with a historical period definable by musical iconography – films such as *Boogie Nights*, *The Last Days of Disco* and *Forrest Gump* – all draw heavily on the commodification of the past through the pop song. Of course, recognising the commercial potential of the past is hardly a recent phenomenon. However the recent opportunities to market retro products through new modes of delivery (the multi-channel television environment, DVD and video) has vastly increased the market for retro products in the last two decades.

Conclusions

Although nostalgia was not in any way new to Hollywood in the 1990s, the nostalgia evoked by 1990s retro-cinema seems to have been specific to this period and was for many critics unimaginable in the 1980s. The comment made by James Monaco that opened this chapter illustrates the perceptual shift that memorialisation can effect. This demonstrates the historical specificity of nostalgia, and the memorialised knowledge of the past that it draws upon. What these observations show is the degree to which our sense of pastness is constructed by mediated forms of memory in the present, such as those evoked in the retro film. Furthermore, if our sense of the past is in part constructed through what Alison Landsberg has called 'prosthetic memory' – memories that are not remembered from personal experience, but which intertwine public memorial knowledge with individual memory – then mediated memories have become increasingly important to how we articulate ourselves and our tastes in the present.[35] Thus we can be nostalgic about, or invest in, an experience that we have not actually had, or a period never personally experienced.

This chapter has argued that 'retro' is a useful concept to consider how history is evoked as a style and feeling in 1990s Hollywood cinema. My analysis has tried to demonstrate how the retro film *performs* the past, offering a selective knowing deployment of a sense of pastness amenable to Hollywood's commercial aesthetic. Retro, then, both describes a structure of feeling and a commercial strategy adopted by Hollywood to market a sense of the past in the present. The pleasure of retro-cinema is not one of (necessary) self-reflexivity or even recreation of the past, but rather its deployment of signifiers of pastness and its exuberant and inventive recycling of the past in new stylistic combinations. The retro perspectives presented in *Jackie Brown* and *Sleepless in Seattle* were, I have argued, able to index a popular discourse of nostalgia through the significant use of music. The deployment of period pop songs in the retro soundtrack of these films, and in other examples of retro-cinema, perform a knowingness, constructing a shared discourse with its audience and highlighting its avoidance of referentiality. Clearly, then, if the retro film is about memory and nostalgia, then the language of memory in retro-cinema is insistently musical as well as visual.

Notes

I would like to thank Ian Craven for his helpful comments and suggestions.

1   James Monaco, *American Film Now* (New York: New American Library, 1984), p. 283.
2   Walter Benjamin, 'Theses on the Philosophy of History', in Walter Benjamin, *Illuminations* (London: Pimlico, 1999), p. 252.
3   David Lowenthal, *The Past is a Foreign Country* (Cambridge: Cambridge University Press, 1985).
4   Lowenthal, *The Past is a Foreign Country*, p. 196.
5   Lowenthal, *The Past is a Foreign Country*, p. 206.
6   Andrew Hoskins, 'New Memory: mediating history', *Historical Journal of Film, Radio and Television*, 21: 4 (2001), 336.
7   Roger Brown and James Kulik, 'Flashbulb Memories', *Cognition*, 5 (1977), 73–99. For a discussion on the validity of the concept see Daniel Schacter, *Searching for Memory: the Brain, the Mind and the Past* (New York: Basic Books, 1996) and Martin Conway, *Flashbulb Memories* (Hove: Erlbaum, 1994).
8   Richard Dyer, 'The Notion of Pastiche', in Jostein Gripsrud (ed.), *The Aesthetics of Popular Art* (Kristiansand/Bergen: Høyskoleforlaget, 2001), p. 82.
9   Dyer, 'The Notion of Pastiche', p. 83.
10 *Ibid.*

11 See, for instance, debates in Kevin S. Sandler and Gaylyn Studlar (eds), *Titanic: Anatomy of a Blockbuster* (London: Rutgers University Press, 1999); Thomas B. Byers, 'History Re-remembered: *Forrest Gump*, Postfeminist Masculinity, and the Burial of the Counterculture', *Modern Fiction Studies* 42: 2 (1996), 41–44; and Jennifer Hyland Wang, '"A Struggle of Contending Stories": Race, Gender and Political Memory in *Forrest Gump*', *Cinema Journal* 39: 3 (2000), 92–115.

12 Hoskins, 'New Memory', 335.

13 Stephen Paul Miller, *The Seventies Now: Culture as Surveillance* (London: Duke University Press, 1999), p. 65.

14 Kennedy Fraser, quoted in Kaja Silverman, 'Fragments of a Fashionable Discourse', in Tania Modleski (ed.), *Studies in Entertainment* (Bloomington: Indiana University Press, 1986), p. 150. My italics.

15 Silverman, 'Fragments', p. 150.

16 See Fredric Jameson, 'Postmodernism and Consumer Society', in H. Foster, *Postmodern Culture* (London: Pluto Press, 1985), pp. 111–25; and 'Nostalgia for the Present', in Jameson, *Postmodernism, or, The Cultural Logic of Late Capitalism* (London: Verso, 1991), pp. 279–96.

17 Jameson, *Postmodernism, or, The Cultural Logic of Late Capitalism*, p. 21.

18 Dyer, 'The Notion of Pastiche', p. 82.

19 Linda Hutcheon, *The Politics of Postmodernism* (New York: Routledge, 1989).

20 Paul Grainge, 'Nostalgia and Style in Retro America: Moods, Modes and Media Recycling', *Journal of American and Comparative Cultures*, 23: 1 (2000), 27–34. For a more detailed consideration, see Paul Grainge, *Monochrome Memories: Nostalgia and Style in Retro America* (Westport, CT and London: Praeger, 2002).

21 Sharon Willis, 'The Father's Watch the Boy's Room', *Camera Obscura*, 32 (1993–94), 48.

22 Willis, 'The Father's Watch the Boy's Room', 48.

23 Raymond Williams, 'Structures of Feeling', in *Marxism and Literature* (Oxford: Oxford University Press, 1977), pp. 128–35.

24 Tarantino in interview at the NFT on '*Jackie Brown*: Collector's Edition Enhanced CD-ROM' (*The Guardian*/NFT/Miramax, 1998). Of course the walk also replays the famous opening scene from *The Graduate* (1967).

25 It is interesting to note that the UK release of the film played down such retro intentions. Its publicity posters, for instance, replaced the two-tone 1970s lettering with a more contemporary font, and emphasised Tarantino's authorship of the film rather than its blaxploitation intertexts, no doubt reflecting the different cultural capital held by the UK audience.

26 Jameson, *Postmodernism, or, The Cultural Logic of Late Capitalism*, p. 288.
27 An exception to this is Annette Kuhn, 'Journey Through Memory', in Susannah Radstone (ed.), *Memory and Methodology* (Oxford: Berg, 2000), pp. 179–96.
28 Jeff Smith, *The Sounds of Commerce: Marketing Popular Film Music* (New York: Columbia University Press, 1998).
29 Erik Bauer, 'The Mouth and The Method', *Sight and Sound*, 8: 3 (1998), 7.
30 Willis, 'The Father's Watch the Boy's Room', 67.
31 Peter Krämer, 'A Powerful Cinema-going Force? Hollywood and Female Audiences since the 1960s', in Melvyn Stokes and Richard Maltby (eds), *Identifying Hollywood's Audiences: Cultural Identity and the Movies* (London: British Film Institute, 1999), pp. 93–108.
32 Source: *MPAA Motion Picture Attendance Study*, 2000 (www.mpaa.org).
33 See, for instance, audience reviews of the film on the Internet Movie Database (www.imdb.com).
34 Ian Garwood, 'Must You Remember This?: Orchestrating the "Standard" Pop Song in *Sleepless in Seattle*', *Screen* 41: 3 (2000), 284.
35 See Alison Landsberg's chapter in this volume. See also, Landsberg, 'Prosthetic Memory: *Total Recall* and *Bladerunner*', in Mike Featherstone and Roger Burrows (eds), *Cyberspace/Cyberbodies/Cyberpunk: Cultures of Technological Embodiment* (London: Sage, 1995), pp. 175–89.

10

Colouring the past: *Pleasantville* and the textuality of media memory

Paul Grainge

When Ted Turner purchased MGM Entertainment in 1986, and then financed a plan to digitally colourise a series of black and white movies from the studio's back catalogue, a beachhead of Hollywood directors, actors, film critics and cinematic guilds vociferously attacked the idea in practice and principle. The crux of complaint focused on the fact that, as a technical process, colourisation did not simply enhance the visual quality and resolution of old monochrome movies, but artfully doctored their entire chromatic character. Believing that colourised films would eventually replace the memory of their black and white progenitors, digital alteration was denounced by the anti-colourisation lobby as a venal process. In transforming a monochrome movie into a digitally re-made spectacle, colourisation was said to mutilate and destroy the visual pastness that could embed original black and white films within the tissues of cultural and aesthetic memory. While specific issues of copyright law and artistic rights were fought over, assumptions of historicist blockage and memory crisis came to infuse the anti-colourisation campaign. Privileging the creative originality and historical temporality of monochrome depth, set against the textual amnesia of colourised surface, the anti-colourisation lobby battled to save an 'authentic', textually untampered, film past. The villain of the conflict was not simply Turner, and his attempt to maximise the profit potential of the MGM catalogue, but the very mutability of postmodern simulacra.[1]

In this chapter, I want to consider a cultural and theoretical development in the discussion of memory crisis, especially as it bears upon the notional 'amnesia' that has been associated with digital technology in, and as part of, the culture of postmodernism. In doing so, I want to examine *Pleasantville* (1998), a film that reframes the relationship between colourisation and cultural remembrance in a period where 'digital cinema' had become, by the late 1990s, a sophisticated media genre. Dramatising the incursions of a colour present into a black and white past, *Pleasantville* creates a narrative based on the cultural apotheosis, 'not everything is as simple as black and white'. Tapping into the spectacular growth of nostalgia networks on cable television during the 1990s, the film uses digital techniques of colour conversion to affect a political allegory about the legacy and significance of the 1960s. I am interested in two related issues. At one level, I want to consider how the film operates in the contested field of meaning that, in the 1990s, came to debate the memory of America's postwar past. This leads to a different, but overlapping, concern: namely, to what effect postmodern technologies and forms of representation impact upon the way that cultural memory is textually figured and articulated. I am interested in questions not only of what, but also of how, cultures (in this case, American culture in the late 1990s) remember.

Addressing the 'what' of media memory requires an engagement with a process that Douglas Kellner has called cultural transcoding.[2] As a type of ideological critique, this describes the way that media cultures articulate a competing array of social discourses within popular representation. In the case of *Pleasantville*, this transcoding centres upon a liberal discourse focused on the rejuvenation of the 1960s. Discursively, the film intervenes in political debates about the status of the 1960s, reclaiming the decade as a positive metaphor against the (supposedly) more reactionary 'memories' of the period advanced in films like *Forrest Gump* (1994). Rather than evacuate history through techniques of digital manipulation and stylistic pastiche – something that Fredric Jameson argues in relation to the postmodern 'nostalgia film'[3] – both *Forrest Gump* and *Pleasantville* inscribe competing visions of the past through an economy of representational retro. As such, my discussion will initially consider *Pleasantville* in relation to that of *Forrest Gump*. Each film demonstrates how a stylised evocation of pastness does not negate, but may textually refigure, the form and locution of memory politics in the semiotic terrain of contemporary culture.

In addressing the 'how' of media memory, it is necessary to consider theoretical revisions that are beginning to negotiate, and rethink, propositions of postmodern amnesia. Whereas theorists of postmodernism such as Jameson have diagnosed a profound waning of historicity in cultural life, linked to what he calls the 'spatial logic of the simulacrum', critics such as Andreas Huyssen, Vivian Sobchack and Jim Collins have begun to look more closely at the bearing of postmodern representation on contemporary memory practice.[4] All three critics explore, in one form or another, the impact of media technologies on structures of temporality and how the quickening pace, and sheer magnitude, of electronic communication has transformed, rather than dissolved, the experience of memory. Huyssen considers the dialectic of memory and forgetting in a rapacious information culture where media technologies – television, film, VCR, cable, computers – have helped create both an evisceration of, and an obsession with, the historical past; Sobchack explores the impact that new representational technologies have had in creating more active and reflective historical subjects; and Collins examines the positive reconstitution of the archive in a culture of accelerated technological innovation and semiotic excess. If Jameson's theory of historicist crisis was commensurate with the fear of amnesia expressed by the anti-colourisation lobby in the late 1980s – both decrying the crass simulation of history within cultural, and especially cinematic, practice – the cartography that Collins gives to 'the information age' perhaps offers a more befitting framework for the colourised memory work of *Pleasantville* at the end of the 1990s.

The politics of pastness: *Pleasantville* and *Forrest Gump*

Pleasantville is based around the transportation of two 1990s teenagers into the world of an eponymous black and white 1950s sitcom. Existing somewhere between the historical time-travelling of *Back to the Future* (1985) and the media voyeurism of *The Truman Show* (1998), *Pleasantville* revisits the 1950s through the auspices of its televisual media, exploring and, ultimately, undoing the constrictive limits of its projected cultural fantasies about domesticity, sexuality, gender and community. *Pleasantville* begins by screen-rushing a catalogue of contemporary afflictions and apocalyptic scenarios: colour news clips and classroom statistics about unemployment, AIDS and ecological disaster. The imaginary world of Pleasantville is the negation of this malaise, a 'kinder, gentler' world where family values and common decency prevail. As a devotee of cable reruns, David (Tobey Maguire) is an arch consumer of 1990s nostalgic camp. His relationship with Pleasantville is not based on longing (at least not in any simple way), but on his command of its plot lines and characters. David is part of what Lynn Spigel describes as the 'young television-literate generation' that nostalgia networks frequently solicit by recontextualising old programmes in new 'reception contexts'.[5] According to Spigel, this process generates a particular ambivalence about the past whereby a romanticised nostalgia for the good old days is mixed with a progressive faith in the enlightened values and attitudes of the present. A combination of longing and ridicule attaches itself to the televisual 1950s, brought out by David and Jennifer, who are never straightforwardly wistful or woeful about the past in any complete sense. Preparing himself for a *Pleasantville* marathon, and a cable quiz based on the sitcom, David adopts a reflexive nostalgia that is suddenly forced in upon itself. Beamed through a magic television remote, David's television literacy is mysteriously transposed and tested in the world of Pleasantville itself. Together with his street-wise and sexually assertive sister (Reese Witherspoon), David and Jennifer are inexplicably confronted with, and literally drawn inside, the monochrome world of sitcom 'gee-whizzery'.

Colour is central to *Pleasantville*'s narrative strategy. Black and white is a visual index of the cultural media *and* the caricatured morality of the 1950s. Monochrome is associated with conventions of sexless, sanitised, nicety; Pleasantville is a place without double beds, working toilets or domestic arguments. However, when present values intrude upon the past, colour begins to appear. As soon as David and Jennifer introduce non-marital sex, rock 'n' roll, modernist art and rebellious literature, colour progressively tints the ersatz monochrome universe of Pleasantville. Beginning with a single red rose, the town and its populace are slowly infused with colour, a chromatic transition that defines a growing youth and community awakening. *Pleasantville*'s chromatic significations are central to the film's shifting registers of reality, fantasy and spectacle. While colour is first associated with realism in the framing scenes that locate the family life of David and Jennifer in the 1990s, it takes on spectacular meaning in Pleasantville. The colour is rich, luxurious and far more intense. The use of colour and black and white is not simply a means of demarcating past and present in the film. Instead, colour is used as a form of spectacular excess in a black and white past that is itself fantastical.

While the spectacle of colour is born of changes brought about by, and that will ultimately effect, the lives of David and Jennifer, this does not happen without protest. Townsmen mobilise against the 'coloureds' in their midst, remonstrating against the irrevocable changes happening to norms of domesticity, fidelity, propriety and pleasantness. Seeing atrophy in colour, the all-male Chamber of Commerce represents a community cabal intent on policing the terms of cultural consensus, of 'separating the pleasant from the unpleasant' through a heady assertion of patriarchal norms and the music of Perry Como. *Pleasantville* revisits themes developed in previous screenplays by the film's director, and one-time Democrat speechwriter, Gary Ross. Like his screenplay for *Dave* (1993), *Pleasantville* evokes a nascent conservatism against which to pit and champion themes of social justice and cultural and political regeneration. While in *Dave*, an honest everyman is displaced into the corrupt world of Presidential politics, changing it with can-do compassion, Daniel and Jennifer are displaced into the regulated mythworld of Pleasantville, transforming it with values and savvy derived from a world of nineties-cum-sixties libertarianism. In each case, a liberal-lite Clintonism seems to be the organising political vision.

In his review in *Sight and Sound*, J. Hoberman criticised *Pleasantville* for its 'exasperating mix of technological wonder and ideological idiocy'.[6] In a more forgiving article, Andrew O'Hehir still called it a 'muddled liberal fairytale about freedom and tolerance in the Frank Capra tradition'.[7] While the visual technique of *Pleasantville* was central to many favourable reviews, the type and degree of the film's quotational referencing became a theme of critical concern, if not explicit complaint. The film invokes a gathering of cultural moments and movements under the aegis of a growing expressive creativity in Pleasantville: artistic Modernism, the sexual revolution, the subcultural radicalism of rock 'n' roll and jazz, the burgeoning impact of feminism and civil rights protest. These libertarian, or maverick, symbols are then set against a rag-bag of right-wing invocations, also played out as part of the community's unfolding civic drama. These range from Kristallnacht and fascist book burning to McCarthyite courtroom battles. Hoberman is fully aware of the ideological stakes of *Pleasantville* in the partisan climate of the late 1990s. He lucidly draws out the film's liberal vision of an inclusive and tolerant society in a period beset by the reactionary moral platform of Christian fundamentalism and the inflammatory jeremiads about aesthetic and educational crises emanating from the cultural right. Complaints about *Pleasantville*'s 'muddle' and 'ideological idiocy' were not levelled at the film's political cloudiness, per se, but rather its narrative style. This refers mainly to the film's over-stimulated quotational practice. There was an underlying assumption in many reviews that the hyperconsciousness of *Pleasantville* simply over-reached itself. By playing excessively in what J. Hoberman calls a 'media hall of mirrors' – a film style dependent on the dizzying mix and self-devouring quotation of historical, mythic and media references – *Pleasantville* left itself open to criticism of narrative confusion and, more seriously, of demonstrating a lack of political and/or historicist depth.[8]

While not argued from the same neo-Marxian position as Jameson, comments of ideological 'muddle' and 'idiocy' share something in sympathy with Jameson's lament about the indiscriminate pastiche of the contemporary 'nostalgia film'. As Philip Drake outlines in the previous chapter, this denotes a film mode entirely dependent on quotational practice, and of the representation of history as 'fashion-plate image'. For Jameson, the nostalgia film concentrates less on the past than on representations and stereotypes of pastness. By this definition, *Pleasantville*'s indiscriminate blending of historical references would be symptomatic of the particular evacuation of historicist meaning and temporal depth that Jameson equates with postmodern culture more generally. However, this pessimistic view does not give reign to the possibilities of postmodern textual practice as it plays with, and reconstitutes, traces of the historical and media archive. Collins provides a different, and I think more enabling, perspective. He describes a certain type of film genre that actively responds to the expanding volume, access, manipulability and circulation of signs in postmodern cultural life. Seen in the context of his treatment of 1990s genericity, films like *Forrest Gump* and *Pleasantville* exemplify less Jameson's 'nostalgia mode' than what Collins has termed 'eclectic irony'.[9] Put succinctly, films that belong to the genre of 'eclectic irony' utilise the sophistication of media culture (its icons, images, sounds, scenarios, conventions and genres), greeting new forms of textuality by reworking traces of the 'semiotic array' in hybrid and ironic combinations. Rather than claim some authentic relation with the past, retreating from and beyond the question of textual mediation (something that Collins relates to an adverse genre he calls 'new sincerity'), films such as *Back to the Future, Thelma and Louise, Who Framed Roger Rabbit?, Forrest Gump* and *Pleasantville* are all defined by their use and

manipulation of the multifarious images and texts that circulate in
the contemporary cultural terrain. This has implications for the
question, and representation, of cultural memory. For Collins,
memory is not a question of unmediated recall or recovery, but of
the reconfiguration of cultural references and textual traces within
the semiotic array. His argument concentrates less on the waning of
historicity than on 'the individual negotiations of the array that form
the delicate process of not just maintaining but constantly rearticulating cultural memories'.[10]

In seeing how this process of articulation can be drawn in different political directions, it is useful to compare *Pleasantville* with *Forrest Gump*. Both films create a period pastness by recycling a diverse
range of media memories, digitally inserting their protagonists into
an archival and textual evocation of (or that begins with) the 1950s.
Forrest Gump rearticulates America's postwar past in a largely iconic
fashion. It replays history through a host of textual traces that
include documentary footage of key national events, archival
vignettes where Gump 'meets' historical figures in digitally altered
footage, and a soundtrack where period lyrics describe the diegetic
events of the film narrative. The film operates through a process of
'zoning', using different film stock, colour diffusions, visual imagery
and musical resonance to index what decade or 'zone' the film narrative is referring to and operating within. Unlike the status of
'docu-fable' that *Forrest Gump* claimed for itself, *Pleasantville* does
not play with boundaries of fiction and history in the same manner.
Instead, *Pleasantville* creates a hyperreal past, entirely defined by,
and within, the fictional conventions of television (sitcom) genre.
Where *Forrest Gump* is based on the archival and historical referencing of 'real' events and peoples – from George Wallace and the
desegregation stand-off to the pelvic gyrations of Elvis – *Pleasantville* creates a satirical iconography of projected cultural values.
This turns ruefully on the aggrandisement of the nuclear family, an
Ozzie and Harriet depiction of the fulfilled wife and mother, the
breadwinning father, and 2.4 compliant children. Set within a culture of material plenty, *Pleasantville* lampoons a set of white representational fantasies of the 1950s established *within* the 1950s.[11]

Despite their differences, the respective protagonists of *Forrest
Gump* and *Pleasantville* are woven into an iconic rendering of his-
torical/representational periodicity. While the character of Forrest
Gump (played by Tom Hanks) becomes the focal link in the film's

textual and narrative development, played out within America's postwar past, David and Jennifer are located squarely within a hermetic textual universe rhetorically drawn from that past. Discussing the escalation in the public sphere of a reflective attitude towards history, Sobchack suggests that *Forrest Gump* is 'absolutely dependent for its humor and irony upon the historically (self) conscious viewers who have been immersed in questions about the boundaries, meanings, and place of history in their daily lives, as well as their own possible place in history'.[12] Similar questions of historical subjectivity are given an added, more explicitly textualised, dimension in *Pleasantville*. Rather than revisit the 1950s, David and Jennifer are placed in an idealised representation of the 1950s. Here, they proceed to challenge, interrogate and deconstruct its ideological assumptions. In some sense, *Pleasantville* makes literal the process of postmodern historicism that Linda Hutcheon identifies when textual traces of the past come into ideological and cultural mediation with the present. *Pleasantville* is less concerned with the degree to which individuals impact upon historical events and happenings (as in *Forrest Gump*), than with the reflective engagement, intervention and re-constellation of history's semiotised traces. Through David and Jennifer's own textual adventure – an adventure that changes the representational and chromatic life-world of Pleasantville as seen and consumed in the present – *Pleasantville* exemplifies what, in the context of postmodern historicism, Hutcheon has described as the 'critical, dialogical reviewing of the forms, contexts and values of the past'.[13]

This takes on a particular significance in the climate of the 1990s. In political terms, *Pleasantville* revisits the instructive mythologies of 'traditional family values' that have underpinned the sanctity and general lauding of the 1950s in conservative rhetoric. According to Stephanie Coontz, these mythologies were most powerfully derived in the 1990s from the countless reruns of television sitcoms like *The Donna Read Show* and *Leave it to Beaver*.[14] Of course, the fate of the family, trammelled in culture war debates, informed much larger questions about American cultural morality, history and identity in the 1990s. These turned centrally upon the pivotal significance and legacy of the 1960s. For conservatives, especially the New-Right coalition that formed around Newt Gingrich in the middle of the decade, the 1960s became a key battleground of cultural memory. As a decade, 'the sixties' emblematised the lapsarian moment from which a diagnosis of contemporary malaise took its form and force. In right-wing rhetoric, symptoms linked to the 1960s could include anything from the breakdown of the family and the rise in violent crime, to the emergence of multicultural separatism and the crisis of university education. The liberal-left response, vociferously argued by the so-tarred 'tenured radicals' of right-wing lore, argued for the crucial importance of the 1960s in rethinking terms of inclusion/ exclusion in American life and society. These frictions and battles of value were duly fought out in the cultural terrain. Ever sensitive to marketable moods and public discourse – and a prime site of ideo-logical contestation – this could not help but include Hollywood film.

No film is *intrinsically* 'conservative' or 'liberal' and therefore representative of any pure ideological position. This is especially true when relating films to the nebulous culture war debates of the 1990s. As Douglas Kellner points out, the texts of media culture often incorporate a variety of images, effects and narrative strate-gies, frequently going both ways, ideologically, to maximise their audience appeal.[15] This flexibility combines with the highly complex and 'structurally ambiguous' way that contemporary films construct meaning and negotiate identity. Jude Davies and Carol Smith suggest that any attempt to carve up Hollywood film in thematic terms, based on what specific texts appear to be 'about', will rarely account for the way that films solicit audience identification on a partial basis, and depend upon overlapping and multidimensional con-structions of identity.[16] *Forrest Gump* is a good example of a film that offered itself up for a conservative reading – celebrating family values and the authority of a white, male redemption figure – while also providing a view whereby conventional values and racial/ gender prejudices appear to be satirised. Despite the ideological ambiguity resulting from the reach for mainstream appeal, popular films *do* inscribe and transcode ideological positions within particu-lar discursive fields. Such is the case, I would argue, with *Pleas-antville* and *Forrest Gump*. Both films combine digital innovation and cultural invocation to allegorise the significance of the 1960s, making alternate claims in the hegemonic battle to control the decade's 'memory' and 'legacy'.

Without wishing to simplify the discursive complexity of either film, I would suggest that *Pleasantville* can be read as a cultural and allegorical response to the residual conservatism of *Forrest Gump*. If, as numerous critics agree, *Forrest Gump* constructs a consensus view of American history based upon the authority of the white father and the marginalisation of black, female, gay and radical 'others',[17] *Pleasantville* assimilates the terms of culture war debate that informed *Gump*'s vision of family idealism, and that underwrote various elements of conservative rhetoric in the early 1990s. While *Forrest Gump* can be set in relation to the high-point of culture war discourse – a period where the 1960s were seen as the cause and origin of a more general crisis of morality and values – *Pleasantville* is focused on the culture war as a political and rhetorical *moment*. The film is less concerned with controlling the popular memory of America's recent past than with addressing conservative 'culture war' mythologies themselves. Specifically, *Pleasantville* puts forward a vision of community – tolerant, enlightened, coloured – carried out from within, and set against, the conservative territory of the stolid, monochrome, and resoundingly fetishised, 1950s.

This interpretation might better explain the type and variety of media invocation in *Pleasantville*, troubling to critics who identify the film's particular 'muddle' and 'idiocy'. Basically, I would suggest that *Pleasantville* turns key elements of conservative rhetoric against itself. The film invokes a variety of issues, images and right-wing bugbears in a fable that responds openly to culture war discourse of the early 1990s. The film dramatises a series of recognised conflict sites fought over art, literature, music, morality, sexuality, family and difference. At the same time, the film also figures, and playfully renders, images and echoes drawn from conservative rhetoric. While the spectral presence of Alan Bloom and Hilton Kramer haunts the film – symbolically drawn in the town's enforcement of a 'non-changist view of history, emphasising continuity over alteration', and in its vociferous policing of art and public display[18] *Pleasantville* weaves into its narrative several incendiary tropes that distinguished media representation of the culture wars in the early 1990s.[19]

One moment in the film that has invited a cautionary, if not openly sceptical, response on the part of many reviewers, has been the invocation of fascist book burning. Responding to the cultural threat of literary and artistic flowering in Pleasantville, represented both by the town's youth and proprietor-cum-artist, Bill Johnson (Jeff Daniels), a conservative mob rampage through the town, smashing windows, creating bonfires of censored texts and sneering at the deviancy of the 'coloureds'. For some, the echoes of Kristallnacht sit uncomfortably within a fable ostensibly dealing with myths of 1950s America. However, fascist invocation was endemic to the kind of rhetoric mobilised in the vitriolic 'political correctness' debates of the early 1990s. From a conservative standpoint, left-wing 'feminazis' and other 'Visigoths in tweed' had come to police cultural value and personal behaviour, representing nothing short of an emergent 'totalitarianism' or 'McCarthyism' of the left. The language of fascism infused the standard bromides emanating from the cultural right. *Pleasantville* replayed these fascist and McCarthyite invocations, but transposed them back onto the black and white burghers of the town, characters who increasingly appear as if within the cartoon grip of New Right moralism.

It should be said that 'political correctness', the lightning rod of culture war debate, created significant rafts between factions of the left and right. This makes it difficult to speak confidently or coherently about discreet left/right positions and standards of moral value. On issues ranging from the emergence of academic theory and the strategic import of identity politics, to campus speech codes and anti-pornographic censorship, discursive territories of left and right were subject to frequent clouding and conflation. In media terms, however, that axis of left and right was fairly well maintained. If, as Jim Nielsen suggests, the 'most striking feature of media representation of political correctness was its consistent identification with fascism',[20] *Pleasantville* used culture war metaphors of political extremism, associated with tenured radicals and their ilk, but repositioned these within and against the prescriptive social regulation of (white, male, middle class) conservative moral guardians.

Collins suggests that contemporary film genre must work within, and should be understood in terms of, a cultural terrain that is 'already sedimented with layers of popular mythologies, some old, some recent, but all co-present and subject to rearticulation according to different ideological agendas'.[21] Through active appropriation of the media and discursive array, *Pleasantville* satirises the fallacious nostalgia of the New Right, attached as it was (and remains) to a prelapsarian order of patriarchal norms and family idealism and absorbed, at some level, within films like *Forrest Gump*. A concerted narrative reading of *Pleasantville* would have to contend with the film's own ideological prescriptions. The film's version of a culturally expressive and socially inclusive community is, in the end, fairly muted. J. Hoberman is surely right to comment that, quite aside from its inclusive pretensions, *Pleasantville* projects a resiliently white, heterosexual version of the redeemed community. The film offers a fairly mainstream dose of Hollywood liberalism. It would be wrong to suggest, however, that *Pleasantville* traffics in a muddled, random or idiotic narrative to advance this liberal positionality. On the contrary, the film rather cleverly weaves elements of culture war rhetoric in and within a media fiction (i.e. the 1950s sitcom) whose myths of family idealism and harmonious community it contiguously deconstructs. Rather than a paradigm of narrative confusion, ideological idiocy or historicist blockage, *Pleasantville* plays reflexively with culture war discourse and its constituent politics of memory.

Colourised memory

Pleasantville is an interesting memory text on a number of levels. I have so far suggested that, through eclectic quotational referencing, the film transcodes a social discourse about the meaning and memory of the 1960s. Specifically, it plays with (and against) conservative nostalgia for the mythic universe of the 1950s domestic sitcom. The film also invokes different kinds of memory debate, however. In significant ways, *Pleasantville* revisits the question of digital colourisation. To its liberal critics in the late 1980s, the process of colourisation created movies that were hollow simulations. They were a crude and stupefying cultural form symptomatic of an emerging digital age, and enabled by a political climate that licensed the re-privatisation of public culture through the enforcement of property rights (in this case, Ted Turner's). While the political climate altered very little in the 1990s – copyright protection becoming a defining issue in the neo-liberal media marketplace – attitudes towards digital culture *did* change. With regard to Hollywood's own output, Andrew Darley suggests that a new modality of mainstream cinema developed, comprised of films defined by sophisticated techniques of computer imaging.[22] Represented in movies such as *Terminator 2: Judgement Day* (1991), *Jurassic Park* (1993), *The Mask* (1994), *True Lies* (1994), *Starship Troopers* (1997) and *Titanic* (1997), the 1990s witnessed the development of an enlivened 'digital cinema' of which *Pleasantville* can be seen to be a part.

In Darley's definition, 'digital cinema' is a movie style characterised by a new regime of spectacle, centring upon the creation of dazzling and spellbinding imagery. Manifest in various genre forms, digital cinema deploys, and is often highly dependent on, the formal excitations created by techniques of computer imaging. Darley writes: 'The growth of spectacle, and the fascination with image as image, in the sense of both visual excitation and technological density (artifice), is one indication that attention to *formal* facets – means and pure perceptual play – are finding a place within mass entertainment forms.'[23] *Pleasantville* engages a distinctive mode of colourised spectacle. Indeed, the film's 'perceptual play' became a selling point in promotional and advertising strategy (posters depicted a black and white audience from the 1950s awe-struck by the projection of a colour world). However, *Pleasantville* challenges Darley's critical assertion that spectacle has brought with it a consequent 'waning of narrative'. If the film's quotational practice constructs a highly reflexive narrative based on the relationship between present and past, digital technology is used to draw out and acknowledge this relationship in textual terms.

In form and style, *Pleasantville* was not without precedent. In 1991, Nickelodeon (the cable network owned by Viacom that operates the rerun programme Nick at Nite) produced a situation comedy where a 1950s sitcom family were re-located in a 'real-life' suburb of New Jersey in the 1990s. Entitled *Hi Honey, I'm Home*, the family appeared in vintage black and white. *Pleasantville* used the same conceit but reversed the terms. In each case, the narrative 'hook' was based upon temporal displacements in and between the real and televisual universe of the 1950s and the 1990s. While themes of time-travel and of mystical transportations to alternate worlds are nothing new in American film (going back to *The Wizard of Oz*), digital technology has opened up new creative possibilities in the representation of these spatial and temporal displacements: of transposing the present in the past, the past in the present, and of recreating mythic and historical worlds on a new and visually spectacular scale. In *Pleasantville*, digital capacities of visual manipulation are used to create a myth-world where *chromatic* difference becomes the narrative lynchpin. Unlike *Forrest Gump*, where the central character is harmoniously transposed into a tableau of American cultural history, colour in *Pleasantville* is used to draw out cultural and temporal disjunctions; the infusion of colour is a device that signifies the unmistakeable trace of the present as it intervenes with, interprets, and transforms, the semiotised realm of the past.

There is, of course, an important difference between the colourisation of old movies – what for Turner became a commercial attempt to maximise the syndication potential of black and white films he'd paid too much for – and *Pleasantville*'s use of colourisation as a narrative device. Accepting the principle that 'colourisation' does not have the same legal, aesthetic and discursive stakes in each case, I would nevertheless say that *Pleasantville* reflects a changing attitude towards the digital re-presentation of the past. To detractors of the colourisation process, colour conversion tampered with the aura (the artefact) and the era (the tradition) of the 'classic' black and white movie.[24] At stake in the colourisation debate, and especially felt by the Hollywood establishment, was the destabilisation of categories of value such as 'authenticity' and 'the archive'; digital technology was seen to challenge the visual and cultural basis upon which these categories have been traditionally grounded and sustained. However, as computer technology has been absorbed within cultural life – most profoundly via the Internet but also within a range of genres in the 1990s including film, advertising and music video – digital imaging/information has become less of a threat and more an intrinsic part of (new) media life.

Describing the forms and features of the contemporary 'information age', Collins links the accelerated rate of technological innovation with a new and particular attitude towards the archive. Not only have digital technologies transformed 'offices and living rooms into instant ad hoc archives where juxtapositions are a matter of perpetually reconfigurable random access',[25] Collins suggests that the art of (cinematic) storytelling has changed in the context of this exponential increase in the volume of transmissible images. Pointing to a new textual hyperconsciousness in cultural life, Collins puts a refreshingly positive slant on the negotiation of identity and memory in the information age. Mapping a cultural shift in the 1990s, he argues that early, technophobic, fears of information glut – manifest in hostility towards representational forms and genres enabled by new digital technologies – have been replaced by 'the more contemporary response of mastering the array of information which now forms the fabric of day-to-day life'.[26] In terms of the interests of this chapter, one might say that while the colourisation debate of the late 1980s was born, in part, from the shock of technological excess – especially as it was felt to impact on the 'authenticity' of the art work and the basis of artistic heritage – *Pleasantville* represents the domestication of colouring technique and the marketable manipulation of 'techno-textuality'.

It would be wrong to suggest too neat a transition from the 'shock of excess' to the 'domestication of the semiotic array'. And yet, some kind of cultural and critical transformation has occurred. This is linked fundamentally to the way that, in the words of Stephen Prince, 'digital imaging technologies are rapidly transforming nearly all phases of contemporary film production'.[27] With the new creative possibilities of computer-generated imagery, notions of authenticity and indexicality have been seriously problematised. As Prince notes, the result in film theory has been to shift emphasis 'away from naïve notions of indexical realism in favour of an attention to the constructedness of cinematic discourse'.[28] Digital technology has raised new questions about the ideology of cinematic representation and referentiality and the status of memory is embroiled in these cultural and critical transformations. In cinematic terms, the transition is usefully brought out by the way that *Pleasantville* revisits and recasts the issue of film colourisation, adopting a highly reflexive attitude towards the discursive intersection of memory and textuality. Unlike the anti-colourisation lobby, which sought to preserve a selection of 'classic' art works under the auspice and designation of a sacral film history, *Pleasantville* makes a point of the means by which texts are refigured, recontextualised and remembered in the contemporary cultural terrain.

It has been my argument that *Pleasantville* uses digital colourisation to illustrate the discursive circulation and rearticulation of the past, in and by the present. Creating its own ironic sense of what Gilbert Adair calls the 'suburban pastoral'[29] – an idealised evocation of small-town Americana in the tradition of *It's a Wonderful Life*[30] – *Pleasantville* deploys colouring technique to recast conservative nostalgia for family values and the glories of small-town community. In doing so, the film transcodes a social discourse prevalent in the 1990s, attempting to recuperate the significance and memory of the 1960s. Writing in 1993, scion of the New Left, Todd Gitlin, said: 'the genies that the Sixties loosed are still abroad in the land, inspiring and unsettling and offending, making trouble'.[31] In *Pleasantville*, David and Jennifer become the figurative embodiments of these 1990s-cum-1960s genies. With their sexual savvy, political sophistication, and demystified notions of identity, gender and family, they question, interrogate and problematise the forms and values of the (media) past caricatured in Pleasantville. Using the infusion of colour to dramatise this process, *Pleasantville* is a pregnant, even indicative, memory text of the late 1990s: it articulates a discourse of cultural remembrance in a moment where the textuality of memory has, itself, become increasingly hyperconscious.

Notes

1 A full account of these issues can be found in Paul Grainge, *Monochrome Memories: Nostalgia and Style in Retro America* (Westport, CT and London: Praeger, 2002).

2 Douglas Kellner, *Media Culture* (London: Routledge, 1995), pp. 93–122.

3 Fredric Jameson, *Postmodernism, or, The Cultural Logic of Late Capitalism* (London: Verso, 1991).

4 See Andreas Huyssen, *Twilight Memories: Marking Time in A Culture of Amnesia* (New York: Routledge, 1995); Vivian Sobchack (ed.), *The Persistence of History: Cinema, Television and the Modern Event* (New York: Routledge, 1995); Jim Collins, *Architectures of Excess: Cultural Life in the Information Age* (London: Routledge, 1995).

5 Lynn Spigel, 'From the Dark Ages to the Golden Age: Women's Memories and Television Re-runs', *Screen* 36: 1 (1995), 16–33. Discussing the popularity of television reruns in the 1990s, Spigel suggests that interest in programmes such as *Nick at Nite* (part of Nickelodeon's evening schedule and a forerunner of rerun programming) has less to do with the endurance of television art than with strategies of recontextualisation. These include programme marathons, theme nights, promotions and ironic guest presenters, all of which help to create a new, essentially playful, 'reception context' for old reruns. See also, Paul Grainge, 'Nostalgia and Style in Retro America: Moods, Modes and Media Recycling', *The Journal of American and Comparative Cultures* 23: 1 (2000), 27–34.

6 J. Hoberman, 'Under the Rainbow', *Sight and Sound* (January 1999), 16.

7 Andrew O'Hehir, 'Pleasantville', *Sight and Sound* (March 1999), 50.

8 For a discussion of these issues, see Jim Collins, 'Genericity in the Nineties: Eclectic Irony and the New Sincerity', in Jim Collins, Hilary Radner and Ava Preacher Collins (eds), *Film Theory Goes to the Movies* (New York: Routledge, 1993), pp. 242–63. An example of the lament for narrative coherence and historicist depth can be found in Jameson, *Postmodernism*, and Allison Graham, 'Nostalgia and the Criminality of Popular Culture', *Georgia Review* 38: 2 (1984), 348–64.

9 Collins, 'Genericity in the Nineties', pp. 242–57.

10 Collins, 'Genericity in the Nineties', p. 255.
11 See Nina C. Leibman, *Living Room Lectures: The Fifties Family in Film and Television* (Austin: University of Texas Press, 1995).
12 Vivian Sobchack, 'History Happens', in *The Persistence of History*, p. 3.
13 Linda Hutcheon, *A Poetics of Postmodernism: History, Theory, Fiction* (London: Routledge, 1988), p. 89.
14 Stephanie Coontz, *The Way We Never Were: American Families and the Nostalgia Trap* (New York: Basic Books, 1992), pp. 23–41.
15 Kellner, *Media Culture*, p. 93.
16 Jude Davies and Carol Smith, *Gender, Ethnicity and Sexuality in Contemporary American Film* (Keele: Keele University Press, 1997), p. 9.
17 See, in particular, Robert Burgoyne, *Film Nation: Hollywood Looks at U.S. History* (Minneapolis: University of Minnesota Press, 1997), pp. 104–19; Thomas Byers, 'History Re-membered: Forrest Gump, Post-feminist Masculinity, and the Burial of the Counterculture', *Modern Fiction Studies* 42: 2 (1996), 419–44; and Fred Pfeil, *White Guys* (London: Verso, 1995), pp. 233–62.
18 Allan Bloom and Hilton Kramer were two arch cultural warriors in the conservative attack on educational and artistic standards, represented in Bloom's 1987 jeremiad on American liberal education, *The Closing of The American Mind,* and in Kramer's various media pronouncements on political correctness in the arts.
19 Troubled by the so-called 'politicisation of the academy', editorials in *New York, The New Republic, The Chicago Tribune, Time* and *Newsweek* spoke throughout 1991 of a new intolerance within universities and in cultural life more generally. The bogey of 'political correctness' became the touch-point for news stories about the tyrannies of the 'loony' left.
20 Jim Neilson, 'The Great PC Scare: Tyrannies of the Left, Rhetoric of the Right', in Jeffrey Williams (ed.), *PC Wars: Politics and Theory in the Academy* (New York: outledge, 1995), pp. 60–89.
21 Collins, *Architectures of Excess*, p. 155.
22 Andrew Darley, *Visual Digital Culture* (London: Routledge, 2000), p. 109. Of course, Hollywood embraced digital technology long before the 1990s. While experimentation with digital-based technologies can be traced to the 1960s, Darley suggests that Hollywood really embraced computer imaging in the middle of the 1980s, pioneered in films using special effects such as *Alien* (1979), *Tron* (1982) and *The Last Starfighter* (1985). It was the commercial success of *Terminator 2* in 1991, however, that 'convinced Hollywood that digital cinema was both aesthetically feasible and potentially highly lucrative'.
23 Darley, *Visual Digital Culture,* p. 114.
24 While the colourisation conflict marked a figurative defeat for those wishing to instigate a legal grounding for the protection of artistic

rights, the brouhaha soon expired when it became clear that colourised films were not, in fact, replacing black and white 'classics' but were often co-existing with monochrome originals in the programming schedules of rerun cable stations such as American Movie Classics. For a lucid summary of the cultural and legal debates surrounding the colourisation conflict, see Stuart Klawans, 'Colorization: Rose-Tinted Spectacles', in Mark Crispin-Miller (ed.), *Seeing Through Movies* (New York: Pantheon, 1990), pp. 150–85; and Craig Wagner, 'Motion Picture Colorization and the Elusive Moral Right', *New York University Law Review* 64: 3 (1989), 628–725. For a discussion of the 'discourse of black and whiteness' in American visual culture during the 1990s, see Paul Grainge, *Monochrome Memories*.

25 Collins, *Architectures of Excess*, p. 3.
26 Collins, *Architectures of Excess*, p. 4.
27 Stephen Prince, 'True Lies: Perceptual Realism, Digital Images and Film Theory', *Film Quarterly* 49: 3 (1996), 27.
28 Prince, 'True Lies', 35.
29 Gilbert Adair, 'It's a Phantasmagorical Life', *The Independent on Sunday* (14 March 1999), p. 5.
30 An indication of *Pleasantville*'s discreet invocation of the colourisation debate – aside from its obvious use of colouring technology – can arguably be found in the film's implicit, or at least atmospheric, reference to *It's a Wonderful Life*. It was Ted Turner's attempt to produce a colourised version of Capra's film that mobilised the anti-colourisation lobby in 1987, liberal directors and film guilds rushing to protect the aesthetic integrity and original status of *It's a Wonderful Life* as an 'American classic'.
31 Todd Gitlin, *The Sixties: Years of Hope, Days of Rage* (New York: Bantam Books, 1993), p. xiv.

11

Memory, history and digital imagery in contemporary film

Robert Burgoyne

Bernardo Bertolucci once said in an interview that the cinema 'is the language through which reality expresses itself . . . to create the language of the cinema, more than with any other form of expression, you have first to put your camera in front of reality, because cinema is made of reality'.[1] He also said that every film is a documentary, including fiction films, for every film carries within it an archival record of the period in which it was made, expressed in terms of lighting style, set design, camera work, make up, and even the behavioural gestures and acting techniques of the performers.

Today the idea that the cinema is the language through which reality expresses itself – an idea that has moulded much of film practice and theory from the time of cinema's invention by the Lumière brothers in 1896 – seems to be increasingly under assault. The widespread use of computer generated imagery in film, which allows filmmakers to fuse photographic and digital images – as well as documentary and fictional footage – in the same composited frame, is only one aspect of a rapid and accelerating movement toward replacing celluloid with the infinitely malleable medium of digital imaging, a movement that has made contemporary cinema the emblematic expression, not of the real, but rather of the hyperreal. The rise of digital morphing techniques, for example, along with other forms of electronic manipulation of images in film, and the certain development in the very near future of an interactive digital cinema in which endings can be changed, and troublesome scenes transformed instantaneously according to audience responses, demographics and tastes makes the once intimate connection between cinema and reality remote at best, a distant memory of a century – the century of film, now past – when the ontology of the photographic image could be celebrated by the theorist André Bazin as the death mask of reality, as the fingerprint of the real.

Perhaps the greatest champion of the realist vocation of the cinema, Bazin argued that the realism of cinema derived from its existential relation to the physical world: the same rays of light that fell onto the objects of the phenomenal world bounced off those objects and into the lens of the camera, there to be imprinted on the photographic emulsion which preserved that very same light like a fly preserved in amber. For Bazin, the realist aspect of the cinema carried almost religious overtones: he likened film to the Shroud of Turin or Veronica's veil – not just a representation of the real, but rather an actual physical impression.[2] In the present day, however, the imprimatur of reality that once stamped the cinema has been replaced by the doubt and uncertainty that accompanies computer generated imagery, in which 'mountains, cities, armies [or the Roman Colisseum in the 4th Century A.D.], can be altered or created whole in a digital snap'.[3] Most importantly, the increasing use of computer generated, artificial visual environments in the movies that we see today appears to threaten not only the certitude and authenticity that we associate with photography, which is often described as a 'visual record', but also the loss of the ethical and moral dimension that Bazin associated with film: its way of insisting on the 'irreducible integrity of people and things beyond ourselves', its way of 'reminding us constantly of our relationship to them'.[4]

This privileged relation to reality that the cinema once enjoyed, and which it appears to have spontaneously sacrificed with its embrace of the hyperreality of electronic image creation, raises particular questions for the way history is represented in film. For films that take history as their subject undertake a dialogue with the real in a way that other films do not. Historical films have real-world reverberations: recent films such as *JFK*, *Braveheart*, *Glory*, *The Hurricane* and *Dances with Wolves* have served as a catalyst for the reevaluation of the historical past; they have provoked governments and led to the opening of secret files; they have inspired national consciousness. In a more general sense, film has played an extraordinarily powerful role in shaping our conception of the history of the twentieth century: the films championed by Bazin, for example – the neo-realist films of Rossellini, Visconti and De Sica – have had a deep and lasting effect on our understanding of the effects of World War Two, as have more recent films such as *Schindler's List* and other films dealing with the Holocaust. The powerful effect of films that deal with war, suffering and injustice is intimately related to the way they connect us to their physical and social environments, to the way they connect us to the world, to history.

The ferocious controversies that surround films such as *JFK* and *Forrest Gump* appear to me to stem not only from the interpretations they offer of controversial historical events, but also, pointedly, from their departure from the conventions of photo-realism through their use of computer enhanced and computer generated images, by their seamless splicing together of fictional scenes and archival footage, and by their use of documentary footage to re-enact events from a fictional or speculative perspective, blurring the boundary between actuality and fiction. In these films, the status of the 'document' – which, as Paul Ricouer reminds us, is the indelible dividing line between history and fiction – is placed in doubt.[5] We can no longer be sure that the documentary images of John F. Kennedy, George Wallace, John Lennon, Lyndon Baines Johnson and other historical figures that appear in *Forrest Gump* and *JFK* are the authentic traces of the past; the archival image can no longer be assumed to be an authentic record of past events. As Thomas Elsaesser writes, 'Future generations, looking at the history of the 20th century, will never be able to tell fact from fiction, having the media as material evidence. But then, will this distinction still matter to them?'[6]

In Elsaesser's view, history itself, partly because of the rise of elec-tronic media, has suffered a serious loss of prestige:

> History, when it is not just what's past, but what's being passed on, seems to have entered a conceptual twilight zone, not least because it has become a past that cinema and television can 'master' for us by dig-itally remastering archival material. While memory, especially when contrasted with history, has gained in value as a subject of public inter-est and interpretation, history has become the very signifier of the inauthentic . . . the false and the falsifiable . . . merely designating what is left when the site of memory has been vacated by the living. With the audio-visual media effortlessly re-presenting that site, however, the line where memory passes into history has become uncertain.[7]

In this chapter, I would like to explore some of the implications of computer generated imagery for the cinematic representation of the past. In particular, I will focus on the most contested and con-troversial area of contemporary fiction cinema's representation of the past – the use of documentary images as a mode of imaginative reconstruction or re-enactment. The shift from documentary images being understood as the trace of the past, as something left behind by a past event, to something available for imaginative and poetic reconstruction through computer alteration would seem to present a particular challenge to historical film's claim to capture a certain truth about the past. For although the representation of history in film is a notoriously vexed subject, typically involving controversies over authenticity and accuracy versus the interpretive requirements of narrative form, the more narrow case of the alteration or embellishment of documentary images for the purposes of dramatic storytelling highlights some new questions. The unprecedented conjunction of archival images and computer generated imagery in contemporary films such as *Forrest Gump* would seem, for example, to directly contradict what Ricouer calls the 'primacy of the referential intention' in historical reconstruction. With its increasing use of morphing techniques and computer generated visual environments, the cinema would seem to be a medium that now refuses history in the traditional sense of origins, authenticity and documentation.

And yet, contrary to expectation, film in the present day appears to have strengthened its cultural claims on the past. The cinematic rewriting of history has, in the present cultural moment, accrued an extraordinary degree of social power and influence. Film appears to have acquired, more than ever, the mantle of meaningfulness and authenticity with relation to the past – not necessarily of accuracy or fidelity to the record, but of meaningfulness, understood in terms of emotional and affective truth. Cinema, in effect, seems to evoke the emotional certitude we associate with memory for, like memory, film is now, to a greater extent than before, associated with the body; it engages the viewer at the somatic level, immersing the spectator in experiences and impressions that, like memories, seem to be burned in.

I will begin by summarising an important argument that has been made by Alison Landsberg, who has coined the striking term 'prosthetic memory' to describe the way mass cultural technologies of memory, such as film, enable individuals to experience, as if they were memories, events through which they themselves did not live. She cites the growing popularity of experiential museums, such as the Holocaust Museum in Washington DC, of historical re-enactments, including the relatively recent D-Day celebrations, and of historical films such as *Schindler's List* as evidence of a widespread cultural desire to re-experience the past in a sensuous form, and stresses the power of what she calls experiential mass cultural forms to make historical or political events meaningful in a personal, local way. The new modes of experience, sensation and history that are made available in American mass culture, she writes, 'have profoundly altered the individual's relationship to both their own memories and to the archive of collective cultural memories'.[8] Defining the concept of prosthetic memory as 'memories that circulate publicly, that are not organically based, but that are nonetheless experienced with one's own body – by means of a wide range of cultural technologies',[9] Landsberg argues that prosthetic memories, especially those afforded by the cinema, 'become part of one's personal archive of experience'.[10] The artificial but real experiences afforded by the cinema 'might actually install in individuals "symptoms" through which they didn't actually live, but to which they subsequently have a kind of experiential relationship'.[11] Although the production and dissemination of memories that are defined not by organic, individual experience but by simulation and re-enactment are potentially dangerous, posing the threat of alienation and revisionism, prosthetic memories also enable a sensuous engagement with past lives and past experiences that, Landsberg argues, can serve as 'the basis for mediated collective identification'.[12]

These arguments appear to have a particular salience for understanding the popularity and the larger cultural significance of films such as *Forrest Gump, JFK, Glory, The Hurricane* and *Saving Private Ryan*. In many ways, these films seem to literalise the concept of prosthetic memory. They explicitly take on the role of offering an experiential relation to history, inserting their main characters and, by extension, their viewers, into what appears to be a physical, literal relationship to actual historical figures and events: in *Forrest Gump,* for example, the film splices the character of Gump into fictionalised interactions with historical figures captured in archival film images – Gump is seen shaking hands with JFK and Richard Nixon, standing on the University of Alabama steps with George Wallace and conversing with John Lennon. And in the case of Steven Spielberg's *Saving Private Ryan*, the film creates a visceral, sensesurround experience of the D-Day invasion with excruciatingly realistic effects. What Landsberg calls the 'widespread desire on the part of Americans to experience and to live history', the desire to experience history in a 'personal, bodily way',[13] is exemplified in these films.

The cinema is thus revealed, in the most emphatic way, to be an instrument that allows individuals to 'experience a bodily, mimetic encounter with a collective past they never actually led', experiences that foreground the multiple and complicated relations between individual and collective memory and history in the age of media culture.

Memory, in the traditional sense, describes an individual relation to the past, a bodily, physical relation to an actual experience that is significant enough to inform and colour the subjectivity of the rememberer. History, on the other hand, is traditionally conceived as impersonal, the realm of public events that have occurred outside the archive of personal experience. But in contemporary media culture, the most significant 'historical' events are often transformed into spectatorial 'experiences' that shape and inform the subjectivity of the individual viewer; with the media continually and effortlessly re-presenting the past, history, once thought of as an impersonal phenomenon, has been replaced by 'experiential' collective memory. Electronic or audio-visual 'lieux de memoire' (sites of memory) have created a kind of second order memory system that is fast becoming a second order reality. As Elsaesser writes,

> we may be deceiving ourselves [if we] contrast too sharply authentic memory with inauthentic (media-) history. A new authenticity may be in the making . . . When we ask: 'Do you remember the day Kennedy was shot?', do we not actually mean 'Do you remember the day you watched Kennedy being shot all day on the television?' . . . Or after the Challenger disaster, when the space shuttle seemed to explode into a starburst of white smoke over and over again, until we could no longer tell the television screen from our retinas?[14]

Elsaesser, however, seems wary of the experiential effects of mass media, arguing that the seemingly physical, experiential relation to the historical event and the historical past that mass technology affords may inhibit the narrative closure that storytelling and narrative history allow. Rather than generating historical amnesia, as is so often claimed, film and media may generate its opposite, an inability to stop obsessing about an event: 'No longer is storytelling the culture's meaning-making response; an activity closer to therapeutic practice has taken over, with acts of re-telling, remembering, and repeating all pointing in the direction of obsession, fantasy, trauma.'[15] In this view, the mass media create cultural memories that resist the kind of narrative closure associated with storytelling, with narrative history. He asks what obscure urge is satisfied by the com-pulsion to repeat that seems to drive the mass media in its continu-ous presenting and re-presenting of historical trauma, a question that has gained in importance and urgency after 11 September 2001. Hayden White has described twentieth-century historical events as 'modernist'; the lack of closure, the fragmentation and dissociation of one event from another, the inability of historians and the public at large to 'master' and contain events in narrative form, may be a consequence, he writes, of the unprecedented scale and compound contexts of 'modernist' historical events, such as the Holocaust, the Vietnam War, the assassination of JFK, and now the attack of 11 September.[16] Taking White's hypothesis one step further, Elsaesser suggests that the lack of closure in modernist historical events may be a property of the mass media itself and its take on history, which tends to create in the spectator symptoms of obsession and trauma. In the optimistic account of prosthetic memory provided by Lands-berg, the somatic powers of mass technology to produce something like symptoms in the spectator create the potential for empathic identification, for new collective frameworks, for public spheres based on memory. In Elsaesser's less sanguine perspective, the burn-ing in of memories via the media – burned in to the point that they create symptoms in the spectator – speak not to empathy and new social alliances but rather to cultural obsession, fantasy, and trauma.

Elsaesser's and Landsberg's suggestion that a new kind of authen-ticity may be in the making, one which includes media events as a form of individual and collective experience, is a striking insight. But although this idea is provocative and persuasive enough as regards memory and the media, it falls short of considering the wild card effect that digital imaging has on this conception of the authen-ticity of mediated experience. For, as Elsaesser says elsewhere, there is a particular kind of postmodern hubris at work in contemporary media culture, expressed most powerfully in the widespread faith that film and video can 'redeem the past, rescue the real, and even rescue that which was never real'.[17] Here, I would like to offer a small counterexample of the cinema's power to inform subjectivity and 'rescue that which was never real'. In a recent Hollywood film entitled *Wag the Dog,* a Hollywood producer in league with the President's closest advisors concocts a fake war with Albania to dis-tract the country from a scandal involving the President and a young girl. The key element in this fake war is phony news footage of the rescue of a young Albanian woman fleeing the smouldering ruins of her village. The news footage that the Hollywood producer concocts for this disinformation campaign, of course, is computer generated, with every detail, including the amount of smoke, the placement of the burning buildings, the small bridge over which she runs and the colour of the cat she rescues from the ruins, created and composited together by computer. Through elaborate devices such as this, the nation comes to believe in the reality of the fake war, which comes complete with a fake hero. Here the cinema clearly 'redeems the past, rescues the real, and even rescues that which was never real'. *Wag The Dog* serves as a dazzling example of the potential of computer generated imagery to create utterly realistic 'events'; it also serves as a strong cautionary tale concerning the faith we place in the cinema as a form of integral realism, as 'a recreation of the world in its own image, an image unburdened by the freedom of interpretation of the artist or the irreversibility of time'.[18]

The realist style championed by Bazin carried a particular message about history and its relation to individual existence: the privileged meaning of the photo-realist style is that it keys the spectator in to the passing of time, to the saturation of space with meaning, and to the organic link between the actor and the setting in which the action occurs. In favouring the long take over montage, for example, Bazin argued that the long take – the unbroken shot of extended duration – accentuated the meaning and value of temporality on the screen; temporality in the photo-realist style is directly related to the spectator's own 'embodied perception of lived time and transformation'.[19] In the long take, and for that matter in the photo-realist style in general, human emergence is accomplished in real historical time, laboriously, with difficulty, and irreversibly. With the ascendance of computer generated imagery in film, however, with its ease of transformation and quick change potential – a potential figured most prominently in the use of computer warping and morphing – there is a radical transformation of the spatial and temporal coordinates of the cinema and its relation to human experience, a transformation, as Vivian Sobchack says, of the 'spatial and temporal grounding of the photo-realist cinema that up until now has been indexically related to human physical existence as it is daily experienced in space and time'.[20]

With the technology of digital compositing and morphing, as exemplified in the digital images of *Forrest Gump*, two or more

temporally distinct moments are composited together. In *Gump*
older 16 mm film images of John F. Kennedy are composited
together with new 35 mm footage of Tom Hanks as Gump, and the
differences between the two are blended together through digital
morphing.[21] Gump now seamlessly appears to be interacting with
Kennedy, whose words to Gump are created from a sampled com-
posite of Kennedy's recorded speech, and whose mouth movements
are synchronised to the words by way of computer morphing. This
sequence of Kennedy, culled from the archives, thus no longer orig-
inates from a fixed moment in history, no longer carries, as
Bertolucci would say, the archival trace of the moment of its shooting: it rather carries a double temporality, conveying its separate
origins – Kennedy from the past of 1962, Hanks as Gump from the
past of 1994 – as well as the resulting morphed single present.

There seems to be little question that computer effects are 'subtly
changing the nature of reality as experienced through moving
images'.[22] Whereas cinema came into being as a way of recording the
real and preserving time, computer generated imagery creates its
own time and duration, its own synthetic spaces, and its own interface between the actor and the background setting in which the
action seems to occur. These developments move cinema away from
the real and away from history in the traditional sense of origins,
documentation, and lived duration. However, despite the loss many
of us may feel over cinema's sacrifice of this essential recording and
preserving function, it is nevertheless the case that computer generated imagery is a key marker of our time; computer morphing, in
particular, has been called the contemporary period's most important trope.[23] In a period defined by the blurring of boundaries of
race, gender, and nation, by the collapse of the clear-cut distinction
between the natural and manufactured worlds, by the merging of
biology and technology and by the uncertainty surrounding the past,
which is now available to be replayed, endlessly, with digital
enhancements, computer generated imagery can be seen as a privileged 'visual demonstration of the boundary fluctuations that
humans and their worlds are experiencing', a privileged form of the
cultural imaginary in the early years of the twenty-first century.[24]

The question that I still consider at issue, however, is whether this
new trope, this new culturally dominant technique of imaging, can be
placed in the service of historical representation and understanding.
Here I will discuss three different films which I feel illustrate both the

negative and the positive potential for the new kind of interweaving of fiction and history that computer generated imagery allows.

One of the most striking uses of digital compositing and morphing in film is found in *Forrest Gump,* which at certain points digitally rewrites some of the most sensitive scenes of the American past. In the first few images of the film, Tom Hanks's face is composited and morphed into an image from D. W. Griffith's *The Birth of A Nation.* The film superimposes Hanks' face onto that of a Ku Klux Klansman from the film. Gump (played by Hanks) then narrates how he was named after the 'famous Civil War general Nathan Bedford Forrest', who 'started up a club called the Ku Klux Klan'. As we watch scenes from *The Birth of a Nation*, Gump talks about how the club 'liked to dress up in white sheets, and act like a bunch of ghosts or spooks or something; they even put sheets on their horses.' Scenes from Griffith's famous film, with Tom Hanks seeming to ride at the head of the Klan, unfold before our eyes. As the film progresses, the history of racial conflict that *Forrest Gump* evokes in its opening scenes intersects with Gump's own experiences, as his image is digitally inserted into newsreel footage of the integration of the University of Alabama. As two black students are seen walking into the classroom building over the protests of Governor George Wallace and under the protection of Federal troops, the figure of Forrest Gump appears, digitally grafted into the newsreel footage, glancing into the camera. Then, in a staged sequence composited into the actual newsreel footage, Gump picks up a book one of the black students had dropped and hands it to her. He waves to the hostile crowd, and then follows her into the schoolhouse.

In effect, Forrest Gump is now inscribed into the historical archive as a figure that ameliorates the history of racial intolerance associated with his namesake, the Ku Klux Klan leader Nathan Bedford Forrest. Digitally inserted into two famous scenes, one from a fictional source – *The Birth of a Nation* – the other the documentary newsreel footage of George Wallace – the figure of Forrest Gump serves the exemplary function of 'redeeming the past, rescuing the real, and even rescuing that which was never real'. In the confrontation on the University of Alabama steps, for example, George Wallace's inflammatory statements about the Federal Government, and his vocal defiance of the court's desegregation order, are omitted; instead, Gump's inability to comprehend what the confrontation is about becomes the centre of the scene. Gump's insertion into the historical archive suggests a kind of reconciliation, a healing acceptance – one prompted, however, not by an understanding of the history of racial oppression but rather by a lack of understanding, by an absence of historical knowledge.

Later, other equally famous documentary images and moments in history are reconstituted for our gaze: Gump shakes hands and converses with John F. Kennedy, Lyndon Baines Johnson and Richard Nixon, he appears on a talk show with John Lennon and he meets Robert F. Kennedy. In each of these encounters, the meaning of the past is decisively changed. In the scene with Lennon, for example, Lennon is shown finding inspiration for the song 'Imagine' from Gump in a way that reverses the meaning of the song itself. Archival footage of Lennon's appearance on the Dick Cavett Show from the 1960s is composited together with Gump talking about his recent visit to China, and expressing amazement about the atheism, collective ownership and antimaterialism that he found there. Lennon appears to respond to Gump's descriptions of life in China with the word 'Imagine!', which he repeats after all of Gump's incredulous descriptions. As with the George Wallace and John F. Kennedy sequences, Lennon's recorded words are culled from the archive, and his mouth movements morphed so that they seem to form the word 'imagine'. In this context, Lennon's morphed response seems to imply that Gump's descriptions of the alien mode of life in China became the genesis of the famous song. Thus, a song that protests against the power of materialism, nationalism, and religion is transformed in *Forrest Gump* into a celebration of American values: the revolutionary message of the song is turned into a statement that seems to endorse the American way.

History and reality are here reprocessed to the point that 'old reality, unmorphed reality . . . begins to look fake and unreal'. Forrest Gump the character, as one commentator says, 'looks more real than any US president – or historical event we have seen'.[25] In *Forrest Gump,* as Joseba Gabilondo writes, 'history is no longer a reality fixed by the truth of mimetic representation . . . history is no longer real, but hyperreal and open to change. Any subject can access history and rewrite it from its own position . . . History can be accessed and then morphed, reproduced, and changed in such a way that one's own position need no longer be marginal or peripheral'.[26] By morphing the character Forrest Gump into the archive of actual history, 'into the record', as it were, *Forrest Gump,* the film, rewrites the social and historical past in a way that dovetailed with conservative and reactionary political movements in the mid-1990s, many of which used the film as a rallying cry for fundraising and for political campaigns.

In the two other films I will discuss here, however, I feel that digital morphing and computer enhanced imagery does in fact give us a deep understanding of temporal process, of change over time, and of the way the past itself changes under the pressure of new perspectives.

A powerful example of the positive potential of this new trope can be found in a short film by Daniel Reeves, entitled *Obsessive Becoming*. By digitally morphing and warping generations of documentary family photographs and home movies, Reeves shows a child changing into an adult, shows the features of the filmmaker's nineteenth-century ancestors morphing into the features of later generations, and shows the elderly seeming to transform again into children, demonstrating in a palpable and astonishing way the physical connection across and within generations, 'the persistence over time of a bloodline and a history'. One critic writes about the film: 'Along with keen hand tintings and other painterly treatments, the hi-tech effect of morphing finally becomes not so much graphical pizzazz as a visual recognition of our seamless linkage to the past',[27] 'a timeless litany of both family dispersion and eternal return'.[28] Here, the temporality of becoming, of one generation flowing into another, of faces and features changing and then reappearing later, in a subsequent generation, in a slightly different key, exemplifies the timelessness as well as the historical nature of human existence. The singular details attached to the individual lives portrayed in this film and the weight of their specific histories and specific events is encapsulated within an overall movement of time flowing onward. The film ultimately gives 'human (not computergraphic) emphasis and value to the lives and times [the filmmaker] weaves together'.[29]

Another film that I feel points the way toward a productive breakdown of boundary distinctions in the representation of the past is Oliver Stone's *JFK*. Although *JFK* doesn't use the type of computer generated imagery – the compositing, warping, and morphing – that *Forrest Gump* and *Obsessive Becoming* employ, it does approximate the effect of compositing and morphing by splicing together documentary footage and staged sequences with great rapidity. It also uses pseudo-documentary sequences – staged sequences made to

look grainy, badly lit, and scratched so as to resemble 16 mm documentary footage – and places existing documentary footage into
new contexts. Thus the film, like *Forrest Gump,* makes it hard to distinguish fact from speculative fiction: as Elsaesser says, a future generation would hardly be able to tell the archival documentary images
from the staged sequences in *JFK.* Here the line between realistic
and imaginative discourses is perpetually crossed and recrossed.

Crucially, however, the famous documentary film made by Abraham Zapruder which records the assassination of Kennedy, and
which Stone uses to immensely powerful effect in the trial scene in
the film, is not computer enhanced or altered by digital effects in any
way: it is, Stone asserts, shown exactly as it is was shot; although the
images are magnified, blown up from the original 8 mm to 35 mm,
and cropped so that the focus is more and more closely drawn to the
President's wounding as the sequence is repeated in the trial scene of
JFK. The Zapruder film as used in *JFK* is essentially unaltered – not
digitally manipulated or subjected to computer enhancement.

Certain scenes do combine documentary, archival images with
staged footage in a nearly seamless way, however, and these scenes
do produce something like a new accentuation, a subtle nuancing of
the historical archive. For example, the scene of Lee Harvey
Oswald's shooting in the basement of the Dallas Sheriff's office is
shown initially in blurry, black and white television style footage;
these images are the actual archival footage of the event from the
television news coverage of that day. Then, Stone introduces a
staged sequence of shots, a series of close-ups, reverse angles and
reaction shots that are photographed in a more vivid black and
white style. Here, it seems as if Oswald and Jack Ruby look at one
another before the shooting, suggesting that perhaps they know
each other, that perhaps they recognise each other. The psychological dimension that is introduced here, as Oswald and Ruby are given
the kind of close-up portraiture and eyeline connection that implies
subjectivity, that implies motivation, orients the historical event of
Oswald's murder in the direction of conspiracy: Stone imaginatively
'enters' the scene of Oswald's murder, rethinks it, presents it from a
psychological perspective and defamiliarises images long established
as part of the historical archive. Then, at the climactic moment of
the shooting, he cuts back to the actual archival footage, showing the
authentic clip of Oswald's murder, which now has a subtle but distinct new message attached to it, a message concerning the strong

possibility of a conspiracy, of a connection between Oswald and Ruby that has turned fatal for Oswald.

The cinematic rewriting of the historical past is here pushed to the level of the historical documents themselves. As in *Forrest Gump*, the audio-visual archive of American history in the twentieth century is quoted, reimagined, and reinterpreted through the use of cinematic techniques that make it difficult to distinguish between archival footage and dramatic interpretation. Stone has said that 'the style of my films is ambivalent and shifting. I make people aware that they are watching a movie. I make them aware that reality itself is in question . . . the movie is not only about a conspiracy to kill President Kennedy, but also about the way we look at our recent history. [*JFK*] calls attention to itself as a means of looking at history – shifting styles, such as the use of black and white and color, and viewing people from offbeat angles'.[30]

Although Stone is careful not to alter or tamper with the documentary images themselves, his imaginative quoting and re-presenting of the audio-visual documents by rapidly splicing in staged footage that seems to flesh out, or elaborate on the material in the archive produces an effect that is similar to director Robert Zemeckis' morphing and compositing techniques in *Forrest Gump*. In both cases, the meaning of the documents is altered: in the case of *Forrest Gump*, by an actual transformation, placing Forrest in photographic scenes with George Wallace, John F. Kennedy, and others in such a way that Kennedy and Wallace, for example, are made to appear to interact with Forrest. In the case of *JFK*, the audio-visual documents are in effect reaccentuated, remotivated, reenacted, by Stone's inventive montage technique, one that brings together factual, fictional, and speculative imagery.

As Robert Rosenstone writes, 'it is possible that such history on the screen is the history of the future. Perhaps in a visual culture, the truth of the individual fact is less important than the overall truth of the metaphors we create to help us understand the past. . . The visual media may represent a major shift in consciousness about how we think about our past'.[31]

I would like now, in closing, to return to a point made by Elsaesser which I quoted earlier in this paper, and which I would like now to consider in a different light. That quote is the following: 'Future generations, looking at the history of the 20th century, will never be able to tell fact from fiction, having the media as material evidence.

But then, will this distinction still matter to them?' I expect most readers will be vaguely troubled by this quote, troubled by the idea that fact and fiction as presented in the media would be indistinguishable to a future generation, but perhaps even more troubled by what seems to be the throwaway line, 'But then will this distinction still matter to them?' But let us consider this point again. Could it be that in the history of the future this distinction will not be so crucial? As Rosenstone writes, 'Fact has not always been the primary tool for telling the past. The truth of facts was never very important to griots in Africa or to history makers in other oral cultures. Perhaps Oliver Stone is a kind of griot for a new visual age.'[32]

To consider the documentary images of the history of the twentieth century, what most people consider to be the audio-visual record of the recent past, as simply part of the image bank, material available for poetic or metaphoric use, challenges our sense of the sacrosanct nature of the document which, as Ricouer points out, 'marks a dividing line between history and fiction'.[33] But in fact, this form of visual history, one that uses documentary images in the service of storytelling that freely mixes fictional, factual and speculative discourses, gives us a history of the future that is in some ways very like the mythic histories of the past. Perhaps, for future generations, the distinction between fact and fiction as presented in the media will no longer matter because a whole new genre of visual history, or history as vision, will have emerged with its own rules, its own regimes of credibility, and its own sort of truth. For them, and perhaps even for us, documentary images may no longer signify the facticity of past events, per se, but rather convey the sense that they are a representation of the past, a representation that may be employed for the purpose of metaphor, irony, analogy or argument, and that may be used in such a way that a certain poetic truth may emerge in the telling. Interestingly, Bazin, the great theorist of realism in the cinema, provides a way of thinking about hyperrealism in film when he writes: 'Every new development added to the cinema must, paradoxically, take it nearer and nearer to its origins.'[34] Although Bazin probably meant that cinema would eventually arrive at a perfect replication of the real, computer generated imagery in fact pushes the cinema's origins back beyond the nineteenth- and twentieth-century dream of the mechanical or electronic reproduction of reality, all the way to premodernity, to medieval or mythic times when the line between fantasy, fact and speculation was not yet clearly drawn.[35]

Notes

1 Geoffrey Nowell-Smith and Ilona Halberstadt, 'Interview with Bernardo Bertolucci', in Fabien S. Gerard, T. Jefferson Kline and Bruce Sklarew (eds), *Bernardo Bertolucci: Interviews* (Jackson: University Press of Mississippi, 2000), p. 248.
2 See André Bazin, *What Is Cinema?* vols 1–2, trans. Hugh Gray (Berkeley: University of California Press, 1967–71).
3 Godfrey Cheshire, 'The Death of Film', www.artswire.org.
4 *Ibid.*
5 Paul Ricouer, *The Reality of the Historical Past* (Milwaukee: Marquette University Press, 1984), p. 1.
6 Thomas Elsaesser, 'One Train May Be Hiding Another: Private History, Memory, and National Identity', *Screening The Past* (May 1999), 2.
7 Thomas Elsaesser, 'Subject Positions, Speaking Positions: From *Holocaust, Our Hitler,* and *Heimat* to *Shoah* and *Schindler's List*', in Vivian Sobchack (ed.) *The Persistence of History* (New York: Routledge, 1996), p. 145.
8 See Alison Landsberg, 'Prosthetic Memory: The Logic and Politics of Memory in Modern American Culture' (PhD dissertation, University of Chicago, 1996), p. 13.
9 See Alison Landsberg, 'America, the Holocaust, and the Mass Culture of Memory: Toward a Radical Politics of Empathy', *New German Critique* 71 (Summer 1997), 63–86, p. 66.
10 Landsberg, 'Prosthetic Memory: The Logic and Politics of Memory in Modern American Culture', p. 24.
11 Landsberg, 'Prosthetic Memory: The Logic and Politics of Memory in Modern American Culture', p. 23.
12 Landsberg, 'Prosthetic Memory: The Logic and Politics of Memory in Modern American Culture', p. 4. See also Alison Landsberg, 'Prosthetic Memory: Total Recall and Blade Runner', in Mike Featherstone and Roger Burrows (eds), *Cyberspace/Cyberbodies/Cyberpunk: Cultures of Technological Embodiment* (London: Sage, 1995), pp. 175–89 and 'America, the Holocaust, and the Mass Culture of Memory'.
13 Landsberg, 'America, the Holocaust, and the Mass Culture of Memory', p. 75.
14 Elsaesser, 'One Train May Be Hiding Another', p. 6.
15 Elsaesser, 'Subject Positions, Speaking Positions', p. 146.
16 Hayden White, 'The Fact of Modernism: The Fading of the Historical Event,' in Vivian Sobchack (ed.), *The Persistence of History* (New York: Routledge, 1996), pp. 17–38.
17 Elsaesser, 'Subject Positions, Speaking Positions', p. 166.
18 Joseba Gabilondo, 'Morphing Saint Sebastian: Masochism and Masculinity in Forrest Gump', in Vivian Sobchack (ed.), *Meta-Morphing*

(Minneapolis: University of Minnesota Press, 2000), p. 185.

19 Vivian Sobchack, '"At the Still Point of the Turning World" Meta-Morphing and Meta-Stasis', in *Meta-Morphing*, p. 134.

20 Sobchack, '"At the Still Point of the Turning World"', p. 138.

21 See Gabilondo, 'Morphing Saint Sebastian', p. 186. See Also Stephen Prince, 'True Lies: Perceptual Realism, Digital Images, and Film Theory, *Film Quarterly* 49: 3 (Spring 1996), 30.

22 Woody Hochswender, 'When Seeing Cannot Be Believing', *New York Times* (23 June 1992), 1.

23 Louise Krasniewicz, 'Magical Transformations: Morphing and Meta-morphosis in Two Cultures', in Sobchack (ed.), *Meta-Morphing*, p. 54.

24 Krasniewicz, 'Magical Transformations, p. 55.

25 Gabilondo, 'Morphing Saint Sebastian', p. 201.

26 *Ibid*.

27 Steven Seid, '*Obsessive Becoming*: The Video Poetics of Daniel Reeves in *Works by Daniel Reeves*', www.mediopolis.de/transmedia/english, 13 May 1999.

28 Sobchack, '"At the Still Point of the Turning World"', p. 143.

29 *Ibid*.

30 Oliver Stone, 'Stone on Stone's Image (As Presented by Some Historians)', in Robert Brent Toplin (ed.), *Oliver Stone's USA* (Lawrence: University Press of Kansas, 2000), p. 53.

31 Robert Rosenstone, 'Oliver Stone as Historian', in Toplin (ed.), *Oliver Stone's USA*, p. 39.

32 Rosenstone, 'Oliver Stone as Historian', pp. 38–9.

33 Ricouer, *The Reality of the Historical Past*, p. 1.

34 André Bazin, 'The Myth of Total Cinema', in *What Is Cinema?*, p. 21.

35 Gabilondo, 'Morphing Saint Sebastian', p. 186.

12

Postcinema/Postmemory

Jeffrey Pence

As technologies of mass entertainment undergo accelerated development, their affiliated institutional complexes likewise inhabit a state of apparently endless transformation. By institutional complex I mean the commercial and social contexts of production and consumption, as well as the forms of textuality and aesthetic experience associated with particular technologies – easy contrasts being between narrative cinema and the fragmentary action and spectacular intensity of music videos or the idiosyncratic variability of interactive web experiences. In technological, textual and structural terms, these different media compete for preeminence, for literal and symbolic capital, in an increasingly global context. This chapter focuses on the agonistic dimension of contemporary technological changes as manifested in cinema.

While its new technical and stylistic possibilities suggested an early potential to contribute to political or aesthetic innovation, cinema actually carried the burden of memory in modernity. In fact, it shouldn't surprise that one of the key transformations cinema wrought involved the restructuring and revising of retrospection. If the process of memory can be linked to remediating experience, the fate of that process largely depends on the context of the 'construct' which available technologies provide as means and models of remembrance. The shape and possibility of meaningful memory, then, are immediately questions concerning technology. Cinema's iconic, even monumental moments, figures and styles offered something like a continuous cultural tradition and set of strategies, a simultaneously public and subjective mnemonics for framing the past and imagining the future. New, competitor technologies seem initially to deliver the same goals, only more efficiently and powerfully. If film's felt ability to model and remake the world seemed to deliver reality to our collective control, newer technologies like video seem to deliver reality to our individual control. This possibility destabilises our notions of what memory might be by privatising its collective form and totalising its subjective form. The instruments, institutions, styles and practices that one would term postcinematic also, by definition, lead us into a state of postmemory.

Not surprisingly, for filmmakers and critics alike memory plays a crucial role in efforts to distinguish between the nature and influence of these different media. To a great extent, recent North American cinema forwards a profound contrast between narrative cinema and the textual forms associated with new technologies as models and modellers of memory. From one point of view, this transformation may lead to panic, as in an entire genre of techno-dystopian films emerging from Hollywood such as *Strange Days*, an example I will return to shortly. From another, it demands sober acknowledgement as an irreversible change for consciousness and cultural practice – as, paradigmatically, in the work of Fredric Jameson. A more interesting and exemplary response, I argue, may be found in the cinema of Atom Egoyan. Here postcinematic technologies and textual forms disappoint, rather than deliver upon, cinema's promises. Specifically, they reveal postmemory as an admixture of longing and forgetting, as the disappointment of that promise to model and remake the world as an expression of will. Rather than merely dying, the memorialising project of cinema lives on, in agonistic balance with the frustration of this project. In this regard, the conjunction postcinema/postmemory may be read both as a symptom of, and as an indispensable strategy for, our new historical epoch of globalisation.

In terms of cultural and institutional dominance, cinema faces a future which, by any measure, will be less than its past. In Hegelian terms, we have reached the End of Cinema.[1] Rather than a sudden death, productive negotiations with competitor media and forms initially characterise film's posthistorical era. Hollywood quickly assimilated new procedures and styles into its repertoire – including computer imaging and animation, miniaturisation and digital developments in sound recording and amplification. This incorporation of video and electronic technologies into the core production processes and values of Hollywood cinema drives such second-generation products of the blockbuster strategy as *Jurassic Park*, *Titanic*, *Independence Day* and so on. The coordinated structuring of pay-per-view, cable, video and network release dates, along with the incorporation of global release planning into every facet of production, virtually renders the larger class of Hollywood releases risk-free. For these sorts of productions, the boundary between film as text and film as event blurs as global forces of promotion and distribution mirror the immense scale of the technology-driven movies themselves. Not only do such films pull cable-ready, video-renting consumers into theatres in staggering numbers, configuring a global public in the process, but the almost-Omnimax scale and volume of their spectacular productions entice repeat viewings at multiplexes and home. From this perspective, the film industry appears unnaturally durable, capable of domesticating any changes in the contours of production or reception.

But these industry practices are only the visible portion of the iceberg. If audiences have begun to ration the attention and investment they give to a medium qua medium – as the simultaneous levelling off of cinema attendance, television viewing and book purchasing seems to indicate – then the clear provocation is the emergence of a variety of alternative entertainment technologies offering a range of cognitive and somatic experiences which can best be described as postcinematic: the illusion of sensory immersion in virtual reality; the varieties of interactivity; multimedia and hypermedia. Cinema faces the crisis of becoming passé. The self-conscious and symptomatic response of cinema to its challengers likewise turns to the register of the past. Film itself is undergoing a displacement from a cultural pre-eminence that, in the wake of modernity, is still figured in being toward the future. Think here of Walter Benjamin's linkage of cinema and revolution. Now dislodged from this privileged position, film moves towards the opposite and marginalised position of being of the past. Many current films can be seen as figuring their difference from other media precisely through a textualisation of film technology's relationship to the past, to human and collective memory, in contrast and competition with the same relationships as mediated by different technologies.

Exhibiting a common tendency to simultaneously imitate and demonise new techno-developments, Kathryn Bigelow's *Strange Days* (1995) elaborates a future which is nightmarish in its contours precisely as it represents a mediascape in which film is increasingly but one medium among many. This future appears salvageable only insofar as a return to past narrative formulas, linked explicitly to film as the form of these formulas, is possible. For example, in the conclusion of *Strange Days* a figure of traditional authority, the Los Angeles Chief of Police, saves the city from complete social breakdown by exercising his authority to punish particular individuals for corruption. That the city seems destined for anarchy if its enormous inequities of wealth and power are not addressed is momentarily forgotten, as this scene coincides with the romantic union of the two protagonists, standing here for a wildly imaginary reconciliation of the city itself under the Phoenix-like power of film. After all, social inequality pales in comparison to the film's true nightmare: the spread of a postcinematic virtual reality technology so addictive as to require criminalisation.

Resistance and anxiety towards competitor media has a long history in cinema, a fact which might seem to militate against the more extremely dystopic visions of other forms presented in David Cronenberg's *Videodrome* (1982), Brett Leonard's *Lawnmower Man* (1992), James Cameron's *The Terminator* (1984) and *Terminator 2: Judgement Day* (1991) and Oliver Stone's *Natural Born Killers* (1994). From Elia Kazan's *A Face in the Crowd* (1957), through Sidney Lumet's *Network* (1976), to Gus Van Sant's *To Die For* (1995), film has constructed a vision of television as destructive of character and community under the irresistible logics of profit, spectacle and saturation. However, to take this history of inter-media tension as simply a cautionary note against techno-phobia is to mistake the extent to which such television-oriented films accurately indexed, if not the exact dimensions of the tube's deleterious effects on the human condition, the specific radical disruption of cinema's relationship to its consuming public, financial infrastructure and entertainment rivals. Furthermore, if these anti-television films can be read, broadly, as retextualising the emergence of a rival in morality tales of individual corruption and redemption, this fact, by contrast, also illuminates the scale of the challenge presented to film by contemporary technological developments. In techno-paranoia films, new technologies threaten to spin away and exceed any effort to renarrativise them in a way that returns at least a measure of cultural prestige to the cinematic medium. Perhaps the best example here is *Natural Born Killers*, in which postcinematic technologies are demonised by association with the inscrutably pathological violence of Mickey and Mallory. These characters' alienation from any coherent or organic notion of memory signals the film's failure to contain their threat in some explanatory narrative. At the same time, the film collapses into the dizzying array of postcinematic effects and affects it conjured up initially as the object of its satire. If *Strange Days*, or even *Lawnmower Man*, with its surprising evocation of a thematic of Christian resurrection, are films about the redemption of cinema, *Natural Born Killers* achieves something like the status of the Book of Revelation. It is a film about the eschaton of film figured as the end of comprehensible time within film; it is thus about the end of film as memory. From this perspective, we can understand that television forced changes upon film, but that the two forms eventually developed a technical, industrial and textual symbiosis, with cinema trading a measure of mass appeal for a relatively greater prestige. The threat of electronic media seems to be of a whole other type, signaling less a future of managed co-existence than the advent of a postcinematic age.

The collapse of the cinematic into its postcinematic other symp-tomised by Stone's film parallels a more widely perceived decline of perspective and critical authority in postmodernity. A fundamental crisis of memory connects and drives these formulations. Jameson explicitly locates the demise of memory through a comparison of cinema and television:

> If anything like critical distance is still possible in film, indeed, it is surely bound up with memory itself. But memory seems to play no role in television, commercial or otherwise (or . . . in postmodernism gen-erally): nothing here haunts the mind or leaves its afterimages in the manner of the great moments of film.[2]

The concept and phenomenological experience of subjectivity depends ultimately upon memory:

> [H]aving a self, it seems, necessarily involves a disposition on the part of an appropriately constituted organism to identify itself with remem-bered states and actions, perhaps also with states and actions it does not remember but may be convinced occurred (as an amnesiac might come to feel guilt over her own unremembered but reliably reported crimes).[3]

Without a memory-enabling narrative, the distinction between spec-tator and spectacle disappears. According to Jameson, the postcine-matic subject becomes 'a quasi-material registering apparatus for . . . machine time . . . and the video image or "total flow"'.[4] Absent a stable economy of memory, extracting any clarifying interpretative vantage fails immediately; such moves mistake the logic of total flow:

a ceaseless rotation of elements such that they change place at every
moment, with the result that no single element can occupy the position
of 'interpretant' (or that of primary sign) for any length of time; but
must be dislodged in turn in the following instant (the filmic terminology of 'frames' and 'shots' does not seem appropriate for this kind of
succession) . . . anything which arrests or interrupts it will be sensed as
an aesthetic flaw.[5]

Jameson extends this concept beyond a specific aesthetic experience,
arguing that the contemporary medium that 'serve[s] as some
supreme and privileged, symptomatic, index to the *Zeitgeist* . . . as the
cultural *dominant* of a new social and economic conjuncture is clearly
video'.[6] Video, on one hand, refers to a discrete set of instruments and
practices. On the other hand, it may stand for postcinematic technology writ large, due to the dispersal of its form into film, computer
networks and television. Egoyan, whose films I shall rely upon to
work through and beyond Jameson's diagnosis, himself argues that
video determines our experience of both older and newer technologies; for him, computer networks only repeat the metaphorics
of video.[7] In general, video's exemplary status as a 'do-it-yourself'
practice presaged and permeates our contemporary valuation of
'interactivity'. In their ubiquity and solicitation of particular subjective dispositions, video images offer a prosthetic alternative to previous models of memory. In this sense, video links the postcinematic to
the postmemorial.

Under the cultural dominant of video, Jameson calls for a criticism more oriented toward reiterating a complete experiential context than explaining singular artefacts. He suggests the anachronism
of memorialising, through interpretation, texts that are themselves
not amemorable. Thus he connects the demise of the 'monumental'
or 'autonomous' work of art to the fate of a subject now 'vanished'
or 'volatilised'.[8] Jameson returns repeatedly to a dictum against discrete hermeneutical responses to video texts, to a dictum against
remembering them:

if we find ourselves confronted henceforth with 'texts'. . . with the
ephemeral, with disposable works that wish to fold back immediately
into the accumulating detritus of historical time – then it becomes difficult and even contradictory to organize an analysis and an interpretation around any single one of these fragments in flight. To select –
even as an 'example' – a single video text, and to discuss it in isolation,
is fatally to regenerate the illusion of the masterpiece or the canonical

text, and to reify the experience of total flow from which it was momentarily extracted . . . What is quite out of the question is to look at a single 'video work' all by itself . . . there are no video masterpieces, there can never be a video canon, even an auteur theory of video . . . The discussion, the indispensable preliminary selection and isolation, of a single 'text' then automatically transforms it back into a 'work', turns the anonymous videomaker back into a named artist or 'auteur', opens the way for the return of all those features of an older modernist aesthetic which it was in the revolutionary nature of the new medium to have precisely effaced and dispelled.[9]

To be fair, Jameson himself immediately breaks his own prescription, suggesting at least the rhetorical necessity of the example. From a Lyotardian standpoint, we might grant his account descriptive value (this is our critical problem) while jettisoning its prescriptive features.

By emphasising criticism's anachronism, Jameson eulogises memory. It seems as if memory, even or especially critical memory, is always already nostalgia in postmodernity. Nostalgia is a disposition more easily assailed than defended. Even in an age that has seen ideological critique turn inward upon itself, nostalgia remains – nostalgically, of course – a sign of false consciousness, of individual and mass delusion leading to commercial, critical and political vulnerability. Beyond the various monuments, *lieux de memoires*, television shills in documentary form, fashion revivals, musical retreads, pop cultural recyclings, political atavisms, religious parochialisms and business enterprises nostalgia props up, it emerges as instrumental memory itself. Not memory of, but memory for, a state of contra-cognitive affect rendering subjects singularly malleable. If nostalgia appears as the antithesis of enlightenment, the low status it often receives amongst contemporary theorists and critics is in its own right a paradoxical instance of nostalgia. If postmodernism demands scepticism towards narratives of progress, how then does the progressive view of temporal consciousness implied by the derogation of nostalgia remain so readily acceptable? Perhaps nostalgia is less a problem here, than the nostalgia implied by negative interpretations of the disposition. It is on this ground of memory that I wish to bring Jameson and Egoyan together. For the latter, memory and technology seem closely related, before instrumental approaches seem to alienate the remembering subject from his or her desire. Nevertheless, the impulse toward memory, the longing to make good imagined or real losses, does not thereby disappear or become any less important. Rather, this desire reveals itself as not only animating potentially regressive forms of nostalgia but also animating affective and cognitive alternatives to the seductive technologies through which it may express itself.

If subjectivity depends upon memory, memory may be inseparable from some degree of nostalgia. Sophisticated critical hostility to nostalgia may, then, strangely echo the fears of dominant cinematic institutions. While holding onto the notion that video represents profound transformations, it is possible to understand that its role in techno-paranoia films or Jameson's criticism is something like that of a guest star. Pre-existing narratives, of institutional self-preservation or the long-running critique of the illusory ego, incorporate video into their workings while denying the possibility of other sorts of engagement. In Egoyan's work, we find a more particularised account of how video changes, but does not destroy, memory, and thus how it changes, without erasing, subjectivity. Postcinema connotes, then, not merely the end of cinema, but its endurance beyond the recognition of the form's limits. In turn, postmemory suggests not simply the demise of memory, but its attenuation beyond the recognition of the impossibility of its totalisation. Finally, we shall see that postcinema/postmemory can serve as 'an index to the *Zeitgeist*', understood not as the dissipation of critical agency but as its modest but irreducible potential in the new cultural structures and processes of globalisation.

Positing Egoyan's work as exceptionally symptomatic of the postcinematic is in itself uncontroversial. After all, his films chart the same technological territory Jameson does, 'dealing with the process of memory and the construct of memory'.[10] In contrast, suggesting that this single filmmaker offers an occasion to achieve a measure of perspective on the postcinematic is a riskier claim. Jameson consigns the auteur to the cutting room floor, as the forgotten avatar of monumental memory. He argues that in video there is no signature as the apparatus is ontologically anonymous and anti-subjective. However, Egoyan suggests that video's democracy of access and application – its ubiquity, simplicity and affordability – may enable rather than flatten expressivism. Speaking of the most banal of video practices, amateur pornography, he says that such particularised and idiosyncratic images 'immediately suggest an allusion to the person who made [them]'.[11] This may be the zero degree of auteurism, but its significance ought not be underestimated. If the agency of the maker is

not wholly subsumed into the apparatus, then even the banal work
may not be inseparable from the overwashing flow of indifferent
texts from which it is assembled and against which it is encountered.
Further, the 'old autonomous subject or ego' for whom monumental works were staged (or restaged, at the level of criticism), may not
have been fully 'volatilised'. By implication, such a subject – even if
it is the zero degree subject – remains capable of shaping a sort of
critical memory out of the not-quite irresistible experience of the
postcinematic.

Capable of linking experiences across time to a consistent ethical
identity, this subject may approach and exceed exactly what Jameson argues is unimaginable:

> A description of the structural exclusion of memory, then, and of 'crit-
> ical distance' might well lead on into the impossible, namely a theory
> of video itself: how the thing blocks its own theorization becoming a
> theory in its own right.[12]

Egoyan explains his own understanding of the relationship between
film and video precisely in terms of memory's exclusion through
externalisation:

> Video images are suggestive of the images that go on inside people's
> heads. [T]here's a profound difference in attitude toward . . . video
> and film. In terms of home movies, everyone using film knows in the
> back of their minds that they are going to have to pay for a roll. That
> means no matter how obsessive they are about recording, they have to
> chose [sic]. With video, the process can be indiscriminate. You can
> record an entire day in real time without any form of selection. That
> experience of time is extremely dangerous. Some people never look at
> what they record but by recording something, they make it a posses-
> sion. It has an effect on the process of memory. We give away respon-
> sibility for memory to a piece of technology. I don't think film was so
> insidious.[13]

If memory becomes a matter of indiscriminate information and
image storage, then its character changes radically. The series of
oppositions and associations that define memory disappear when
retention becomes infinite, retrieval a function of electronic pros-
theses, and communication instantaneous. Memory's other, forgetting or oblivion, recedes as the distinction between past and present
fades. Rather than unfolding in a horizon of temporality with mir-
rored vanishing points of past and future, experience becomes a

matter of continuous recollection, which is to say that it is simultaneously a continuous performance of and for recollection:

> in terms of how this works with the patterns of memory and the pat-
> terns of our shared experience . . . we have to be able to see our lives
> are artifacts which can be exchanged . . . the extension of that is for me
> to somehow imagine every moment of my life, every word that is
> coming out of my mouth as being suitable for the process of docu-
> mentation, because the process of documentation defines our modern
> sense of what it means to lead a truly rich experience.[14]

Where once modernity and the cinematic could be seen to break the
grip of history on the present – precisely through disciplining the
past by monumentalising it – and redirecting action and sociality
toward an unmade future, postmodernity and the postcinematic
seem initially to wrest the present from the domination of the future
in a process by which the here and now becomes identical with the
there and then. In this light, documentation no longer serves as a
useful means for recording actualities in order to enable discourse
based on empirical authority. Instead, documentation becomes an
end in itself, a goal of self-fashioning for ongoing retrospection.
Such a degree of mnemonic arrest produces a melancholic culture in
which progress is marked by the increase of intimacy with the past:
whole libraries available through a home terminal; lives video-
graphed from birth through toddlerhood, graduations through
sexual encounters, surgeries through testaments. Rather than Benjamin's Angel of History, the figure for this condition might be Lot's
wife. Fleeing the traumas of history, the flight to the future itself
becomes traumatic. She turns back, not fearing death but loss and
transformation. She desires to transform memory into the memorial, to fix the past and future in a permanent present. Literally
becoming a monument satisfies her desire.[15]

Egoyan's work manifests these processes of self-reification in a
number of ways. Typically, the diegesis consists of repetitive character interactions with different mediations of memory. The reliance
on prosthetic memories results in increasing figurative and literal
alienation, as signified in the frequent physical isolation of characters who primarily relate to the world through technological devices
– phones, tape recorders, microphones, video or photographic
images – and are thus regularly framed in hermetic spaces, whether
the empty rooms in which they dwell or the screen itself. Above all,

'Video is everywhere – recording experience, mediating experience, "surveilling" experience, reducing reality to replica'.[16] While the registers and modes vary across the films, a general trajectory holds true. First, the attempt to record, manipulate and control experience reveals itself as an effort to transfer the burdens of memory to postcinematic technologies. Next, in the wake of the arresting malfunction of these controlling gestures, the persistent and powerful attraction of a seemingly authentic, if ultimately unavailable, form of memory forces itself upon the characters and viewers. Finally, there emerges an impulse to renarrate the films in such a way that these contradictory desires are neither met nor cancel each other out. Instead, they are held in an agonistic balance that simultaneously reflects the paradoxes of consciousness in global culture – postcinematic, postmemorial – and provides a critically and ethically astute perspective on them.

The postcinematic effort to manage memory through denaturalised representation aims to ameliorate the traumas of subjective, familial and social life. Egoyan's larger exploration of cultural identity in postmodernity gathers these otherwise diffuse examinations. Specifically, he investigates the question of identity in the context of Canada, in so far as the problems posed therein are understood to stand for postmodernity generally. A nation without an epic story of origin, whose identity is a resolutely open question, Canada emerges here as a definitively postmodern state.[17] The fabricated and antiseptic interiors of Egoyan's work foreground the *sui generis* character of their national and historical setting. For example, in *Next of Kin*, Peter's sterile home of origin, where his fantasies provide the only sign of life, parodies an affluent Anglo-Canada dissociated from a meaningful sense of the past or future. *Speaking Parts'* hotel figures as a symbol for metropolitan Canada, with fugitive figures moving throughout its transitory spaces while being recorded by surveillance cameras. In transfer to film stock, this footage degenerates and begins to lose its indexical function; as the images morph, their abstract circulation resembles the flow of commodities through markets. Noah Render's home in *The Adjuster* varies this logic of commodified simulation: a prototype in an abandoned suburban development, the borrowed space includes fake furnishings and a *faux* family.

Against this sort of simulated existence, Egoyan elaborates the attractions of an 'authentic' Other, an object of desire through

which characters imagine they might transform themselves. Compared to the pale and washed out images of Anglo-Canadian spaces
and faces, other ethnic locales and bodies are presented as warm and
vibrant (the Armenian family in *Next of Kin*), rooted in unattainable
tradition (the silent grandmother in *Family Viewing*), or sexually
irresistible (the 'other' men with whom Thomas trades opera tickets
for sex in *Exotica*). By *Felicia's Journey*, the attractions of origins
have become worn – mostly indicated by sequences of Felicia's
father hectoring her about ethnic treason in a ruined Irish fortress –
but nevertheless powerful, as Felicia pursues the absconded father of
her child. Like cultural orphans, caught between an unhomely present and an inaccessible past, characters perform rituals of appropriation and self-transformation to acquire a new identity.

Characters enact a self-memorialising process by becoming consumers of their own spectacular performances. What Lipman writes
of *Exotica* could be said of virtually every character in every film:

> Almost every member of this group mythologises who and where they
> are through play acting and ritual. Zoe plays the part of the dispas-
> sionate matriarch. Christina is crystallised into the schoolgirl she acts
> onstage. Francis turns his mourning for his dead daughter into a
> fetishistic, psychosexual relationship through Christina's striptease
> character. Thomas, a pet shop owner, would rather see himself as a
> smuggler of exotic goods.[18]

Here we might think also of the father in *Family Viewing*, method-
ically revising the family romance by overdubbing home videos of
his first marriage and son's childhood with pornographic footage
which he and his partner are coached through by a phone sex
worker. Despite these characters' attempts to transform and exoti-
cise themselves, their alienation from such idealised identities
remains foregrounded. Egoyan's actors perform in a deliberately
awkward manner. Their stiff and muted delivery and motions provide neither the normative expressivity or transparency of screen
acting, nor the affected naturalism of direct cinema. Rather, the
actors appear as functions without interior motivation, or at least
none they recognise or communicate. The dialogue suggests a flat-
tening of affect and minimising of connections between characters
and within their own psyches, compounding their isolation even
from an assumed identity. No matter what lengths they go to, the
desired revision of the self seems impossible.

Some form of sexualised self-othering provides the chief vehicle for such efforts at transformation, as characters attempt to link identity to substitute somatic experiences. Their obsessive rituals of commodified sensation effectively instrumentalise the body, making it into an extension of the technologies, broadly defined, that promise a liberation from their pasts. The Armenian father in *Next of Kin* belies his dogged traditionalism by visiting strip clubs; burdened with the care of her invalid, immigrant grandmother in *Family Viewing*, Aline works as a phone sex dominatrix and an escort; Clare in *Speaking Parts* sublimates her grief and frustration with a mediated relationship with Lance, really a consensual onanism as the two perform before their respective digitised images on a videophone. The motives are various, but tend in all cases to be lost in the very process of externalising identity in the form of commodified memories. The father in *Family Viewing*, for instance, a videotape salesman, is initially moved by guilt over his sadistic treatment of his first wife, whom he drove to abandon the family; but his guilt has been taped over to the point that he no longer knows its origins, as when he fails to recognise his mother-in-law, whom he earlier institutionalised as part of his effort to erase memory.

Whereas these characters use technology to avoid the ethical burden of memory, other figures seek to use technology to invent a past they never had. In *Next of Kin*, Peter's ability to gain access to the history of an Armenian family through the video tape of their therapy sessions permits him to insert himself into the vacant role of their long-lost son, put up for adoption when the family struggled upon their immigration to Canada. A particular postcinematic equation of representation with the real permits this family to accept that Peter/Bedros looks like (one is tempted to say 'is', but that would miss the point) a fair-skinned WASP. Likewise, Van in *Family Viewing* absconds with the videotapes his father has not yet overdubbed and with his invalid grandmother, also an Armenian immigrant, in order to reinvent for himself a family history and unity which he has never in actuality experienced.

All these cases enact a sort of rolling fabrication of the past while foregrounding this very process:

> not only does technical memorization replace the factuality of beings and things when we seek confirmation of our own remembrance in a second look at certain images; even more, this technical recall actually becomes a new part of our memories.[19]

As memory and the real become fully mediated and externalised this image field offers itself as the field of action in which subjects may search for or construct a self that has never been and will never be. Yet this field is more properly a screen for projecting artificial identities while blocking access to a new reality. In *Felicia's Journey*, for example, Hilditch obsessively re-enacts an Oedipal romance with a mother who lives only in the footage of her television show, videotapes the confessions and murders of the stray young women he takes into his care, all while framed in a carefully photographed film self-consciously saturated with elements of a prime cinematic genre, the psychological suspense film. Less a vehicle for authentic self-fashioning, video here delivers us to a psychoanalytic labyrinth in which Film the Father and Television the Mother produce neuroses in the Video Child. Video's heightened powers of editing and retention promise greater intimacy and agency; they actually deliver greater irrationality and alienation. If the desires evoked by video now appear unattainable, in contrast, Lisa emerges at the end of *Speaking Parts* with her desired relationship with Lance, a relationship significantly enabled by her failed attempt to learn to use video technology.

Up to a certain point, Egoyan's films depict a familiar scenario in which technology has simultaneously obliterated textuality, memory, and agency. Like techno-paranoia films or Jameson's analysis, such a dystopian line depends upon idealising the technologies in question as a monolithic and irresistible set of forces.[20] However, Egoyan escapes such determinism through his rigorous attention both to video's rhetorical power and to its limits. Video's conspicuousness and omnipresence undercuts its own power. While video may bear with it certain dangers it also solicits subjective action in a way film may not. In contrast with his description of video's tendency toward reification, Egoyan describes video as exceptionally susceptible to criticism:

> the video image has associations which are far more quotidian, far more domestic and less mystified. There is still a mystification which exists around the filmmaking process. When people see a projected image, they're seeing something which is beyond them and therefore invites a very specific type of identification. When people see a video image, the first response is that it is something that *they themselves* could make ... therefore it is far easier to be suspicious of a video image.[21]

Video is a domesticated technology: with a videocam and two VCR's or a digital camera and an iMac any home can be a site for production. Egoyan seems to want to transfer the skepticism such domestication enables to viewers' reception of films. As he says, 'The most important thing is to be open about the process, at every opportunity to demystify the process of making films'.[22] The palpable dysfunctions of technologised memory in Egoyan's work encourage suspicion in viewers towards the images and actions before them. In turn, this suspicion revives a putatively defunct hermeneutic impulse that reverberates across our understanding of the film.

In a manner typical of other films, the retrospective re-evaluation of previous mausoleum scenes in *Speaking Parts* engages our own awareness with the tenuous nature of our construction of sense in the film, a mediated image ensemble which we relate to in the manner that characters relate to the own image rich milieu. Here, Clare's entry into the oft-repeated video-mausoleum images of her brother, who died while donating an organ to her, is undercut by the revelation that her own torso is unscarred; the original traumatic wound that drives the film never occurred. The echoes of association that ensue from such a jarring exposure – such as Nicole's decision to lie at her deposition in *The Sweet Hereafter* – redirect and substitute for the specular and exteriorised desires which the films initially establish as the stakes for both characters and viewers. The obtuseness of such redirections of spectatorial investment from the image, due to its exposure, is in direct proportion to the stakes at hand. As Lageira writes, 'memory is the final rampart against the depersonalization carried out by machines and the media. But it is the most fragile as well, for the terrible effort involved . . . often veers dangerously toward the absurd'.[23]

The absurd moment when image becomes manifestly derealised is not a danger but a relief, freeing characters and viewers from an illusory and debilitating repetition compulsion. The effort to maintain stilted, hermetic and morbid connections with a technologised past fails. Spectatorial attention is shifted away from the transfixing image toward a reexamination of the stakes behind characters' efforts at self-transformation. Writing in terms of the image, Daniele Riviere argues that Egoyan's films are 'interactive':

> For in fact, the image that interests Egoyan is the one projected by our gaze, redoubling the image of the world . . . [He] focuses on this

ambivalence of the image in which the spectator, redoubled on the
screen, watches himself projecting his mental images onto the images
of the world . . . the image extracted from ourselves materialized,
becomes incarnate, and now begins to regard us.[24]

Precisely the same argument of interactivity, I think, can be made in
regards to the chronotype of narrative, of memory, as viewers
become aware of their projections of causality and connection. The
films, therefore, tend to engage viewers in a retrospective engagement with their images and narratives in a temporality which is quite
literally postcinematic. After the film, that is, we must remember and
reorganise the images, repetitions and juxtapositions in order to
make sense of them. This effort, crucially, depends on the willful forgetting of the melancholic performances of self-memorialising that
have constituted the films thus far. This retroactive narrativisation,
therefore, binds recollection to oblivion, the limiting force which
makes memory coherent. As Virilio reminds Egoyan in a citation of
Norman Spear, 'The content of memory is the function of the speed
of forgetting'.[25] By self-consciously abandoning the pretense to monumental totalisation implicit in the cinematic, or the intimate totalisation seemingly promised by the postcinematic, such an enduring
and delimited mnemonics can be understood as postmemory.

   The stakes in this elaborate play of technologised memory and
willful forgetting are not simply subjective, but connect with issues
of identity and agency on a collective, even global scale. Egoyan continuously contrasts an acculturated, technologised metropole with
the residual attractions of an organic cultural identity. Cosmopolitan
and consumerist Toronto is identified with the commodification of
the past. In contrast, the remnants of an ethnic identity, the memory
of Armenia, is defined by its persistent attractions: stability, meaningful community beyond the imploded bounds of the nuclear
family, the attenuated temporality of place and history embodied in
the landmark. Given the profound appeal of Egoyan's Armenia –
from the party at which Peter decides to remain in the role of Bedros
in *Next of Kin*, with Egoyan himself smiling into the camera,
through the variety of romanticised grandmothers, to the interpreter's decision to re-emigrate to Armenia in *Calendar* – we can
understand how easily the anomie of metropolitan life under the
postcinematic could seem to be resolved by similar movements.
However, the draw of deep identity Egoyan evokes is as dangerous
as it is appealing. After all, a response to contemporary cultural

changes quite opposed to Egoyan's reveals itself in the flowering of a thousand fundamentalisms across the contemporary world. The emergence of a variety of atavisms, precisely akin to the ethnic particularism that resulted in the Armenian genocide and dispersal, can be read not as a regressive echo but as a response to the disruptions of traditional schemes for framing contemporary experience in relation to a continuous past and future. Given the dichotomy between the contours of identity available in the technologised metropole and the native land, Arjun Appadurai convincingly argues that 'the central feature of global culture today is the politics of the mutual effort at sameness and difference to cannibalize one another and thus to proclaim their successful hijacking of the twin Enlightenment ideals of the triumphantly universal and the resiliently particular'.[26] Egoyan elaborates a possibility for an alternative to these equally unappealing antinomies.

Egoyan's cinema embodies and explores globalisation, using the postcinematic technologies of these developments to examine the consequences for subjective and collective identity when peoples are relocated and autochthonous traditions begin to circulate and collide with others. Armenia offers a locus of desire, a figurative alternative to the tempting unreality of global life. That this nostalgic desire cannot be satisfied in no way decreases its value. Quite the opposite is true. From his perspective, one of the attractions of Armenia is its metaphorical status, the way it stands for all sorts of desires for a replete past. The most obvious film in this sense is *Calendar*. 'In conceiving *Calendar*', Egoyan notes, 'I wanted to find a story that would deal with three levels of Armenian consciousness: Nationalist, Diasporan, and Assimilationist'.[27] The photographer (Egoyan), interpreter (Arsinée Khanjian, Egoyan's spouse and collaborator) and native guide (Ashot Adamian), all in fact can be defined this way. Born in Egypt, Egoyan has only a scant knowledge of Armenian and a second- or third-generation relationship to this cultural legacy. Khanjian, meanwhile, grew up in the midst of a first-generation immigrant community, and her familiarity with the language and culture figures in many of the films. An Armenian actor hired on-site, Adamian spoke no English, the latest global language. Throughout the film, the photographer relates to the landscapes, indeed all of Armenia, strictly through videotape. Likewise, he only relates to the interpreter who chooses to repatriate, and later her call girl proxies, through mediating technologies. However, after a certain point of repetition, both his reviewings of the videotapes and the rejection ritual, the photographer emerges into something like real time. As the calendar with his photographs becomes outdated, he finally writes about his perspective on his experiences. In the act, he achieves a measure of linkage between interiority and the world of others and objects, with the communicative act of writing standing for both the non-imagistic and tenuous nature of this connection. The photographer remains in postmodern Toronto, but is fully aware of what he has lost and why, and to what extent it differentiates him from his acculturated surroundings. Here, in miniature, is Egoyan's alternative to acculturalisation and nativism, two varieties of memorial excess: by inhabiting the in-between space, neither the metropole nor the particular, it is possible to imagine a future, however difficult, for critical memory.

Writing of the transnational dispersals of peoples and traditions, Appadurai notes that:

> the central paradox of ethnic politics in today's world is that primordia (whether of language or skin color or neighborhood or kinship) have become globalized. That is, sentiments whose greatest force is in their ability to ignite intimacy into a political sentiment and turn locality into a staging ground for identity, have become spread over vast and irregular spaces as groups move, yet stay linked to one another through sophisticated media capabilities.[28]

By coupling an awareness of globalisation with an understanding of the seductions of both the technological and its apparent opposite, the autochthonous, Egoyan invites us to direct a critical forgetting in two directions at once. Technologised memory and nationalisms are both instrumental in a strong sense and produce, in his films and the world itself, the irrationalities of any totalising system. In order for memory to have meaning in postcinematic culture, Egoyan could be seen to invite us to occupy the transitory consciousness of the migrant, to guide us toward an Armenia of the mind in which the true past is already somewhat lost. But lost as well are any fantasies of total memory.

Notes

1 Arthur Danto provides the model for this point. He translates the Hegelian dialectic to the terms of contemporary visual art. If we conceive of artistic history as progressive, he argues, we are operating

under the aegis of Hegel's historicism. The dialectic, however, demands that we accept the inevitable dissipation of progress in any particular field: 'Hegel's thought was that for a period of time the energies of history coincided with the energies of art, but now history and art must go in different directions, and though art may continue to exist in . . . a post-historical fashion, its existence carries no historical significance whatever'. Arthur Danto, *The Philosophical Disenfranchisement of Art* (New York: Columbia University Press, 1986), p. 84. In its combination of mass appeal and aesthetic development, cinema is arguably the supreme art form of the last century. This chapter explores how cinema negotiates its transition to a posthistorical status.

2 Fredric Jameson, 'Reading Without Interpretation: Postmodernism and the Video-Text', in Nigel Fabb (ed.), *The Linguistics of Writing: Arguments Between Language and Literature* (Manchester: Manchester University Press, 1987), p. 202.

3 Steven Knapp, 'Collective Memory and the Actual Past', *Representations* 26 (Spring 1989), 137.

4 Jameson, 'Reading', p. 206.

5 Jameson, 'Reading', p. 218.

6 Jameson, 'Reading', p. 201.

7 See Jonathan Romney, 'Exploitations', *Sight and Sound* (May 1995), 6–9.

8 Jameson, 'Reading', p. 208.

9 Jameson, 'Reading', pp. 208–9.

10 Paul Virilio, 'Video Letters: An Interview with Atom Egoyan', in Carole Desbarats *et al.* (eds), *Atom Egoyan*, trans. Brian Holmes (Paris, Editions Dis Voir, 1994), p. 106.

11 Virilio, 'Video', p. 108.

12 Jameson, 'Reading', p. 202.

13 Amy Taubin, 'Memories of Overdevelopment: Up and Atom', *Film Comment* (November/December 1989), 28.

14 Virilio, 'Video', p. 112.

15 The story of Orpheus also resonates with this condition. 'In the Orphic underworld the dead must avoid the springs of oblivion; they must not drink the waters of Lethe, but on the contrary drink from the fountain of memory, which is a source of immortality', Jacques Le Goff, *History and Memory*, trans. Steven Rendell and Elizabeth Claman (New York: Columbia University Press, 1992), p. 64.

16 Peter Harcourt, 'Imaginary Films: An Examination of the Films of Atom Egoyan, *Film Quarterly* (Spring 1995), 6.

17 For a brilliant analysis of the construction of Canadian national identity through the wiring of its vast and underpopulated spaces with the world's most complete telephone and broadcasting network, along

with Canada's peculiar dominance of techniques of satellite imagery, see Jody Berland, 'Mapping Space: Imaging Technologies and the Planetary Body', in Stanley Aronowitz, Barbara Martinsons and Michael Mensa (eds), *Technoscience and Cyberculture* (New York: Routledge, 1996), pp. 123–37. For broader discussions of Canadian self-perception, under the rubrics of postmodernism and cultural studies, see Valda Blundell, John Shepard and Ian Taylor (eds), *Relocating Cultural Studies* (London: Routledge, 1990).
18 Amanda Lipman, 'Exotica', *Sight and Sound* (May 1995), 45.
19 Jacinto Lageira, 'The Recollection of Scattered Parts', in Carole Desbarats *et al.*(eds), *Atom Egoyan*, p. 33.
20 For a persuasive detailing and critique of techno-determinism in contemporary criticism and theory, see Richard Gruisin 'What Is an Electronic Author? Theory and the Technological Fallacy', in Richard Markley (ed.), *Virtual Realities and Their Discontents*(Baltimore: Johns Hopkins University Press, 1996), pp. 39–54.
21 Virilio, 'Video', p. 106.
22 Romney, 'Exploitations', p. 9.
23 Lageira, 'Recollection', p. 34.
24 Daniele Riviere, 'The Place of the Spectator', in Desbarats *et al.* (eds), *Atom Egoyan*, p. 96.
25 Virilio, 'Video', p. 114.
26 Arjun Appadurai, 'Disjuncture and Difference in the Global Cultural Economy', in Bruce Robbins (ed.), *The Phantom Public Sphere* (Minneapolis: University of Minnesota Press, 1993), p. 287.
27 Farah Anwar, 'Calendar', *Sight and Sound* (February 1993), 49.
28 Appadurai, 'Disjuncture', p. 285.

Index